SEEDING SUCCESS

The Story of Olds College Since 1913

by

Barry Potyondi

OLDS COLLEGE
100 years

1913-2013

It gives me great pleasure to introduce *Seeding Success*, the story of our first one hundred years.

This comprehensive history owes a great deal to generations of Olds College students, instructors and administrators who always appreciated the importance of the past, preserved records and photographs of their time here and, in many cases, willingly shared their recollections with the author.

They understood, as we all must, that a centennial is a time to take stock, a time to reflect on our roots — How deep are they? How widespread? How strong?

These are important questions. Their answers not only ground us in the rich legacy of our forebears but also guide us confidently as we begin our second century as a leading educational institution.

As this fine book shows, Olds College was founded on a solid and lasting base of admirable values that bind us together as a community, inspire our students, staff and faculty, and support us in the face of any challenge.

Our traditions, which bring together academic excellence, hands-on learning and unselfish service to the community, have contributed greatly to the sustainability of land management in particular and to the betterment of rural society in general.

We are justly proud to be associated with such enduring values and the important achievements that have come from them.

In the years ahead, Olds College will continue to pursue the vision of our founders as we strive to serve Canada and the world as an integrated learning and applied research community specializing in agriculture, horticulture, and land and environmental management. And we'll do it while remaining true to our heritage and our values.

That's the real importance of a history like *Seeding Success* — in reminding us of our deep roots, it affirms that our practical, down-to-earth values will carry us successfully through our next century of achievement. That, too, will be worthy of celebration.

Dr. H.J. (Tom) Thompson
President
Olds College

Acknowledgments

No book is the work of one person. In fact, none would be written at all if it were not for the help and guidance of many people. This book is no different.

I am grateful for the thoughtfulness of dozens of Olds College alumni, administrators, instructors and industry partners who had the foresight to contribute their written records, photographs and memorabilia to the Olds College Alumni Museum. As the book shows, their generosity over the years has been remarkable.

Equally gratifying was the assistance provided by all those who agreed to talk with me about their experiences while attending or teaching at the College. In addition to offering insight into College events large and small, they provided me with a heart-warming sense of the abiding values and tremendous spirit of community that have pervaded the College since 1913. My thanks to each of you for making this stranger feel at home.

Archivists and librarians in Olds, Calgary, Edmonton and Ottawa facilitated my research every step of the way with a skill and efficiency that I can only envy. Garry McCullough of the College Alumni Museum not only gave me the run of the place, but eagerly shared his own findings with me time after time. Jeffery Kearney, Archivist of the Mountain View Museum and Archives, was generous with his knowledge of local sources and events. And the peerless Paulette Shoemaker of the President's Office made my research much easier and more comprehensive with her wealth of experience and her unflagging enthusiasm.

Olds College President Tom Thompson proved a strong, eager and active supporter of the centennial history from the beginning, as did Vice President of Advancement Jordan Cleland. I thank them for allowing me to undertake this delightful project and to play a small role in celebration of this momentous event.

For the past two years it has also been my distinct pleasure to work closely with 2013 Centennial General Manager Kerry Moynihan, the best project manager I have encountered in several decades of consulting.

Finally, I wish to dedicate this book to my wife, Brenda Maunders, the love of my life.

Barry Potyondi
Peachland, British Columbia
September 2012

Table of Contents

Message From the President – page 4

Acknowledgments – page 8

Chapter One: Foundations – page 12

Chapter Two: A Practical Education – page 46

Chapter Three: Heart of the District – page 82

Chapter Four: Traditions in the Making – page 122

Chapter Five: Depression and War – page 164

Chapter Six: A Period of Uncertainty – page 210

Chapter Seven: The Vocational College – page 244

Chapter Eight: Alberta in Transition – page 292

Chapter Nine: Community Partner – page 328

Epilogue: Coming Full Circle – page 404

A Note on Sources – page 412

Endnotes – page 416

Foundations

Standing ankle-deep in a field of golden stubble, Christena Marshall placed her elegantly gloved hands firmly upon the rough wooden handles of the breaking plough and turned her face to the camera.

1

Breaking Ground

It was nine o'clock in the morning on Saturday, the 21ˢᵗ day of September, 1912. The day was clear and slowly warming — it would reach 60° F by early afternoon — and Christena had chosen to wear a light coat as she attended to her important duties in the crisp autumn air. Her head was crowned by an enormous haystack of a hat set off by a single stylish feather. The few other women in attendance were equally well turned out.

The men presented a more motley appearance. The politicians, including Christena's husband Duncan, wore their customary stiff-collared shirts, sackcloth suits and narrow, four-in-hand ties. These could not have been more different from the cotton bib overalls of the farmhands who held the draught horses. One of the hands, the one entrusted with the reins of Mrs. Marshall's team, had had the presence of mind to add a neck-tie to his usual work clothes. The Marshall son in attendance — Christena and Duncan had three children, all boys — stood stiffly in short pants by his mother's side, looking for all the world like he would rather be off playing than trying to keep still while the photographer went about his business.

Christena Marshall broke ground for the Olds School of Agriculture and Home Economics on September 21, 1912. Her husband, Duncan, was Alberta's Minister of Agriculture and largely responsible for developing the Province's network of agricultural schools.

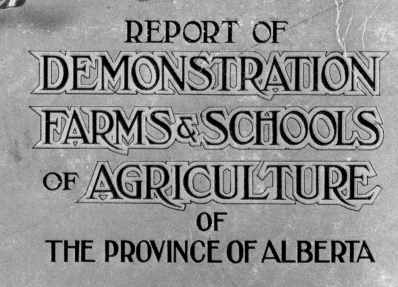

REPORT OF
DEMONSTRATION
FARMS & SCHOOLS
OF AGRICULTURE
OF
THE PROVINCE OF ALBERTA

ISSUED BY THE DIRECTION OF
HON. DUNCAN MARSHALL
MINISTER OF AGRICULTURE

The photographer took his time, for this was not just any photograph. It captured, as the reporter for the *Olds Gazette* was pleased to note,[1] the momentous first step in construction of what he called the Government Agricultural College. The College was to be erected on the Demonstration Farm near the foot of Second Street — today's 49 Street.

The fragrant black loam that Christena Marshall's ploughshare turned over on that lovely September morning was nothing like the sandy red soil she had grown up with on Prince Edward Island. This topsoil blanketed some of the finest arable land in the Province of Alberta, perhaps in all of Western Canada. To those attending the sod-turning, that dark, sweetly rotting earth was a powerful symbol of economic prosperity and a glorious future in which the farmer's way of life would receive the attention it so richly deserved.

These were people who believed firmly in the rural way of life. They saw it as the wellspring of economic strength, political liberty, moral rectitude and healthy living, in contrast to the despised dissipation of urban life. As immigrants came to Canada in record numbers and settled in thin ribbons along the railway lines that had begun to cross the vast western prairies, it seemed to agricultural promoters that the day of the farmer had finally arrived. Greater numbers gave them courage and a sense of political solidarity and strength.

They also believed that knowledge of the best farming practices would provide settlers with a better living and an effective way of keeping their children on the farm. Those exemplary practices came to be referred to by a catch-all phrase, "scientific agriculture," or what is now called agronomy. Many things fell under this umbrella, but at the turn of the last century it usually meant a deep knowledge of soils, moisture, animal and plant breeding, and appropriate cultivation techniques. Those present at the sod-breaking were zealous converts to the gospel of scientific agriculture.

In their view the Olds School of Agriculture and Home Economics, as the college was called when it opened late in 1913, would be responsible for teaching their sons and daughters how to draw lives of comfort, dignity and purpose from the soil. Moreover, the students' understanding of the tenets of scientific agriculture would make them leaders of the community, responsible citizens who could be counted upon to build a better country by living in accordance with agrarian ideals. This unalloyed faith in the importance of farming, expressed so confidently at the sod-turning, imbued the new school at Olds with the clear sense of purpose it would always retain.

As the title of this 1914 pamphlet suggests, Duncan Marshall always saw Demonstration Farms and Schools of Agriculture as two sides of the same coin.

The Olds Demonstration Farm

Christena's husband, Duncan McLean Marshall, was largely responsible for establishing agricultural schools in Alberta. He was also a key influence in the decision to erect one of the schools immediately east of the Town of Olds.

Born into a farming family in Elderslie Township, Bruce County, Ontario, in 1872, Marshall seemed destined for a life in politics and a career as a passionate advocate of farm life. His parents, like many in Bruce County, supported the Patrons of Industry, a radical farm organization that co-operated with the urban labour movement against what they saw as the growing power of big business.

When still in his teens, Marshall became a County organizer for the Patrons. On one occasion this gave him the chance to debate a well-known Liberal politician about the issues of the day. Marshall proved so articulate and charismatic that everyone in the audience was convinced he would make his mark in politics. As a reporter later said of the debate, "a head-on collision with Mr. Marshall invariably results in wreckage, and in this particular instance the astonished intruder went back to Ottawa and never showed his face in Bruce County again."[2]

After teaching school briefly in Gillies Hill and then editing small-town newspapers across Ontario, Marshall headed west in 1905 to become editor of the *Edmonton Bulletin*. The *Bulletin* was owned by Frank Oliver, Alberta's first Member of Parliament and the powerful Minister of the Interior in Prime Minister Wilfrid Laurier's 1905 cabinet.

Ambition, ability and personal connections served Marshall well. He contested the provincial election of 1909, winning the new Olds electoral district for Alexander Cameron Rutherford's Liberal Party over Conservative candidate George McDonald.

His bid for local office coincided with his purchase of a farm northeast of town, which he called Elderslie in honour of his Ontario birthplace. At about the same time, he acquired *The Olds Gazette*, which was a relief to some residents who thought the weekly paper had acquired a socialist tone under former owner Tom Buckton.

Premier Rutherford was so impressed by the 37-year old Marshall that he appointed him Minister of Agriculture in the Cabinet. Marshall retained the portfolio in the government of Liberal Premier Arthur Sifton that was elected in 1910, and would remain Alberta's Minister of Agriculture until 1921.

This was an important Cabinet position. Alberta, like the rest of Western Canada, was experiencing a settlement boom of unprecedented proportions. Between 1901 and 1905, more than 40,000 homesteads were granted in what would become the Province of Alberta in 1905. Those homesteads were concentrated along the mainline of the Canadian Pacific Railway through Calgary and northwards along the Calgary and Edmonton Railway

that was built in 1891. Not surprisingly, the first business in the village of Olds opened its doors in the same year to serve the settlers who were rapidly taking up land along the line. By 1911, Alberta could claim more than 60,000 working farms.

The thousands of settlers who poured into central Alberta before the Great War of 1914-18 came from eastern Canada, the United States, England, the Scandinavian countries and many other places. As a result, few were familiar with local growing conditions. Their farms were rarely run as efficiently and profitably as North American agricultural experts thought they might have been.

The Olds Demonstration Farm, established in 1911, showing the Manager's house in the foreground. The Farm operated separately from the Olds School of Agriculture until 1919.

Alberta's Department of Agriculture tried to remedy this lack of local knowledge in several ways. It helped to organize annual summer fairs and exhibitions throughout the Province so farm families could see the finest examples of local livestock and produce. It sent staff to host short courses on topics ranging from the raising of livestock and poultry to the identification and eradication of noxious weeds. It partnered with local farmers willing to conduct long-term experiments with test plots of everything from cereal crops to fruit trees in the hope of identifying those crops with the greatest potential for production in Alberta conditions. At every opportunity, government officials stressed the value of mixed farming as a hedge against the economic downturns that recurred within the farming community.

Duncan Marshall, aware of the success of the Dominion government in establishing experimental farms and illustration stations at locations like Brandon, Indian Head, Lacombe and Fort Vermilion, decided to set up Alberta's own version. In 1911, he authorized the development of six Demonstration Farms, which he hoped would be the first of many across the Province.

In 1911 the Demonstration Farm at Olds, which was located considerably downwind of the town's 1,200 residents, consisted of 320 acres of raw prairie. Although heavy willow brush covered much of this land,[3] the farmhands managed to clear and then break 130 acres between spring thaw and September. Oats and barley were sown for both seed and feed.

They also put up many buildings in that first year: a manager's house for Joseph Clements, a house for the farmhands, dairy and horse barns, a hog pen, four hen coops, a shed, a root house, an ice house, a milk house, a pump house and some corrals. The cost of this construction was $15,000. By the end of 1912 the farm boasted 105 steers, 10 registered Holstein cows, two heifer calves and one bull, 18 grade Holstein cows, 13 horses and two colts, 36 hogs, and 35 Barred Rock hens. The Government's total investment exceeded $46,000.[4]

In addition to the Olds operation, the Government established nearly identical farms at Medicine Hat, Claresholm, Sedgewick, Stony Plain, Athabasca Landing and Vermilion. H. A. Craig, a graduate of the Ontario Agricultural College in Guelph who was later to serve as Deputy Minister of the Department of Agriculture, became Alberta's first Superintendent of Demonstration Farms.

These farms were not merely agricultural showplaces, although their fields and pens and plots soon attracted thousands of visitors annually. On the contrary, the Government wanted them to be practical in nature, exhibiting fine cattle and produce that any farmer could raise with a bit of advice and some hands-on instruction. As Superintendent Craig said,

The farms thus become the channels of conveying to the farmers concretely the results of investigational work instead of leaving them to get these through experimental farm literature, which does not reach many people

and is not always diligently read and applied by those
who are hard driven by the details of farm work.[5]

In other words, these farms were intended to teach by doing. They also sold purebred livestock and registered seed grain to Alberta producers.

Over the years, the Demonstration Farm at Olds would grow larger but its essential purpose would stay the same; it would act as a practical example of the concept of scientific agriculture that captured the attention of farmers across North America in the early years of the 20th century.

Ontario-born Duncan Marshall, a Liberal who served as Alberta's Minister of Agriculture from 1909 to 1921, established six Demonstration Farms designed to showcase the principles of scientific agriculture and serve as outdoor laboratories for agricultural school students. Following spread: This panoramic winter image, from around 1914-15, shows the first three school buildings on the left (Main Building, Livestock Pavilion, and Carpentry/Blacksmith Shop), and the Demonstration Farm to the right. Bottom left: Arthur Humphreys breaking land at Demonstration Farm. Bottom right: The carpentry and blacksmith shop in the foreground was built, in part, by the School's first-year students as a hands-on project. Visible in the background are the dairy barn of the Demonstration Farm and the Farm Manager's house.

SCHOOL OF AGRICULTURE AND DEMONST

The Agricultural Instruction Act came with few restrictions. Basically, it provided $10 million to the provinces to be spent on projects related to agricultural instruction and the advancement of rural social welfare between 1913 and 1923.

Burrell asked C. C. James, former Deputy Minister of Agriculture in Ontario, to visit all the Provinces and report back on the educational needs and wishes of each. James met with Duncan Marshall in Edmonton and apprised him of the Government's intentions. Marshall replied, "I want an agricultural school in Alberta. We have six Demonstration Farms, and I would like eventually to have an agricultural school at each of these farms."[8] Immediately after meeting with James, Marshall called his Cabinet colleagues together and won their agreement to start work at once on not one but three schools. The Provincial budget estimates of February, 1912, set aside $40,000 for that purpose.[9]

The Agricultural Instruction Act came with few restrictions. Basically, it provided $10 million to the provinces to be spent on projects related to agricultural instruction and the advancement of rural social welfare between 1913 and 1923.[10] Allocation of the funds was based on population. By 1917, the Province of Alberta was receiving nearly $67,000 annually. The lion's share of that ($40,000) was given over to rural education, while the rest was spent on the promotion of school fairs, the work of Women's Institutes and on extension work. While the Province of Alberta agreed to pay for construction of the School buildings, most of the federal grant was used to outfit the structures with equipment and to cover operational costs for the first decade of their existence.

The grant was highly unusual, in that federal aid to agriculture was usually only provided in response to crop failures or economic depression. The legislation that made the grant possible also came at a time when crop production and receipts were very high. While Borden's Conservative government was undoubtedly sincere in its appreciation of the farming sector, there is no doubt it was also conscious of a rising tide of rural discontent in the country.

Many farmers felt ignored by Ottawa and treated unfairly by the banks, railway companies, line elevator companies and farm machinery manufacturers. As a result, they were beginning to organize politically. Farm women, for their part, started to form local clubs called Women's Institutes to promote better rural living conditions and help stem the tide of young people to the cities. No one on the farm thought governments were doing enough about these matters. In passing the Agricultural Instruction Act, the Government was not just supporting primary producers; it was also shoring up its political support.

Olds students received training in academic subjects, such as chemistry, alongside more practical lessons in animal husbandry and judging.

28

Creating a Campus

Whatever its complex political origins, the federal money was quickly put to good use. Throughout the spring, summer and fall of 1913, three nearly identical schools arose at Claresholm, Vermilion and Olds from a common set of architectural plans.

In each case a two-storey, wood-frame Main Building housed classrooms for animal husbandry, science, dairying, household science, two lecture rooms, a large assembly hall, administrative offices and a library. This was the only building fully finished at Olds by the fall of 1913 when the first classes began, so it temporarily accommodated mechanical and metal-working classes as well. A room on the north side of the basement was even used for stock judging classes for a time.

No sooner was the Main Building at Olds completed than it nearly burned to the ground.[11] Early on the morning of December 9th, Theodore Moe, the School janitor, was on his way to light the classroom stoves when he noticed smoke billowing from one of the main floor windows. He sounded the alarm and soon every resident of Olds was awakened by the sharp clang of the fire bell that hung from the tower of the town hall. Volunteers quickly hauled the chemical fire engine to the School but found, to their dismay, that it refused to function. They then turned their attention to the windmill that pumped water to the campus, but with no wind blowing that particular morning this source was of no use to them. In desperation, some residents and students formed a bucket brigade while others took turns pumping water by hand from a nearby well. Half an hour of pouring water into the south wall from the second and third floors did the trick and the $40,000 building was saved.

Suits and ties gave early classes a sense of formality that lasted until the Second World War. Note the boys proudly wearing sweaters emblazoned with the original "O.S.A." crest.

Completion of the second campus building provided an early lesson in practical education.[12] When the New Year began, the first-year boys unexpectedly received more than they had bargained for in their carpentry class as their instructor expected them to complete work on a two-storey structure south-east of the Main Building. Begun in the fall of 1913, this building housed a carpentry shop upstairs and a blacksmith shop with 18 forges below. The electrical generation dynamo was next to the blacksmith shop. The third structure to be constructed held a livestock judging ring and the agronomy classroom upstairs. Contrary to the original grant agreement, monies available through the Agricultural Instruction Act were used to build the farm mechanics and stock judging buildings.[13]

The look of the School yard and nearby fields changed rapidly, too. At first, there was no grass, no trees and no shrubs, unless you counted the abundant willows. Those were concentrated around a large slough on the southwestern corner of the yard; it was a favourite with all the local ducks. In October, the School and Demonstration Farm staff worked day and night with two four-horse teams on fresnoes to fill the slough and grade the yard so it could be seeded to grass and used as a sports field by students and staff for games like baseball and football. Frank Stevenett, among the first to enrol at the School, recalled that,

The school grounds were hewn out of heavy willow brush, and our first winter being fairly open, the students had the opportunity of picking roots and leveling the grounds, part of which was used for a football field. This sport was the main feature the first year, and some excellent players showed up both from the staff and students. Some spectacular games were played between the Olds Bankers team and the O.S.A.[14]

Other parts of this new lawn were reserved for the planting of ornamental hedges, shrubs, trees and flowers that could serve as an object lesson for the students.[15] A length of wooden sidewalk was also installed along the road allowance on the west side of the new campus to make it easier for students to avoid the swampy ground.[16]

In the spring of 1914, the School started work on a shelterbelt of sorts on the northwestern corner of the grounds. On the north side they planted Russian poplar, cottonwoods, maple and willows; to the west they put poplars, spruce and pine.[17] Many years later Frank Grisdale remembered ordering a few hundred seedlings of Jack Pines, Lodge Pole Pine and White Spruce.[18] Twenty acres north of the School buildings were prepared as test plots that would help determine the best grains, grasses and root crops for the district. Even before classes ended for the summer in 1914, the School yard had acquired a remarkably tidy and organized appearance.

Hiring a teaching staff was the next task before Duncan Marshall and his colleagues. This proved difficult.

The Search for Instructors

Few institutions in Canada prepared students for agricultural teaching careers. The two main schools were the Ontario Agricultural College in Guelph and Macdonald College near Montreal. Traditionally, if graduates of these schools wished to teach, they had to move to the United States because there were so few positions in Canada. Now, complicating things further for Marshall, there was a sudden demand for agricultural instructors as province after province took the Dominion Government up on its offer to help fund agricultural education. The federal largesse, doled out to every province at the same time, was both a blessing and a curse.

In June of 1913, 38-year-old William James Elliott was named to head the Olds School. Born in Huron County, Ontario, Elliott had graduated from the Ontario Agricultural College with a Bachelor of Science degree in Agriculture in 1895. Within a few years of completing this degree, he became manager of a large creamery in Minnesota. By the fall of 1903 he found himself in Bozeman, Montana where he directed the departments of Dairy and Animal Industry at the State Agricultural College. Within five years, he had become the Dean in charge of agricultural short courses. He retained that title until 1910, when he accepted a job with the Canadian Pacific Railway as Superintendent of Agriculture in their Natural Resources Department. Through that position, based at Strathmore, he quickly became a familiar figure in Alberta. Securing his services as Principal cost the Provincial Government $2,700 a year,[19] at a time when most farmers earned less than $500 annually.

The first Principal, William James (Pops) Elliott, was a stern disciplinarian who exemplified the strong moral values, academic rigour and extracurricular participation that he expected of all Olds students. Right: Principal Elliott, flanked by Miss Marjorie Goldie (left) and Miss Nan Lawson (right), and the other instructors at the Olds School of Agriculture and Home Economics in the winter of 1913-14. Frank Grisdale, who would become Principal in 1919, is in the back row on the far right.

This undated photograph, likely from the 1920s, shows the remarkable determination of the School staff to enhance the campus landscape with ornamental plantings, demonstration plots and thoughtfully designed roadways.

Courtesy Glenbow Archives NA-2637-7

I had shot at; however, that might have been, the noise of the gun and the dust it kicks up in the plowed ground has given the coyotes the idea that it is dangerous to come near my buildings. A pair that were always hanging about during the winter have quit the place entirely and I have seen only one on the place in the last month and he was a half mile from the house just as far away from the house as he could be and be on the farm.

The most pleasing part of it is that I have not had a hen taken by a coyote during the summer. It seems that a gun big enough to kill a coyote is a protection from them even though one can not hit them.

Alta.   "OBSERVER."

THE FARMYARD BEAUTIFUL

Written for the FARMER'S ADVOCATE
by H. E. VIALOUX

Listen! kind readers of "THE ADVOCATE" to a little tale, a really true story, of how an energetic woman grew flowers for pleasure and profit on the plains of Manitoba without the friendly aid of a shelter belt or bluff of trees, mastering the art of making waste places beautiful.

We well know it is blessed to make two blades of grass grow where only one has been, and the culture of beautiful flowers appeals to all and surely brings a rich blessing with it even if it is only the patch of bright-hued, fragrant flowers in front of the lonely prairie home smothered in wheat fields.

Mr. and Mrs. Drumbril homesteaded some years ago in the Rainy River dis-

In Mrs. Drumbril's Garden

Picking Flowers for Market

An Interested Visitor

Showing Wire Fence

THE ALBERTA
Provincial Government Schools of Agriculture
At CLARESHOLM, OLDS AND VERMILLION
WILL OPEN OCTOBER 28

The course covers a period of two years leading to a diploma.

Courses of study are offered for men in field husbandry, animal husbandry, veterinary science, farm mechanics, farm dairying, horticulture, elementary chemistry, physics, botany, bacteriology, geology, poultry, farm management, mathematics and English.

Courses of study are offered for women in household science including foods, hygiene and sanitation, sewing, laundry work, home care of the sick, gardening, poultry, home-dairying.

The aim is to give practical training for the farm and the home. The theoretical work will be closely associated with the work of the demonstration farms.

Age for admission, for boys 14, for girls 16, no entrance examination is required.

For calendar and further particulars address, Principal W. J. Stephen, Claresholm; Principal W. J. Elliott, Olds; Principal E. A. Howes, Vermillion.

This print advertisement, which appeared in newspapers and farm periodicals throughout Alberta, was one element of a very successful campaign to fill the classrooms of the new Olds School of Agriculture.

George Holeton, Instructor in blacksmithing, carpentry and engine repair. He taught at Olds from 1913 to 1944 and was the leading light of the school fairs program.

Miss Marjorie M. Goldie, Household Science Instructor and bread baking authority.

Following Spread: Formerly a large slough, the first School sports field was filled, levelled and seeded through the volunteer efforts of the first class. Courtesy Glenbow Archives P-1023-2

The rest of the initial staff arrived in October. All men, they included soils and crops expert Frank S. Grisdale, a graduate of Macdonald College who had spent the previous two years as assistant superintendent of the Dominion Experimental Farm at Lethbridge; George Holeton, an authority in farm mechanics from Wisconsin who took charge of the blacksmithing, carpentry and gasoline engine courses; and Scotland-born and trained James Fowler, a specialist in the application of chemistry and physics to agriculture who would teach elementary science and English. They received $100 per month for the five months of the school year and assurances of paid summer work.

At first, the School had no women on its teaching staff. Instead, Miss Marjorie M. Goldie and Miss Nan Lawson, respectively Instructor and Assistant Instructor in Household Science, rotated from one School to the next as the school year progressed. This was because the household science program, which focused on cooking and sewing, was taught for only eight weeks during the first year of the Schools' operation.

Both women were well educated. Miss Goldie, a native of Guelph, Ontario, had received a degree in home economics from Macdonald College before continuing on to graduate work in flour testing and bread baking. After a time lecturing to Women's Institutes in Ontario, she became the director of household science in an Eastern Canadian school. Miss Lawson, who was born in Scotland, moved with her parents to Winnipeg and then to Calgary. She trained at the prestigious California State Normal School of Manual Arts and Home Economics in Santa Barbara and taught there before returning to Alberta. She was renowned for her dressmaking and millinery skills.

In addition to having a permanent teaching staff, each school benefitted from periodic instruction from travelling instructors. In the first year of operation, two provincial Dairy Branch employees, Alberta's Superintendent of Poultry, and the Provincial Veterinarian toured the Schools. There were special lecturers as well. These included H. A. Craig, the Superintendent of Demonstration Farms; S. G. Carlyle, a Special Instructor in Dairy Farming; W. F. Stevens, the Provincial Livestock Commissioner; C. P. Marker, the Provincial Dairy Commissioner; and Alex Galbraith, a renowned horse breeder and stock judge.

While the teaching staff was being assembled, and work on the buildings completed, the Department of Agriculture launched a formal advertising campaign to recruit students via community newspapers and the agricultural press of the day. The offer was tempting:

> Free Agricultural Education for Young Men & Women
> *Including: field husbandry, horticulture, the scientific study of live stock, dairying, cooking, sewing, sanitation, household administration and tuition in every branch of practical scientific agriculture and household science.*

The only expenses that a farm family would have to meet were for room and board, books and entertainment, estimated at $125 for the school year. Even at that, the School was clearly a place for the better-heeled youth of the Olds district.

To sweeten the offer, the Government advertisements proclaimed that students did not have to pass any sort of entrance qualification. It did not matter what level of education they had attained, if any. As long as they possessed good health and a sound moral character, they were more than welcome to attend.

Principal Elliott proved tireless in his own efforts to recruit students. In the fall of 1913, he travelled extensively to towns and villages throughout central Alberta, extolling the benefits offered by his School. There are even stories of him pumping his way down the railway tracks on a handcar in order to deliver his message.[20]

Sometimes he and George Holeton would take Elliott's Model T Ford and drive from farm to farm or address farmers' meetings and other community gatherings to convince sceptical parents that their sons and daughters deserved this kind of education. On one occasion, when

Elliott had driven to Innisfail by himself, a young man named Harrison stole the parked automobile and headed south with two local men in hot pursuit.[21] Nearing Olds, Harrison abandoned the car and set out on foot but not before firing several shots in the direction of his pursuers. Word quickly reached Constable Martin at Olds, who managed to corner Harrison and force him to surrender at gunpoint. He was taken to Innisfail on the next train and imprisoned to await trial.

As the Government had not voted funds sufficient to build a students' dormitory, Elliott regularly used the columns of the *Gazette* to cajole town residents into providing room and board for the students as well. Some students, he noted, would be pleased to do light chores morning and evening in exchange for a break on the rent.

They had chosen well in hiring Principal Elliott and an excellent group of instructors. Elliott was, as Frank Grisdale once said, a man of boundless enthusiasm with "an abiding belief in the great importance of the work of the agricultural schools. He inspired staff, students, and many others with the same spirit."[22]

Opening the Doors

Residents of Olds marvelled at the throngs that crowded into town on Friday,

November 21, 1913, to witness the grand opening of the School.

The Olds Gazette called it one of the best public gatherings ever held in town. All afternoon farmers and their families filled the hallways of the Main Building and then spilled out into the nearby yard and test plots. They had come from Edmonton, Leduc, Lacombe, Red Deer, Penhold, Crossfield, Didsbury and places farther afield. Interest in what these schools could bring to rural Alberta was running high.

In the evening, everyone gathered in the School's assembly hall to get a glimpse of the dignitaries and listen to their congratulatory speeches. There was Frank Oliver; Henry Marshall Tory; Duncan Marshall; Deputy Minister John Ross of the Department of Education; and even Alberta's Lieutenant-Governor George Bulyea, himself the son of prosperous New Brunswick farmers. Several members of the Official Opposition attended as well, carefully telling anyone who would listen that their support for such a school had never been a matter of party politics. So many people came to listen to these esteemed visitors that the 400 chairs in the auditorium were quickly taken and many others had to stand in the stairwells so that they, too, could claim to have been a part of this momentous occasion.

Of all the speeches made that night — and most did go on at great length — none summed up the situation better or made people laugh more than that of John Blue.[23]

Blue was Alberta's Legislative Librarian and a man with a deep sense of history. He began by saying he had spent part of the afternoon watching a student assess a sample of milk for butterfat content using the Babcock test. In that brief moment, Blue noted, the youth had demonstrated a greater grasp of chemistry than Blue had acquired during an entire year of study at the University of Toronto. This was a perfect example of the practical aspect of the School that everyone wished to see.

Just as importantly, as Blue watched the young man apply experimental science to everyday agriculture, he glimpsed a future that would belong to the farmer. The cities may have claimed the last century, he said, but the 20th century would belong to agriculture because at last "the farmer's boy was to have a chance." Unfortunately, he concluded mischievously, the equally practical household science classes had not yet started at Olds. That probably meant the assembled guests would find "nothing but empty pie plates in the pantry."

Discussing the finer points of a chicken.

A Practical Education

The boys began to arrive by train on Monday, the 27th day of October, 1913, one day before the official start of classes at O.S.A., as the Olds School of Agriculture soon became known. Six trains passed through Olds every day except on Sunday, when there were only four. The boys coming from the north had booked a coach seat on the 522, the 524 or the 526; those from the south chose from among the 521, the 523 or the 525.

C.P.R. Stat
Olds. Alf

"Applications are coming in every day"[1]

There were Thomas Sigurdson and Swain Sveinson from Burnt Lake, Robert Gratz of Sunnyslope, Raymond Figarol of Leo, Harold Braseth from Bashaw, Gordon Flack from Lacombe, John and Samuel Elsinger from Mayton, Lloyd Danford from Ponoka, Frank Stevenett and Thory Johnson from Innisfail, William Rogers from Penhold, Howard Pierce from Daysland, and many more. The C.P.R. Station had rarely seen so many arrivals in so short a time.

Three dozen students, give or take a few, stepped off the train or arrived by car between Monday morning and Tuesday night. They came from 18 different districts in the Province — from Langdon in the south to Wetaskiwin in the north. The Innisfail district contributed the greatest number of freshmen, with the Olds district coming second. This degree of interest greatly exceeded Principal Elliott's expectations, and he was very pleased to receive telephone calls from a number of Olds residents offering their congratulations. In truth, he had thought that the school would be doing well if it succeeded in attracting 15 to 20 farm boys for the first year of studies. As it was, he still had another 12 applications on his desk from boys who had had the courtesy to let him know that they could not make opening day because harvest was not yet completed on their home farms. Most planned to be in Olds within a week. Their arrival would bring enrolment up to the maximum capacity of the classrooms.

That left Elliott to wonder how he might respond best to other interested boys who had not yet completed their public schooling. One curiosity about the Schools of Agriculture was that there were few barriers to admission. In fact, an expression of interest and the ability to pay for books ($5 to $7 for the year) and room and board (from $5 to $5.50 per week) were nearly all that was required of an applicant. Students must have celebrated their 14th birthday as well. In the end, Elliott decided to advise the parents of these younger boys to keep them in school until they graduated and then have them reapply for admission. Elliott believed that a firm grounding in the three Rs would make it much easier for students to pass the School's rigorous course of studies.

The boys who arrived on October 27th were, in fact, hardly boys at all, although that was how Elliott and the staff usually referred to them. Most were 19 or 20 years of age. All were farmer's sons, although the School's insistence on the wearing of suits and ties to most classes (even blacksmithing!) tended to obscure the boys' rural origins. Their combination of comparative maturity and practical experience made them ideal candidates for admission. In the ensuing weeks, more boys arrived, eventually bringing their number to 65 for the 1913-14 school year. Officials in the Department of Agriculture were reprtedly "intensely delighted"[?] with the first year's enrolment. Principal Elliott, who would soon have many of the boys calling him Pop, could not have been more pleased.

The boys were expected to be formally attired for every class, including carpentry, blacksmithing and stock judging.

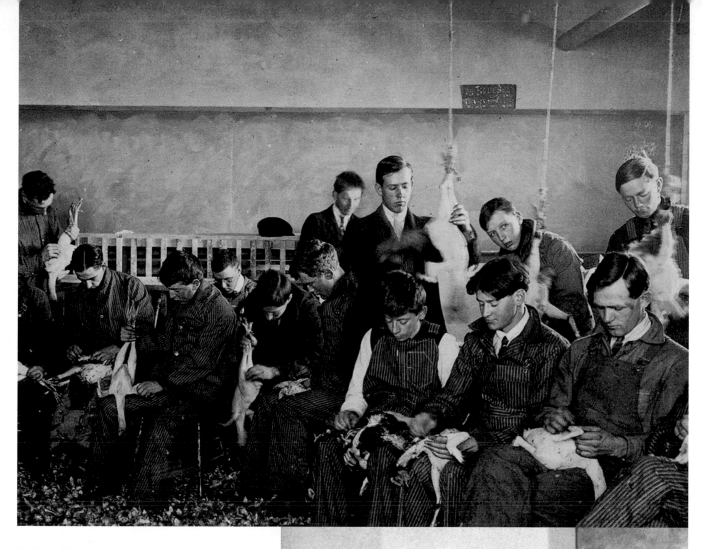

Top left: The makeshift judging ring in the basement of the Main Building. Below left: Hard at work in the 1913 blacksmith shop, the second building completed at the School. This structure housed the carpentry shop on the upper floor. Above: Learning the fine art of chicken plucking and pin-feather removal. Right: Judging grain samples for quality. Note the lone woman in the back row of desks.

The chemistry lab. In 1922 J. A. Anderson lost an eye when a flask exploded in this lab. Declaring that chemistry owed him a living, he went on to a career of international renown as a cereal chemist.

Course Content: The Details

Field Husbandry

(1) The Soil – Kinds of soil, their origin and properties; different methods of cultivation; irrigation and dry farming as pertaining to the province.

(2) The Plant – General structures; relation to air, moisture, heat and light.

(3) Farm Crops – Their history; nature; culture; adaptation to Alberta conditions.

(4) Seed – Work with the score card; comparative judging and grading; germination tests; purity tests.

Animal Husbandry

(1) Necessity of live stock in good farming.

(2) Breeds – History; classification; characteristics; adaptability.

(3) Feeds and Feeding.

Veterinary Science

Structure and functions of the animal body; common ailments of farm animals, diagnosis, treatment and prevention, simple surgery, care of animals, stable hygiene.

Farm Dairying

Milk production; market conditions; keeping of records; butter making; cheese making.

Poultry

Breeds best adapted to Alberta conditions; egg production; incubation; care; feeding; marketing.

Farm Mechanics

(1) Mechanical drawing.

(2) Woodwork.

(3) Blacksmithing.

(4) Building.

(5) Cement.

Horticulture

(1) Floriculture – Culture of flowers and bulbs for house and garden.

(2) Vegetable Gardening – Staple garden vegetables – planting, cultivation, harvesting and storing.

Elementary Science

(1) Physics – The fundamental principles.

(2) Chemistry – Elementary principles of chemistry and their relation to agriculture.

(3) Geology – Formation of the earth and movement of soils.

(4) Botany – Parts of plants, their forms and uses, food supply of plants; pollination; identification of weeds and weed seeds.

Farm Management

The whole purpose of this course is to show how to run in a common sense way a western farm, following mixed farming methods.

English

(1) English composition.

(2) Dictation.

(3) Public speaking – debates.

Mathematics

Arithmetic – Practice in simple rules; commercial arithmetic; mensuration.

Courses for Women

Duncan Marshall and his colleagues always intended the Schools of Agriculture to offer the daughters of Alberta's farmers a superior education as well.

It, too, would be practical in nature. "It is emphatically stated," said *The Olds Gazette*, "that the domestic science work is not designed to teach young ladies how to do fancy cooking, but the purpose is to teach them how to handle the ordinary things in the ordinary home, so as to make the home table as bright and wholesome as possible."[4] Although the household science program would be only eight weeks in length during the first year of the Schools' operations, Marshall indicated that his Department hoped soon to be able to provide a five-month course equal to that of the boys.[5]

The pre-war era was the time of the suffragette, a time when a growing number of middle-class women were organizing to improve their social, economic and legal status. The men behind the Schools of Agriculture were not focused so much on female equality and emancipation, however, as they were on improving the lives of rural women so they would be less likely to be lured from the farm by the domestic conveniences and social circles of the city. As Marshall once said, to great applause,

> *If we are going to have a successful province we must have contentment and happiness in the home. Men, before you spend $150.00 on a binder, look in the kitchen and see if your wife needs a $15.00 washing machine. Unhitch that gasoline engine from the pump and use it on your wife's churn.*[6]

If women continued to find rural life oppressive, as many did, their husbands would be more inclined to leave farming behind for wage labour in the city. Or so the thinking went. By using education as a social lever, male advocates of the Schools hoped to arrest the growing tide of rural depopulation.

The men were not entirely alone in this attitude of farm wives as supportive helpmeets. This was also the view taken by many contemporary domestic science instructors. Men and women had their separate, but complementary, spheres on the farm and in the farming district. Miss E. Cuming, who served as Household Science Instructor at Olds in 1916-17, said, "Nowadays it is looked upon as the man's duty to provide or produce the means for livelihood for the family, but even though the man provide [sic] for the house it is for the woman to make the home. It is her duty and privilege to provide health, comfort and happiness not only in the house but also in the community." Even as late as 1957, O.S.A. alumnus and then Principal J. Everett Birdsall continued to believe that, "If a young woman can meet the challenge of helping her husband to be a successful farmer she too can be classified as a success."[7]

As farmers began to form buying co-operatives to improve their economic situation, influential agricultural journals like the Winnipeg-based *Grain Growers' Guide*

An early cooking class. Note the variations in the women's School uniform that the students were required to sew prior to arrival for the fall term.

urged rural women to organize for the betterment of themselves, their families and the wider farming community. With cash perennially scarce, the *Guide* argued, many farm families would continue to live in poor housing with few modern conveniences while their children would have few chances to attend school beyond the first few grades. Their labour was often needed just to keep the farm afloat. In such circumstances, rural society would never advance; in fact, it might perish. This was a blunt recognition of the precarious financial situation in which many farm families lived.

Plucking, singeing and cooking a chicken was something every young farm woman needed to do several times a week in an era of tight money and no refrigeration.

Alberta farm women, including those in the Olds district, embraced the cause of a better rural society. Taking their cue from the actions of Ontario farm women, they began forming Women's Institutes across the Province and then women's locals of the United Farmers of Alberta. The first local of the United Farm Women's Association (UFWA) began at Alix in the summer of 1913 as an offshoot of the district Women's Institute. Another UFWA local soon followed at Edgerton. In 1915, women from all over Alberta would meet in Edmonton to form a provincial association to promote their interests. Later that year, 100 delegates, representing 1,400 UFWA members, attended the first provincial convention. That convention was hosted by the Olds School of Agriculture and Home Economics.[8]

The issues that concerned these women were the rural issues of the day. They wanted better health care for their families and better education for their sons and daughters. They wanted libraries and restrooms in their communities. They wanted better approaches to homemaking, less drudgery in their lives, and courses about farm bookkeeping and first aid. And they wanted get-togethers that would end their chronic social isolation and allow them to share their problems and their solutions on a regular basis. None of this was surprising, as many Alberta farm wives had emigrated from countries where they took good medical facilities, schools and other social institutions for granted. As these women saw it, they were full partners in the management of their farm operations — not least because of their labour — and needed more modern ways of fostering better homes and communities.

The Government of Alberta was already acting as an advocate for some of these objectives. For example, in creating a domestic science curriculum for the Schools of Agriculture, the Board of Agricultural Education was extending its existing classes for farm women to the next generation. In February of 1912, short courses in cooking and baking had been offered at Olds by two female representatives of the Department of Agriculture, Miss MacAdams and Miss Perkins. The courses proved popular, with more than 100 women in attendance.

Top right: In addition to mastering the domestic arts, all female students were expected to learn the rudiments of carpentry to enable them to do basic repairs around the house. Below right: Sewing clothes for the whole family was an inescapable part of women's work on early Alberta farms.

Still, there was no mistaking the limited nature of the Department's initial offer to young women at the School. Apparently the household science program was not even worthy of Principal Elliott's attention — all applications were to be sent instead to Miss Georgina Stiven, Superintendent of the Alberta Women's Institute and Domestic Science Branch of the Department of Agriculture in Edmonton.[9] As far as we know, Elliott's only roles with regard to female students were to advise on their curriculum and to solicit safe lodgings for them in town. It is also telling that none of the speakers at the grand opening celebrations mentioned the domestic science program at all, except to lament the lack of freshly baked goods.

Based on the experience of the Claresholm School, Elliott and his colleagues thought that Olds would likely attract 25 to 35 young women. As things turned out, 39 enrolled. Most were from the Olds district. Their classes began on January 6th and concluded on February 28th. These dates marked the arrival of Miss Goldie and Miss Lawson from the School at Claresholm and their subsequent departure for the Vermilion School.

Goldie and Lawson focused the attention of the girls on cooking and sewing, basic household skills that just happened to be their teaching strengths. In the cooking classes, Goldie aimed for "good, plain, economical dishes as well as the planning, preparation and serving of various meals."[10] Not one to rely on cookbooks, Goldie taught the girls how to improvise tasty recipes based on an understanding of ingredients and appropriate proportions.

For Miss Lawson's sewing class, each girl was expected to supply her own materials and fashion them into undergarments and a simple dress. While the girls bore the costs of the cloth, they got to keep their creations when they returned home at the conclusion of the course. Lawson also taught them proper laundering techniques for woollens, linens, cottons and silks, as well as how to remove a variety of common stains from the different fabrics.

The classes did not end with cooking and sewing. Goldie and Lawson also teamed up to deliver a series of lectures on home nursing, sanitation and disease, gardening and basic English composition. Other School instructors were drawn upon as needed to speak about dairying (cream separating, butter- and cheese-making, etc.), gardening, and poultry raising, killing and processing.

Just as the boys were expected to wear suits and ties to their classes, the girls also had a uniform of sorts. This was a plain blue dress with a white collar and short sleeves. They also needed to provide three long white aprons, to be worn during the cooking classes.[11]

The facilities for instruction in the domestic sciences were completely modern. The kitchens, located in what were called the Household Science flats, were outfitted with burners and utensils sufficient to accommodate 24 students at a time. Separate rooms were set aside and furnished as dining rooms; this was where the girls practised their table decoration and serving skills. The sewing rooms contained the latest sewing machines set upon small tables. The dairy classes, which used the same facilities as those available to the boys, provided all the equipment needed for milk testing, separating and churning. All the leading manufacturing firms, such as De Laval, were good enough to install their latest separators

for the use of the students. This is the earliest known
relationship between the School and corporate sponsors.

Caring for clothes was as important as knowing how to sew.
Every student learned stain removal, proper washing methods
(using the latest equipment shown here) and appropriate ironing
techniques.

How the O. S. A. Girls
        Made Their First Cake

They measured out the butter
        with a very solemn air,
The milk and sugar also,
        and they took the greatest care
To count the eggs correctly,
        and to add a little bit
Of baking powder, which,
        you know, beginners oft omit.
Then they stirred it all together,
        And they baked it for an hour—
But they never quite forgave themselves
        For leaving out the flour.

A. S. A. Magazine, March 1915

Butter-making class involved more than separating cream from milk and churning; every student had to demonstrate her ability to turn out the perfect block of butter with a wooden butter press.

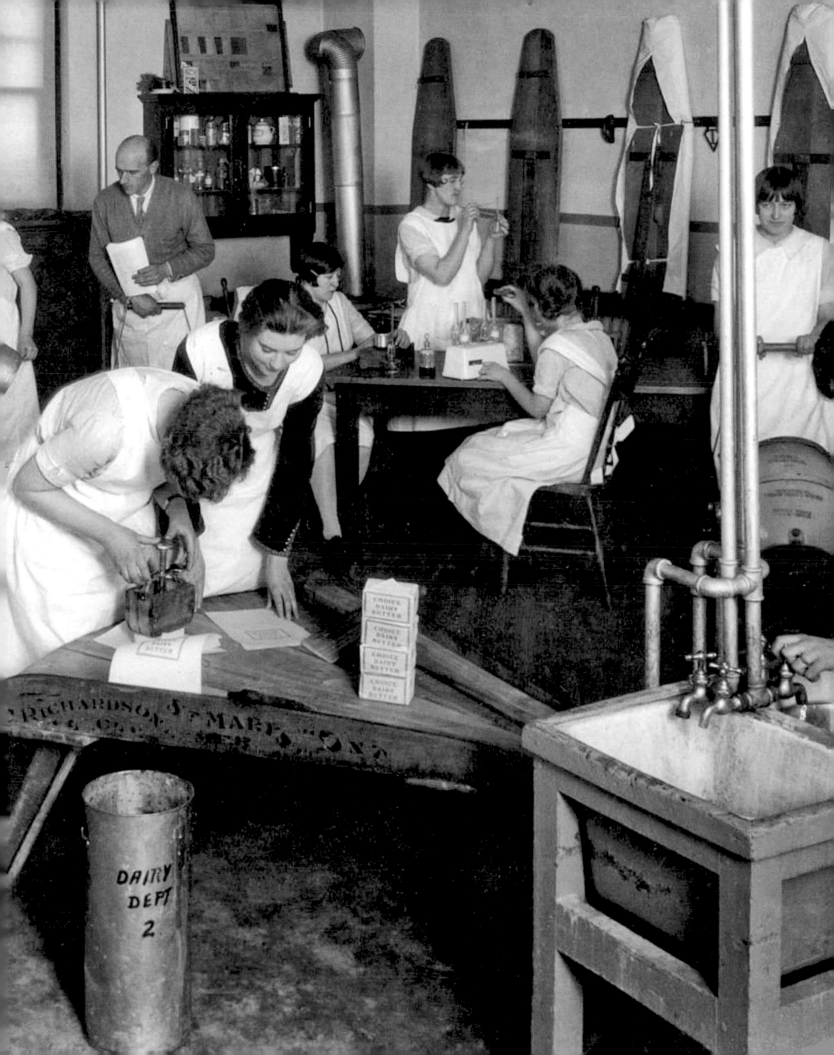

Left: Culinary skills were a central part of the Domestic Science curriculum. In this early photograph, the girls appear to be cooking on kerosene-fueled, one-pot burners, a far cry from their wood-burning cast-iron stoves at home. Above: The 34 students of the 1915 O.S.A. graduating class. Boys outnumbered girls about 2-to-1.

The Great War and Its Aftermath

When Great Britain declared war on Germany in August 1914, Canada, as a Dominion within the British Empire, was at war, too. Albertans signed up to "do their bit" for King and Country at a rate that was among the highest in Canada.

J. Gordon Taggart, Instructor in Science from 1914 to 1918, was one of the first from O.S.A. to enlist in the war effort.

There was great support for the war effort in the Olds district, especially among settlers of British origin, and young men started flocking to the colours almost at once. While the district men volunteered for service with various units, by 1916 it was reported that some 50 had joined the 187th Battalion (Canadian Expeditionary Force), which was also known as the Innisfail Battalion.[12]

O.S.A. students were among the recruits. The first to join were R. Georges-Figarol and Raoul Simon, who left for the trenches of France as soon as the call for troops came. By 1916, 38 students had enlisted, four had been seriously wounded and two had been killed. Arthur "Skipper" Kemp, who would later join O.S.A. as an instructor and achieve a well-deserved reputation as a groundskeeper, was among the 1916 student recruits. One result of this overseas exodus was that the average age of male students at the School dropped to between 17 and 18 years. Before the Armistice was declared in November, 1918, a total of 87 O.S.A. men joined the services. Principal Elliott proudly reported that the figure represented 27.4 per cent of the School's registered men. Twelve were wounded and eleven died in action.[13]

At least one instructor enlisted as well. J. Gordon Taggart, a graduate of the Ontario Agricultural College who had worked as a county agricultural agent in Ontario before joining the Claresholm School of Agriculture faculty in 1913, was Instructor in Science at Olds between 1914 and 1918. His patriotism proved no match, however, for the determination of the Dominion Government to maintain high levels of farm production during the war. Exempted from service so that he might continue to teach agricultural students, Taggart became a favourite at the School. He was known as much for his philosophical discussions with students outside the classroom as for his breath-taking grasp of pure science. In 1919 he would leave Olds to become Principal of the Vermilion School of Agriculture.

The School offered a special class for returning war

veterans who wished to receive agricultural training. Principal

Elliott is third from the left in the front row.

J. Gordon Taggart

Taggart did not stay a teacher. After two years at Vermilion, he was appointed Superintendent of the new Swift Current Experimental Farm. There he contributed much to the understanding of soil erosion, tillage equipment, range management, and forage production. He also perfected his rendition of "Home on the Range." In 1934, he ran for office in Saskatchewan and became the Province's Minister of Agriculture, a post he held until 1944. He then became Food Administrator of the Wartime Prices and Trade Board at Ottawa, Chairman of the Meat Board, and Chairman of the Agricultural Prices Support Board. In 1949 he was appointed federal Deputy Minister of Agriculture and served in that position until retiring in 1959. The University of Saskatchewan awarded him an honorary doctorate of laws in 1956 for his many contributions to agriculture.

The war had another immediate effect upon O.S.A. In 1917, Elliott and his staff initiated a special agricultural course just for veterans of the conflict. The course was created under the terms of the new federal Soldier Settlement Board. The intention was to make practical farmers of returning servicemen so that they might qualify for loans to establish their own farms. The course was ten months in length. Twenty-two veterans enrolled.

Some returning soldiers brought more than a thirst for agricultural knowledge back with them from the front. As the railway cars filled with veterans moved from east to west, incidences of a deadly influenza followed in their wake. Its first symptoms seemed like nothing more than the onset of a bad cold. But the sneezing and coughing quickly changed to sudden weakness, pain and chills. Victims then coughed up blood, their tongues turned brown and dry, their skin took on a bluish cast, their body temperature fell rapidly and many soon died from respiratory system failure. Healthy individuals between the ages of 20 and 40 were most likely to perish. Many of the survivors lived with Parkinson-like tremors for the rest of their lives. Between 1918 and 1920, the Spanish Flu, as this affliction was called, had claimed the lives of some 50,000 Canadians from coast to coast – more than all the Great War battlefield deaths. Worldwide, the death toll was somewhere between 50 and 100 million people.

The epidemic was devastating beyond the loss of life. Quarantine laws restricted mobility, keeping family members apart and disrupting businesses to the point of bankruptcy. Community life broke down as churches, schools and theatres were closed by public order and public gatherings were banned. People donned white cotton facemasks in the hope they might ward off the disease. Some, like Mechanics Instructor George Holeton took up pipe smoking as a germ deterrent; he worked closely with many victims with no ill effects. So many people were sick that labour shortages were experienced everywhere. The loss of parents brought a surge in the ranks of orphans across the country. Doctors, ill equipped to deal with the disease in the era before antibiotics, worked countless hours to the point of exhaustion in their futile effort to save lives from a disease they did not understand.

Olds first felt the impact of the flu in October, 1918, shortly before the School of Agriculture was to open with record attendance. The administration chose to postpone the start of classes for a few weeks, not realizing how serious matters were to become. As the magnitude of the epidemic became clearer, the entire School staff volunteered to help. Soon the Domestic Science staff were using the School kitchen to prepare meals for the invalids, while other instructors used the School automobiles to deliver meals to quarantined farm families within a radius of some 15 to 25 miles.

By the first week in November, the disease was raging throughout the town and the countryside. It became obvious that medical treatment needed to be centralized if it was to be more effective. Because the Main Building of O.S.A. was large and physically separate from the Town of Olds, local health officials commandeered it as a temporary hospital. The Board of Health then asked Dr. H. P. Kenney, Principal Elliott, and Gordon Taggart to direct matters at the School. The staff cooked meals, brought in beds and bedding and medical supplies, and ferried patients to and from the School. Separate wards were established for men, women and children. Public school teachers from throughout the rural district volunteered to nurse the sick. Homemakers from both town and district contributed greatly to this relief effort as well, providing bedding, meal ingredients and their own cooking skills.

The incidence of the disease peaked in the week before Christmas, when 71 patients required care at the School. Seventeen-year-old Gladys French recalled attending a skating party on Cloakey's Lake, about a mile and a half southeast of town, in the weeks before Christmas; almost every skater subsequently came down with the flu. In all, the School of Agriculture treated 144 patients during the winter months.

The seriousness of the flu outbreak caused the Board of Agricultural Education to cancel the 1918-19 School year completely. A well-attended two-week session of short courses was held in February, 1919, but that was the extent of agricultural instruction in Olds during that school year. This was the first and only time that the School did not offer regular classes in its long history.

Two-in-Ones and Third Year Matrics

The curriculum set out by the Board of Agricultural Education proved equal to the needs of students only during the first decade of the Schools' existence.

By the early 1920s, the economic, social and political situation of the Province was changing rapidly. A serious economic recession, which hit farmers particularly hard, followed the Great War. The weather changed for the worse, too, and in several years crop yields dropped markedly. It grew harder and harder to make a good living off the farm. Mature returning veterans competed with green, poorly educated farm kids in a declining job market. While unemployment drove some farm youth to continue their schooling, others were lured away from the countryside by the glitter of new urban recreations such as billiard rooms, bowling alleys and dance halls. Suddenly, the social fabric of rural Alberta seemed tattered and in need of repair.

Understandably, Albertans expressed their concern politically. In 1921, the electors turned their backs on the old-line Liberal and Conservative parties and voted in a provincial government led by the United Farmers of Alberta (UFA). Its strength concentrated in rural ridings, the UFA focused its attention clearly on rural concerns. Those concerns included education. Women's Institutes in particular were lobbying hard for an expansion of secondary education in the countryside, where historically only about two per cent of students finished high school. They wanted better-trained teachers who would be able to prepare students for the uncertain post-war world. They asked for provincially-funded scholarships to help keep rural students in school. And they pushed for an increase in what were called vocational programs that bridged the gap between education and the needs of the job market. Training in scientific agriculture fell into the broad vocational category.

The first clear sign that change was needed at the Schools of Agriculture came during the fall term of 1921-22. Enrolments dropped sharply. At Olds, the total number of students fell from 163 in 1920-21 to just 114 in 1921-22, a decrease of nearly 30 per cent in one year. In light of this and the new climate of fiscal restraint, the UFA administration responded with drastic medicine. Where there had been six Schools by 1920 – at Claresholm, Raymond, Olds, Gleichen, Vermilion and Youngstown – by the start of the 1922-23 term only Olds and Claresholm remained in operation.

In 1921, the Department of Education introduced broad curriculum changes in all secondary schools. These changes included the inauguration of new courses in manual training, domestic science, health and physical education. While the Schools of Agriculture continued to offer their traditional programs in agriculture and home economics, they sought to boost attendance by offering what they called the two-in-one option.

The two-in-one option was intended for rural students who had already graduated from high school. There were not many of them. At O.S.A., prior to 1922, that represented only six per cent of the student population.

Because of the graduates' achievement, they were exempted from taking the customary academic courses at the Schools. Instead, they concentrated solely on their agricultural or home economics courses and were eligible to graduate after a single school term. The option proved increasingly popular until the beginning of the Great Depression.

A second change followed rapidly, as the University of Alberta raised its standards for admission to degree programs, including those in agriculture. The Schools of Agriculture responded by creating what they called a Third Year Matriculation course, designed to provide students with high school standing after they had passed the regular diploma program. This initiative reflected the generally

Attendance at Olds College

School Year	Total Students
1913-14	104
1914-15	119
1915-16	161
1916-17	135
1917-18	145
1918-19	School closed due to Spanish flu epidemic
1919-20	159
1920-21	163
1921-22	114
1922-23	149
1923-24	132
1924-25	191
1925-26	194
1926-27	210
1927-28	274
1928-29	243
1929-30	180

Source: Annual Reports of the Alberta Department of Agriculture.

poor standard of rural educational achievement in the Province, as many mature farm youth had nothing but a few years of formal schooling. In 1922, fully four-fifths of O.S.A. students had never gone beyond primary school.[14]

Six months in length, and offered during the winter months when farm work slowed, the Matriculation course allowed School graduates in agriculture or home economics to matriculate without returning to high school or going to high school at all. School administrators felt that those who enrolled had already proven their intellectual capacity by graduating from the normal program. Moreover, they usually possessed the maturity to apply themselves to their studies.

They were required to take a total of 10 courses in arithmetic, constitutional and ancient history, mathematics, algebra, geometry, composition and English literature, and then write the customary departmental examinations. Until 1933-34, the Third Year students attended classes with the other students; subsequently, they were taught separately. In the early years, these classes were taught by J. J. Loughlin, the English instructor who had been at Olds since 1918, and E. L. Churchill, who possessed a Master's degree in mathematics. The students also received a firm grounding in public speaking, debate and dramatics. Those who passed the course were automatically granted admission to second year

agriculture or home economics at the University of Alberta. Even if Matriculation students chose not to continue at the university level, they unquestionably benefited from these foundation courses.

Those who took the course found it daunting. One 1924-25 student said that it was "very intense," easily demanding 10 hours of studying per day.[15] Even allowing for exaggeration, the statement is probably not far off the mark. *The O.S.A. Magazine* told its readers how easy it was to identify Matriculation students "by their staggering under loads of books, hollow eyes, and pale faces."[16] Another reporter, referring to students named Smith, Downey and Rhodes in 1928-29, noted that, "their chief point of concentration, especially in the afternoon, seems to be the middle of their desk. They solemnly proceed in this task with closed eyes and drawn breaths."[17] Many students found they needed to drop a course or two and then return to take those during the next fall term. Another student claimed that only half "survived its rigors."[18]

Two-in-One Attendance to 1930

School Year	Boys 2-in-1	Girls 2-in-1
1922-23	9	0
1923-24	3	0
1924-25	3	2
1925-26	8	2
1926-27	12	4
1927-28	10	3
1928-29	14	9
1929-30	17	4

Source: O.S.A. News, 1 October 1934

MATRICULATION CLASS..

1925.

1926.

M.Welsh.

C.C.Keller.

L.S.Cooper.

S.Graham.

J.M.Gilchrist.

J.A.Wetmiller.

J.G.McQuarrie.

J.T.T.Parker.

E.G.Tyson.

F.S.Grisdale. B.S.A.~
(Principal)

E.L.Churchill.B.A. M.A.
(Mathematics)

R.E.Stewart.B.A.M.A.
(English)

Provincial School of Agriculture.~
OLDS ALBERTA.~

R.Newcom.

L.W.Bateman.

Cram.William.W.

Holloway.Sydney.

Burgess Photos.

Third Year Matriculation to 1930

School Year	Boys	Girls
1923-24	2	0
1924-25	22	9
1925-26	13	2
1926-27	14	5
1927-28	16	7
1928-29	16	5
1929-30	29	7

The Third Year Matriculation class was introduced to allow regular diploma students to obtain their high school standing.

Opposite Page: E. L. Churchill, Instructor in Mathematics, Third Year Matriculation program. He was later instrumental in setting up the first School library.

Source: O.S.A. News, 1 October 1934

Hoadley's Boys (and Girls)

Although Elliott left the School in 1919 his days of recruiting for Olds were not yet finished. At the request of George Hoadley, the new Minister of Agriculture, Elliott travelled to England in the early 1920s to recruit British boys who wished to learn farming in Canada.[19]

This revived a scheme that had been floated as early as 1913. In that year John Reid, Alberta's Agent General in London, proposed that the Provincial government sponsor the agricultural education of British boys with the thought that they would settle and farm in the Province after their course of studies.[20]

While the start of the Great War quashed Reid's proposal, George Hoadley resuscitated it under the terms of the Empire Settlement Act of 1922. Hoadley, who was born and raised in England, where he trained as a tea taster, had emigrated to Canada in 1890 to become a horse rancher in southern Alberta. Always interested in politics, he ran for office several times before being elected to the Legislature for Okotoks in 1909. He subsequently became leader of the Conservative Party of Alberta, a position he held from 1917 until he was drummed out by his caucus colleagues in 1920. He then switched his allegiance to the United Farmers of Alberta and retained his Okotoks seat in the 1921 election. Herbert Greenfield, the new UFA Premier, appointed the experienced Hoadley as his Minister of Agriculture.

The British government hoped that the Empire Settlement Act, which subsidized the costs of emigration, might alleviate the economic distress and unemployment besetting the country after the Great War. The Province of Alberta, now led by a farmers' government, was so taken with the idea that it agreed to bear more than half of the costs itself. Between 1924 and 1928, Alberta underwrote this scheme to the tune of nearly $68,000, while the British government paid only a little more than $32,000.[21]

The first 64 boys (out of a total of 277) arrived in 1924. They were between the ages of 16 and 23. In exchange for a fee of £50, each was to receive full instruction at the School and a guaranteed position on a local farm for the summer months. While all boys in this first group attended the Vermilion School of Agriculture, those who followed were distributed among Vermilion, Olds and Claresholm. The Olds School is known to have welcomed 21 Hoadley boys in 1925-26 and 16 in 1927-1928.[22]

James Charlton was one of the Olds Hoadley boys.[23] He departed Liverpool on a Canadian Pacific steamship, the *Montrose*, in October of 1925. Upon arrival at Olds, he and his chums were delighted to be fêted by the community at large. Church congregations and other community groups welcomed them with a round of social functions that allowed them to strike up acquaintances immediately. The boys were then billeted with local

families, two to a household, which gave them a further introduction to the ways of Canadian families.

Once in school, Charlton and the other boys received not only their academic lessons but also more basic instruction in how to harness and drive horses, milk cows and feed livestock. As almost all the boys were from English cities, they knew none of these things. Their good-natured antics did, however, provide much amusement for the local students and endless grief for Principal Grisdale, who could find no effective way to reprimand them since he was unable to raise the matter of their misbehaviour with their parents or send them home for breaking school rules.

Above: The Hoadley Boys of 1927, British lads recruited to study scientific agriculture at O.S.A. Few stayed in farming.

SCHOOL OF AGRICULTURE
GLEICHEN, ALBERTA

REPORT OF STUDENT'S FINAL MARKS IN AGRICULTURE,

First 1921-'22 Year

Name...... S. Rodbourne, ...

Address...... Crowfoot, Alta...........

	CREDITS	
SUBJECTS	POSSIBLE	OBTAINED
Animal Husbandry -	300	243
Bacteriology - -	—	—
Botany - - -	100	75
Chemistry - -	200	158
Civics - - -	—	—
Dairying - - -	200	158
English - - -	200	152
Entomology - -	100	79
Farm Book-keeping -	—	—
Farm Management -	100	79
Field Husbandry - -	300	240
Horticulture - -	100	69
Mathematics -	200	148
Mechanics -	300	213
Mechanical Drawing -	—	—
Physics - - -	200	142
Poultry - - -	100	75
Soils - - -	—	—
Veterinary Science -	200	172
Irrigation	100	79
Total - - -	2700	2082

Class Standing Second.... ....

O.S.A. report cards were probably identical to this excellent one from the Gleichen School of Agriculture, 1921-22.

In 1925-26, they put on a special night of entertainment that consisted of a concert, supper and dance. The concert part of the evening included a play on the topic of spiritualism that apparently frightened many in the audience.[24] But without question the highlight of the British boys' involvement with the School came in the winter of 1927 when their production of Dickens's *A Christmas Carol* proved the hit of the season.

In 1929, the Alberta government also tried to recruit 200 young women between the ages of 23 and 33 for its domestic science program. The Olds School hosted nine British girls in two groups during June and July of that year.[25] They spent most of their short stay studying the domestic arts and horticulture. Reportedly, they were baffled by the dampers on Canadian stoves and the treadles on the classroom sewing machines. In addition, they learned the rudiments of household administration, laundry, dairying and poultry. Each also got a crash course in how to drive a left-hand-drive automobile. After four weeks of training, each was placed on a different district farm where she undertook practical training as a "hired girl".

When all was said and done, the urban roots of the Hoadley recruits and their lack of genuine interest in farming showed only too plainly. Although many remained in Alberta, few stayed with farming. Charlton was an exception. He completed his training, spent time with the Brooks Experimental Farm, and eventually served with the Special Areas Board at Hanna. In 1930 the Alberta government, having learned its lesson, wisely discontinued support for the failed Hoadley scheme.

But the happy-go-lucky British boys with little interest in

becoming farmers were the exception at Olds. Between 1913-14 and 1929-30, O.S.A. saw 2,673 students pass through its portals. Seventy per cent were boys and 30 per cent were girls. About one-quarter of the boys went on to higher education,[26] usually at the University of Alberta Faculty of Agriculture, but most stayed on the land, either as farmers or rural extension workers. This was as the School founders had intended.

Writing from the vantage point of 1937, Duncan Marshall felt justifiably proud to claim the Schools of Agriculture as "my first real achievement in a life long desire to bring Agricultural Education within reach of the average girls and boys on farms."[27]

Viewed from the southeast, the well-equipped School farm and its adjacent fields offered the Hoadley boys lessons in practical Canadian farming that few had a desire to learn.

Heart of the District

Education at the Olds School of Agriculture did not stop at the campus fence line. From the opening of the Demonstration Farm in 1911 to the present, extension work in the farming and scientific communities has been part-and-parcel of the School's significant contribution to the wider world.

The Origins of Extension Work

Arthur (Skipper) Kemp, O.S.A. alumnus and Instructor in Biology and Horticulture, turned the campus into a horticultural showpiece that lured thousands of visitors each year.
Courtesy Wallace Kemp

Most of this work, which historically fell to the teaching staff, took place during the summer months when school was out.

As early as 1916, some instructors were expected to work as district agents, fair judges, school fair organizers and lecturers; others were expected to continue their experimental work on plots at the School farm. Principal Elliott, for example, presented lectures on a variety of topics during the summer of 1916 at Olds, Trochu, Bowden and Derbytown.[1] Similarly, the domestic science instructors spent their summers addressing locals of the Alberta Women's Institute (AWI) on everything from more nutritious cooking to handling medical emergencies on the farm. Horticulturalist Art Kemp, on the other hand, spent most of his summers beautifying the grounds and tending the grain, grass, vegetable and tobacco plots immediately north of the campus.

Duncan Marshall insisted on such a collaborative approach to education. This was in keeping with the prevalent belief that betterment of the farm community would only come about through direct exposure to the benefits of scientific agriculture. And to people like Marshall, the word "scientific" implied experimentation. While the Minister stressed that the degree of experimental effort would vary among the Schools of Agriculture, he also voiced his expectation that each would work directly with local farmers to conduct practical farm experiments. In 1914, he was particularly pleased to note the work being done with forage crops:

> *When the ranges are broken up into farms the production of fodder is of paramount importance. No better feed than alfalfa can be grown; but in many localities the growing of alfalfa is still problematical, hence co-operative experiments aiming to ascertain the best methods and conditions for successful alfalfa production represent a splendid means for service by a School of Agriculture.*[2]

So great was interest in these forage trials that three different lumber companies sponsored a competition among the three Schools of Agriculture in 1915 to see which could produce the highest yield of alfalfa seed.[3]

The point of these trials, and of other contemporaneous experiments with potato crops, oats, barley, fruit and grasses, was to "illustrate the very practical manner in which the schools are being conducted."[4] In rural Alberta, talk was cheap; bringing about real change on the farm meant *proving* the advantages of scientific agriculture with results in the field. Marshall knew his audience well.

Marshall himself aided the cause directly each summer when he hosted a Farm Day at Elderslie, his showcase farm northeast of town. Those usually in attendance were staff members from the Faculty of Agriculture at Edmonton, School instructors, constituency supporters, Town dignitaries and good friends. Marshall would have his farmhands erect a huge tent that served as a canvas-

covered banqueting hall, for which his farm supplied the food, and a rain-proof auditorium in which guests could listen to speeches by the experts in attendance on the latest farming trends. Mrs. Marshall and the co-opted Home Economics instructors from the School saw to the preparation of an elaborate luncheon. Inevitably, the special day ended with speeches of appreciation from prominent local citizens and inspection of Marshall's purebred Shorthorns, of which he was justifiably proud. These Farm Days continued annually until Marshall was defeated at the polls in the provincial election of 1921.

Above: Working closely with the national railways, the Department of Agriculture brought education to rural Alberta aboard special Mixed Farming Demonstration Trains. Olds staff like Demonstration Farm Manager Joseph Clements (back row, second from left); Domestic Science Instructor Marjorie Goldie (back row, third from left) and Carpentry Instructor George Holeton (back row, fifth from left), were often among the lecturers.
Courtesy Glenbow Archives NC-4-59

To spread the influence of the Schools throughout the Province, the Department of Agriculture worked closely with the national railways to prepare and tour what was known as the Mixed Farming Demonstration Train. Agricultural colleges on wheels, these trains usually ran in July, offering farmers a brief, entertaining respite from their haying. O. S. Longman, an early Olds Field Husbandry instructor, left a description of the demonstration train from around 1914:

> *The train consisted of about ten cars, about three box cars of livestock, including horses and cattle. Baggage cars from which the interior fixtures had been then removed [sic], and decorated, contained the displays prepared by the Agricultural Schools, the dairy branch, the game branch, the livestock branch and poultry branch. In addition there was a seated passenger car used as a lecture car for the women, plus dining and sleeping car. The train schedule usually, provided for two stops per day, one in the late forenoon and the midafternoon [sic]. The train would be pulled along side of a loading platform, where the livestock could be unloaded and stairways would be lowered from the display cars and the waiting visitors were directed into and through the display cars and the officials in charge would comment on the exhibition and answer questions. Following the examination of the displays, lectures were given to the ladies in the lecture coach and to the men in the open air, on various agricultural and Home Economic subjects, intended to be appropriate to the district in which they were given. The lectures to the men usually began with the livestock which became the center of attention for the visitors. These lectures would be followed by discussions on land cultivation, weed control and allied subjects.[5]*

Demonstration trains were a common sight on railway sidings throughout Western Canada for more than a decade. The partnership worked well. While the Department found them an excellent way to encourage more mixed farming and better farming practices, the railways hoped for increased freight shipments to and from the farm community.

Top right: Canadian Pacific Railway station, Olds, Alberta Courtesy Glenbow Archives NA-1946-2

Below: A metalwork and carpentry exhibit prepared by Agricultural School students for one of the boxcars on the Mixed Farming Demonstration Train.

As Longman noted, the trains also catered to the interests of farm women. Georgina Stiven, who had relieved Principal Elliott of the task of sifting through the first girls' applications at Olds, worked on the train in 1912 and 1913 to establish Women's Institutes locals and to offer domestic science demonstrations and lectures to rural residents. Following Stiven's marriage in 1914, Mary MacIsaac assumed this travelling role as the new Superintendent of the Alberta Women's Institute (AWI). During her six-year tenure, she accomplished a great deal:

> She established short courses in the areas of home
> nursing, child welfare and household science. She added
> two cars to the Mixed Farming Special Train just for the
> use of women: one of these was organized as a nursery
> so that women could concentrate on the lectures and
> demonstrations offered in the other car. She travelled
> the province with the equally enthusiastic and able
> president of AWI, Isobel Noble, organizing as many
> branches as possible. By 1918, their work was finding
> tangible results in 212 branches and approximately
> 8,000 members. In 1919 alone, MacIsaac had arranged
> for 139 short courses and 503 demonstration lectures,
> as well as distributing 30,000 bulletins on home
> Nursing, Sewing, Canning and Child Welfare and food
> cards for infants and small children...[6]

O.S.A. was involved directly in these demonstration trains as early as 1914. The Department of Agriculture asked Olds instructors to make models of barns, blacksmithing tools and other mechanical work; prepare exhibitions of grains and weed seeds; and install household science exhibits that would showcase home nursing, the sewing arts and cooking.[7] Thereafter, this sort of preparation for the summer tour would become a normal part of life at the School.

In the early 1920s the School embraced film technology as another way of reaching out to the farm community. Silent motion pictures, while still an immature medium, were starting to take North America by storm. This was even the case at fall fairs and exhibitions, such as the one in Toronto in 1921, where crowds stood in line to see a film captivatingly entitled Co-operative Marketing of Eggs.[8] The first O.S.A. foray into this means of instruction came in 1920-21, when the Olds school fair judges carried a portable moving picture projector with them as they travelled the fair circuit. They showed both educational and comic films to the school children, many of who had never before seen a moving picture.[9]

The Alberta Department of Agriculture then decided to launch a series of educational films of its own. Beginning in 1923, it either filmed or obtained the distribution rights to more than two dozen 16-mm shorts on farm-related topics. Some of these films were shot at Olds, including one that promoted the Schools of Agriculture themselves.

One example was From Egg to Cooking Pot: Artificial Hatching of Chicks. Beginning rather slowly with a detailed demonstration of the use of an egg incubator, it moved on to feeding, live-action plucking, and then ended dramatically with a shot of the glistening birds turning on a rotisserie.

The district agents were probably glad to take these on their summer tours of the Province, for the films greatly reduced the amount of talking they had to do. As the Department hoped, film proved very popular with Alberta farmers.

OLDS, ALTA.

OLDS

School Fairs and Swine Clubs

When the Department of Agriculture appointed its first district agents in 1916, their role was limited to encouraging an interest in, and appreciation of, farming among rural school children.

The thinking was that this appreciation, when planted in fertile young minds, would be sustained, resulting in more youth staying on the farm and farming better. As Principal E. A. Howes of Vermilion said, "All logical education must begin with the child. Teach the child things agricultural and when he is older he will not depart from them."[11]

The annual fall school fair was the means by which this would be accomplished. Under the provisions of the Agricultural Instruction Act,[12] the generous sum of $8,500 was allocated for this purpose. Responsibility for the work fell to School instructors who acted as district agents during the summer months. The program at Olds began modestly with 22 rural schools taking part in 1916. In 1917 the number tripled.[13] By 1919, Olds instructors were overseeing the organization of fairs at 166 schools in central Alberta.[14] As instructors only went out to those schools that requested their help, it can be seen that the program was a phenomenal success.

The work of the instructors began in April when the O.S.A. school year concluded. During the spring and summer months they travelled through the countryside, providing not only advice but also instructional circulars, mounting materials for plant and insect collections, entry tags, prize lists, seed and a grant of $25 towards the winners of the livestock competitions. Typically, the fairs offered exhibits of garden vegetables, grains, livestock, cooking, canning, sewing, artwork, the manual arts, penmanship, map drawing and plant, insect and weed collections. The instructors served as judges whenever requested by a school. In most cases, the fair was held in October so the instructors could return to Olds before the fall term began at the School.

School fairs were a popular fall event, so popular that the Department of Agriculture created and printed a uniform method for organizing, staging and judging them.

ALBERTA
SCHOOL FAIRS

An Outline of the Plan under which
School Fairs are Conducted, together
with Directions to Local Committees,
Teachers, and Pupils regarding their
respective parts in such Fairs

Prepared by the Provincial Schools
of Agriculture

Issued by Direction of the Hon. Duncan Marshall
Minister of Agriculture

January, 1921

Miss Christine McIntyre, a Domestic Science Instructor at O.S.A. for many years, remembered her participation in the summer of 1921:

When spring came, and the (O.S.A.) students had gone, we began to prepare for school fair work. One of the "jobs" assigned to us was the filling of the paper seed bags to be distributed to various schools in our part of the province. Then one day we started out in the old Ford on our safari armed with the said seeds, Mr. Holeton's red box carrying the rope for the knot instruction and other teaching aids...In spite of delays because of bad roads and all that entails we managed to have a lot of fun through the years.[15]

While many instructors were recruited into service on the school fair circuit over the years, it was George Holeton, more than anyone else, who was responsible for the program's success. He seemed to have the personality for it. A patient, warm and funny man, he managed to make every student, whether in his O.S.A. classroom or in a one-room country school, feel special. When he retired from O.S.A. in 1943-44, his unflagging contribution to organizing and judging at the school fairs was noted above all else.

Above: Each summer O.S.A. staff judged tens of thousands of school fair exhibits across central Alberta and awarded prizes for the most proficient exhibitors.

94

Above: The top male and female exhibitors from each fall school fair received a free week-long course at O.S.A. during the following summer. The course was intended to boost attendance at the School.

The school fairs program at O.S.A. peaked in 1931 with the participation of 35,270 students. Together, they assembled 160,000 exhibits for the judges. While the program continued on a more limited basis after 1931, it did so without funding from the Provincial Government and the services of the Olds School staff. In the midst of economic depression, the government had other priorities.

George Holeton was also in charge of the scholarship short courses held at Olds each July. An annual event that started in 1922, the short courses were offered to two award winners (one boy and one girl) from each rural school that put on fall fairs. The students had to be at least 11 years of age and no two could be from the same family. They were able to attend O.S.A. for a week-long summer course at no cost.

The School administration made no bones about the purpose of the scholarship short course: it was clearly intended to convince both students and parents of the merits of an education at O.S.A.

> *The girls get some instruction in sewing and cooking and are introduced to the grounds and the gardens so that they may have a mental picture of the School and its purpose. The boys get acquainted with the livestock and poultry, and are shown something of the grass, clover and grain crops. They get some practical work in rope work and in carpentry, and take home with them samples of their handicraft.* [16]

The boys were housed in the library and one of the classrooms, while the girls occupied the sewing and dining rooms. All they had to supply was a straw-filled bed-tick on which to sleep. Their busy days consisted of reveille at 6:30 am, physical training at 7, classes from 9 to 4:35, evening games and entertainments, and lights out by 10 pm. No doubt they slept well.

At first, some farm families had to be persuaded to let their youngsters attend. Principal Grisdale reported that

> *Being a new venture and fearing that some parents might have misgivings about sending their boys and girls away from home, a personal visit was made to each home and the scheme was fully explained in detail. After this assurance that the children would be well looked after, they [the parents] were with one exception quite willing for their children to attend.* [17]

To make things easier for the families at a time when both crop yields and commodity prices were low, the Provincial Government paid all related transportation costs. The administration felt the scholarship program was an excellent way of promoting the benefits of the School at a time when these young people were in a receptive frame of mind.[18] Grisdale enthused that those children who attended — more than 100 in number by 1930 — constituted a "band of missionaries for the School Fairs and for the Schools of Agriculture who will assist in no small way the advancement of this work in the province."[19]

In 1916 Principal Elliott created swine raising clubs that became the basis for today's 4-H Clubs. Preparing to show livestock at exhibitions quickly became a popular activity for school children throughout Alberta.

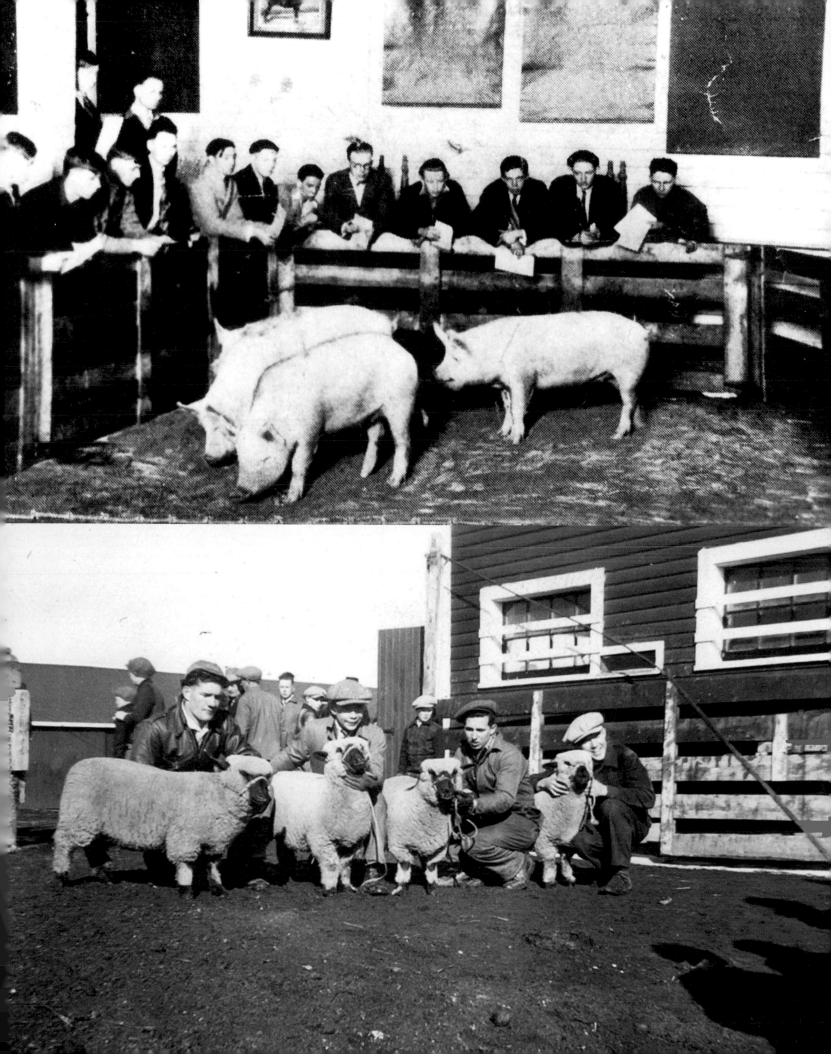

Some who attended the summer program at O.S.A. were likely winners of the annual swine club competition. Started by Principal Elliott in 1916 as part of the Town of Olds school fair program, this proved an exceptionally popular event and quickly spread throughout central Alberta. Hog products were much in demand, in part because of the war, and Elliott embarked on this venture with the clear goal of increasing the quantity and quality of Alberta-raised pork. He started separate clubs for boys and girls.

Each club member was obliged to purchase two registered gilts, one to be sold in the fall and the other to be used as breeding stock. To remove the obstacle of financing, Elliott talked the manager of the local Bank of Commerce into providing each swine club member with a loan. His intention was that the loan would be repaid, with interest at six per cent, in the fall when the club members sold their pigs. In that first year, 24 students signed up. Each purchased either Berkshire or Duroc Jersey gilts. News of this activity spread like wildfire, and in 1917 there were 15 swine clubs in central Alberta with a combined membership of 225. This was the beginning of the 4-H movement in Alberta.[20]

Other boys' and girls' clubs soon proliferated. In 1919, the O.S.A. staff got poultry clubs off the ground by supplying hatching eggs along with detailed instructions for the care of the chicks. Like the swine clubs, these proved very popular. Beef, lamb, dairy, grain, field crop, grass seed, legume, and garden clubs soon followed. Most were established by the district agents in accordance with local requests. By 1926 O.S.A. extension workers had managed to ease the increasing burden on themselves by creating standardized typewritten instructions on topics as diverse as making a dress, milk drinks, poultry culling, beekeeping, laundry, and sheep raising. These were distributed to district school fair organizers.[21]

Left: Near the end of term, as a routine part of their coursework, O.S.A. boys prepared and exhibited everything from iron-working to carpentry. Similarly, the girls showed off their prowess in skills such as dress-making and baking.

Experimental Unions

O.S.A. instructors were not alone in their efforts to take the gospel of scientific agriculture to the wider community. They swiftly found dedicated allies among their school charges.

In the spring of 1914, 40 students banded together under the leadership of R. Georges-Figarol to form what was called an "experimental union" that would extend O.S.A. demonstration farm trials to their home farms during the summer months. The idea was to introduce and test new crop varieties to see which were best suited to the soils and climate of central Alberta. This was very important, as there had been little local field experimentation to that point.

The Union members likely modelled their initiative on The Experimental Union of Canada, the Ontario-based organization of agriculture students and farmers that had conducted joint experiments for years in order to determine the best crops for individual farm locales. Field Husbandry Instructor Frank Grisdale served as the first secretary of the Olds Experimental Union.

In their first year the Union members tackled a great deal with much enthusiasm. They demonstrated how to create one-third acre plots, each dedicated to testing the potential of different strains of barley, oats, alfalfa, grasses, or small fruits. Grisdale travelled about the countryside in the summer of 1914, offering advice about plant breeding, cultural methods, seed selection, potato culture, root seed growing, growing alfalfa for seed, and sheep breeding.[22] While Union membership was initially restricted to O.S.A. students, in the 1930s it was opened up to all farmers with an interest in crop experimentation.

When Grisdale relocated to Vermilion in 1915 to serve as Principal, O. S. Longman assumed these responsibilities, although not with the same degree of success. In fact, with Grisdale's departure, the Union foundered. It did not revive successfully until after Grisdale's return in 1919. In 1922, it was formally reconstituted through affiliation with the O.S.A. Alumni Association. Art Kemp, the Horticultural Instructor who had joined O.S.A. in 1922, became the driving force behind the success it would enjoy during the next two decades or more.[23]

The great accomplishment of the Experimental Union was the establishment of an annual seed fair. The first took place in January of 1922 with the close co-operation of the Pure Seed Branch of the Provincial Field Crops Commission. Fifty contestants vied for the honour of having produced the best seed. In 1923, the University of Alberta donated a trophy to encourage student competition at the seed fair. By then, the concept had spread to the other Schools of Agriculture. Teams competed from Claresholm, Vermilion and Olds, with O.S.A. carrying the day.[24] By 1926, there was a Provincial Seed Fair at which the O.S.A. winners were well represented. In 1926-27 the Experimental Union flirted briefly with

List of Entries to Seed Fair
Held by
The Boy's Experimental Union Jan 4, 1925.

Class 14 - White Potatoes	" Roy Redford, Olds Alta.	?
" 15 - Imp E. Ohio.	Jack Baker, Olds.	?
" 14 - Carters E. Favorite	J. A. Moe, Olds.	
" 13 - N.W. Dent.	R. A. Meeks, Mannville.	
" 13 - Minnesota 13.	Chas. Meeks, Mannville.	
" 13 - " 13.	W. McKenzie Treece, Purple Springs	
" 13 - " 13.	A. E. Treece, Purple Springs.	
" 13 - " 13.	D. W. Treece, Purple Springs.	
" 12 - Squaw	Mrs. A.W. Norris, Castor.	
" 12 - Dakota N. Flint.	W. McKenzie Treece, Purple Springs	
" 12 - Squaw	E. J. Norris, Castor.	
" 12 - Gehu	A.E. Treece Purple Springs	

the idea of introducing a ploughing competition as well.

In the 1923-24 school year, the O.S.A. girls formed their own Experimental Union. While the boys focused on grain production, the girls competed in cake baking, dressmaking, and household efficiency. The instructors were dubious about its chances at first, but they soon came around, saying, "We are now very optimistic about the future [of the Union]. The girls proved there was a place for it with the [alumni] association, by exhibiting many useful articles at the last summer reunion..."[25] Those articles included cakes, bread, candies, cookies and clothing.

By 1930, the Experimental Union had 900 members. Through their efforts, a total of 4,542 sample seed packets were assembled and mailed out to former students and other interested farmers across Alberta. Those samples included wheat, oats, barley, peas, perennial flowers, potatoes, and seeds of various shrubs and trees. In return for the free seeds and planting instructions, members were supposed to submit written reports on their trials at the end of the growing season. Some did; most did not.

An excerpt from the seed fair entry log of the O.S.A. Alumni Association Experimental Union, 1925.

Books for Farmers

By the mid-1920s O.S.A. extension work in the farming districts
of central Alberta had enlarged far beyond its original scope.

In addition to offering advice to individual farmers and presenting numerous lectures to community organizations, O.S.A. instructors judged dozens of school and agricultural fair competitions and ploughing matches, sponsored and organized seed fairs, consulted about Experimental Union test plots and their results, provided free milk testing, distributed blackleg vaccine doses, and inoculated soil with the nitrogen cultures that were all the rage then. These were, quite rightly, practical means of addressing the common farm issues of the day. But in 1925, the Olds School of Agriculture turned its attention to the culture of rural society itself.

It did so through the creation of a lending library. The library was the brainchild of Mr. E. L. Churchill, M. A., who taught mathematics at O.S.A. and sometimes assisted district farmers with their budgeting. Churchill's intention was to assemble a collection of books and periodicals that would stimulate readers intellectually, culturally and spiritually.[26] Its motto would be "Good reading provides good thinking."[27]

He quickly got the students to participate. Together, they approached the Lit Society and the Student Council for support. Both were enthusiastic. They agreed to underwrite the set-up costs and the initial purchase of 156 books. These went into circulation in July, 1925. Other students built much of the furniture, including desks, chairs and bookshelves for the reading room, which was nothing more than space carved out of the north-west corner of the main floor in the Main Building. Other volunteers, both students and instructors, gave their time to the creation of a card catalogue based on the Dewey Decimal System. Then the Alumni Association chipped in, which increased the size of the library to about 1,000 volumes that same summer. Included were works of literature, natural science, philosophy, fine arts, practical arts, fiction, history and sociology books, as well as periodicals, newspapers and agricultural bulletins. There was scarcely any room left on the shelves. Principal Grisdale was impressed and commented that "it already has a

reputation and a prestige that cannot fail to develop it still further."[28]

He was right. The library was an instant success. In fact, so great was interest in it that by early 1926, it was practically self-supporting. In addition to the funds it received from student groups and the Alumni Association, it charged one dollar per year for membership. That modest membership fee entitled off-campus holders of library cards to borrow as many as three books at a time for a one-month period. Library volunteers spent many hours wrapping parcels of books for farm families all over Alberta. They also assembled travelling libraries that they took to rural schools, which typically had few reading books.

External circulation grew apace. What started as the mailing of 46 books per month in the summer of 1925 swiftly turned into the movement of more than 1,000 volumes per month by the following January. Five hundred posters were sent out to postmasters in central Alberta to advertise the service, and soon 10,000 books were being circulated annually. School administrators soon thought it best to formalize the endeavour, and in early 1926 the fledgling library was incorporated under provincial legislation as the Olds School of Agriculture Extensive Library Association. In 1927, it would relocate to a large and well-lighted room in the new students' dormitory. For many years, this remained the only lending library available to the people of Olds, and the Town generously contributed funds for its upkeep and expansion.

The well-stocked O.S.A. library in 1927. In addition to serving the needs of students, it provided reading material to rural families throughout much of Alberta and became the first lending library in the Town of Olds.

"The project," said Grisdale, "is a splendid demonstration of what may be accomplished by co-operation. The work of administration has been carried on by students almost entirely, under the supervision of a staff member of the library committee." Even better, he could report proudly that not a single book had been lost.

If William Elliott established the Olds School of Agriculture on firm academic and moral principles, then it was Frank Sidney Grisdale, whom many respectfully called "Chief", who nurtured it into

Above: Each month School volunteers wrapped and mailed hundreds of parcels to Alberta farm families craving a good book. Left: Frank Grisdale, the second O.S.A. Principal, put the School's extension work and scientific research on a firm footing during his tenure (1919-1930).

maturity as an institution that successfully combined practical education and scientific research.

Quebec-born in 1887, Grisdale was raised near the village of Ste. Marthe, south of the Ottawa River in Vaudreuil County, some 40 miles west of Montreal. He was one of 12 children of A. B. Grisdale and Elizabeth Simpson. As farmers, they supported his decision to leave home to attend the first class of the new Macdonald Agricultural College when it opened in 1907. Grisdale received his Bachelor of Science degree, with a specialization in livestock, in 1911.[29]

Two years later, Grisdale found himself in Western Canada. He had landed the position of Assistant Superintendent of the Dominion Experimental Farm at Lethbridge. There he conducted cultural and crop rotation experiments on both dry and irrigated land. He stayed a year before moving to Edmonton to become associate editor of the *Nor'-West Farmer*, a leading agricultural journal of the day.

Still apparently footloose, Grisdale moved to Olds in 1913 to join the first staff as the instructor in Field Husbandry. In the following year, he married Amy Klein of Olds. Obviously a competent academic and administrator, he was appointed Principal and field husbandry instructor at the Vermilion School of Agriculture in 1915, replacing E. A. Howes, who became Dean of the new Faculty of Agriculture at the University of Alberta. Four years later, however, Grisdale was back at Olds, this time as Principal and as Director of Experimental Work for all six of the Province's Schools of Agriculture. He was 32 years old.

One of the first important changes during Grisdale's tenure was amalgamation of the Demonstration Farm with the School of Agriculture. This was done at all existing Schools, where the two organizations had previously been administered separately, as well as at the three new schools at Raymond, Gleichen and Youngstown. The amalgamation integrated classroom education closely with field experimentation for the first time, thus ensuring a deeper appreciation of applied research among those students who returned to farming after graduation or went on to teach others.

E. S. Hopkins, who was a science instructor at Vermilion, relocated to Olds along with Grisdale in 1919 to oversee the provincial soils investigations that would be based there. Sixteen acres were added to the Olds farm, mainly to facilitate his work. This research focused on crop rotations and water use by different crops. Hopkins's view of the importance of applied research in agriculture probably summed up that of his contemporaries at Olds. "The basis of success in agriculture," he wrote,

> is the success of the individual farmer. The farm must pay. But to make the farm pay many problems must be solved which the farmer alone cannot solve. Scientific study is necessary and this study should include not merely our present problems but what may become problems sometime in the future, so that troubles may be avoided rather than corrected after they have happened.[30]

Although instrumental in setting up soil studies at Olds, Hopkins would soon move to Ottawa to work at the federal Department of Agriculture, where he would thrive and eventually become head of all Dominion Experimental Farms. Art Kemp, the horticulturalist whom Grisdale hired in 1922, took Hopkins's place.

It is not surprising that Grisdale and his staff placed such emphasis on soil studies. Commenting on the farms around Olds in 1915, Alberta's Superintendent of Demonstration Farms noted particularly that few district farms had any system of crop rotation in place.[31] As such, they left themselves open to the depletion of soil nutrients that inevitably followed from the typical pattern of cereal crops in one year and summerfallow in the next. By 1921, the soil experts at Olds were saying that soil depletion was becoming obvious in the district. They were not yet ready to make any pronouncements about the most suitable crop rotation, but told any farmer who would listen that grasses had to be planted in rotation with cereal crops to boost the fibre content of the soil.

To test crop rotation theories, O.S.A. more or less divided the Demonstration Farm into two sections. There was a six-year rotation on the north side of the farm, while the south side was given over to a four-year cycle. They experimented with the timothy hay, a highly successful local crop that gave Olds its earlier name of Hay City; brome grass; western rye; and meadow fescue.[32] Grisdale felt this was some of the most important work being done at O.S.A. As early as 1925 he was able to say that,

Art Kemp took to his assignment at the Demonstration Farm like a fish to water. Believing that O.S.A. could make its mark with its rotation studies, he imported grasses, clovers and alfalfas from Sweden, England, Scotland, the United States and Eastern Canada, and planted them side-by-side with locally grown varieties so that visitors could readily appreciate the differences.

Because the Olds district had limited experience with cereal crops before the Great War, Kemp also brought in new varieties like Garnet and Reward and planted them next to the popular Marquis and other strains. He did the same with oats and barley, although he left their cultivation to Pete Erickson, a 1924 Third Year Matriculation graduate who had a keen interest in experimental work.

Top left: Colourful perennial borders like this, another example of Art Kemp's skill, enticed many farm women to plant more elaborate flower gardens in their own yards. Kemp never tired of telling them, "It isn't a home until it is planted."

Above: Agricultural test plots bordered the north and east sides of the campus, especially after 1920. These experiments contributed to the understanding of local soil conditions and allowed farmers to see the comparative viability of crops for themselves.

107

Not content to stop there, Kemp field-tested peas, vetches, millets, flax, lentils, green feed mixtures and silage crops. He sowed more than 50 varieties of corn, root crops, potatoes and sunflowers. Everywhere you looked, there were carefully maintained rows of tomatoes and pumpkins and marrow and melons and squash. He even planted a variety of tobacco plants. He was nothing if not enthusiastic.

Kemp spent as much, if not more, time on the campus landscaping. Coming as he did from the south of England, he thought the prairies barren and much in need of beautification. "When we view some of the homes in Alberta," he said, "our heart fairly sinks at the sight of desolation — not a tree nor a shrub, no flowers nor fruits to make the home a real home."[34] Realizing that farmers needed to wrest a living from the land before they concerned themselves with beautification of their yards, Kemp decided to convert the Olds campus into an inspiring floral showcase. Beginning in July of 1925, he supervised the laying out and planting of numerous beds in which he planted sweet-smelling roses, showy perennials by the score and more than 6,000 annuals, mostly asters. He bordered these beds and the campus roadways with a variety of trees and shrubs. Near each type of planting, he placed little sticks identifying the species. For the first time, the School's yard was a riot of colour and a treat for the senses each summer. This was Art Kemp's quietly practical way of teaching by example.

By the mid-1920s, O.S.A. had more than 2,000 experimental plots in use. Half were devoted to crop rotations, the others to cultivation of various crops. The volume of this experimental field work, claimed Grisdale, dwarfed the research by the University of Alberta Faculty of Agriculture or the Dominion Experimental Farms throughout the Province. O.S.A. field-tested cereals, grasses, forage crops, root vegetables, potatoes, flowers and shrubs. New varieties were obtained from Europe and across North America to see how they might fare in central Alberta, while standard varieties were culled annually to maintain purity and high yields. Grisdale instituted a policy of giving out seeds and seedlings to anyone who wanted them as a way of maintaining pure varieties of high-yielding strains. Every year O.S.A. shipped out as many as 20,000 small fruit plants and thousands of four-pound bags of potatoes and cereal crops.

"It isn't a home until it is planted."

Former students of Arthur Kemp vividly recall his injunction "Now don't forget this!", as he good-naturedly hammered home a point about the importance of horticulture in creating more attractive farmsteads. Arthur, whom his colleagues called Skipper, was born the son of a railway plate-layer in Droitwich, Worcestershire, England, in 1889. He worked as a gardener on several large British estates, including the Royal Gardens at Windsor, before emigrating to Canada at the age of 22. In 1914 he enrolled at O.S.A. On the day before his graduation in 1916, he enlisted in the 195th Battalion and was soon sent to northern France. There he was hit by shrapnel and given up for dead. According to Principal Frank Grisdale, who knew him well, Kemp suffered from these wounds for the rest of his life. While convalescing in England, Kemp studied agriculture at Edinburgh University. Returning to Canada, he enrolled at the University of Alberta and received his Bachelor of Science in Agriculture in 1922. He immediately joined the O.S.A. as Instructor in Biology and Horticulture, became a champion of the Alumni Association and the Experimental Union, and made his mark by overseeing the experimental plots on the Demonstration Farm and laying out and caring for the campus grounds. According to Isobel Townsend, who was active in the Farm Women's Week held annually at O.S.A., Kemp "knew every flower, shrub and tree by its first name, family name, and Latin name." Ill health forced Kemp to give up his teaching position in 1947. To lessen his burden but allow him to keep working, the Deputy Minister of Agriculture created the position of Assistant District Agriculturalist for Kemp. He died in March of 1948 at the age of 58. Today, his contribution is marked by an Alumni Association plaque in his honour and the Art Kemp Memorial Garden. But, as Grisdale said, "The grounds today are his memorial."

Another example of Art Kemp's work. Note the markers near each bed that identified the different flowers.

Soil rotation and crop cultivation work was only one part of the new O.S.A. research mandate. The Demonstration Farms attached to the Schools of Agriculture had always been intended to stand as classic examples of the principles of mixed farming. This meant an equal emphasis on cereal crop production and livestock. As the Superintendent of the farms said,

The farms will all be operated on the mixed farming principle — dairying, hog-raising, sheep-raising, poultry farming, as well as the raising of horses, and the feeding of beef cattle will be carried on at the farms. Accurate records will be kept so that not only the students but farmers throughout the province can get first-hand information as to actual results along different lines of agriculture in the province. These farms will naturally become live-stock centres, and the breeding of good live-stock will be carried on at each farm, so that the young stock of different breeds and of pure breeding can be offered for sale to farmers at reasonable prices. The keeping of good live-stock on these farms will also stimulate the live-stock industry in that locality, and in this way very materially assist the development of agriculture in the province.[35]

The Farm was stocked with purebred cattle as early as 1912. Holsteins were the preferred dairy cattle, although Guernseys and Ayrshires would come later. By 1915, there were 45 Holsteins at the Farm, one-third of them purebred. Shorthorns (Duncan Marshall's favourite breed) made up most of the beef stock. The manager and his hands undertook steer feeding experiments and sold breeding stock to district farmers "with an eye to not disrupting the existing business of local breeders."[36] They also showed cattle each year at the Edmonton and Calgary summer fairs.

The School, meanwhile, supervised a dairy competition on behalf of the Department of Agriculture, which offered prizes to the winners. Its purpose was to assist farmers in determining the best milk producers in their herds so the rest might be culled. The 1914 competition was a bona fide hit: 35 local farmers entered 266 cows. O.S.A. also hosted a dairy convention during its first school year.

In 1915, the farm acquired a small flock of grade Shrop-shires. These sheep did quite well, grazing on oats and rapeseed pastures in summer and eating prairie and tame hay, straw, roots and whole oats in the winter months.

Horse breeding did not take place at Olds until after Grisdale became Principal. By 1923, the farm had 13 purebred Clydesdale mares and two purebred geldings. The choice of Clydesdales reflected the conventional belief that this was the breed most suited to the diversity of farm work on the prairies.[37] The breed was also a favourite of Marshall's.[38] As almost all work on the farm was done by horsepower, these animals were treated as ordinary draught horses, working from about 7 am to 6 pm with one hour in the barn around noon. Percherons would become more common in the late 1920s.

In the teens and early 1920s poultry production was on the rise in Alberta, growing by some two million birds in just 10 years, so it was not surprising that O.S.A. invested in a flock. In 1920 the School purchased 500 chickens "to teach men and women by practical experience, the importance of poultry keeping on the farm and also to make it possible for farmers in the district to procure purebred egg record birds for stock purposes, day old chickens or eggs for hatching."[39] Morley (Mal) Malyon, a Guelph Agricultural School graduate who joined O.S.A. as Instructor in Mathematics and English in 1920, assumed management of the poultry plant and all instruction about chicken-related matters. He soon became well-known in town as owner of Malmur Marathons, offering brooder chicks for sale. During the 1929-30 school year, a 20-by-60-foot poultry house was built to care for a flock of some 300 Barred Rocks.

Top left: Out for a spin on a winter's day in 1920. Although up-to-date farm equipment like these tractors was common on the Demonstration Farm, students seldom operated them outside of the October-March school year. Opposite below: Holsteins, popular in the Olds district, were the preferred dairy breed on the Demonstration Farm.

111

Top left: Flocks of sheep, first raised on the Demonstration Farm in 1915, were integral to teaching practical lessons about livestock management on campus. Left: Judging the comparative merits of Percheron colts. This photograph, from 1943-44, captured the final days of horsepower on the farm. Horses would not regain a position of importance at the School for nearly another half century. Above: Beginning in 1920, O.S.A. offered instruction in the care and raising of poultry. Chickens and turkeys were considered important elements of a proper mixed farming operation. Following Spread: Raymond Ure with a team of Percherons when he served as a student assistant on the Demonstration Farm. While Clydesdales proved popular at first, by the late 1920s Pecherons had more or less displaced them as the breed of choice on the farm.

Morley (Mal) Malyon, B.S.A.

Truly a jack-of-all-trades, and an enthusiastic one at that, Mal Malyon taught at O.S.A. for 34 years. Born at Saintfield, Ontario, in 1892, he enrolled at the Guelph Agricultural College in 1914 only to have his studies interrupted by two years of overseas service with the 1st Canadian Tank Battalion. After the war, he finished his degree and moved west to work with the Soldier Settlement Board that assisted veterans in becoming farmers. In 1920, Malyon joined O.S.A. as Instructor in Mathematics and English. Almost immediately, he also became responsible for teaching dairying and poultry, which he later said were his favourite subjects. He carried out summer extension work in these areas, as well as in pest control methods and Junior 4-H. He also served for years as an athletics coach at O.S.A., most notably with the girls' basketball team. A fun-loving man well liked by students, Malyon was perhaps best remembered for insisting that each of his dairy classes finish their year by making ice cream for everyone on campus. He mentioned this in a free-verse poem he wrote for the O.S.A. Golden Jubilee in 1963:

Looking back over the years it gives me great pleasure to recall: those who excelled — those who did not; those I expelled — those I locked out. Those who bounced me in football, tripped me in hockey, but couldn't outshoot me in basketball. Those who stole hens, swiped butter, ate lbs of cheese, and quarts of ice-cream, but couldn't kill or dress a chicken.

Those who entertained me at Lits; taught me to dance; knew I was Santa Claus; but never what part of Pa Holeton's reindeer. Those who were Hoadley Boys —those who were Veterans and those who came far from overseas places. Those who appreciated my classes, thought I was witty, asked my advice and forthwith forgot it. Those who drop in, on me and my Gal, to Staff and Alumni who still call me sincerely: "Mal"

In 1921 Malyon became the first O.S.A. staff member to address the important issue of pest control in the district. It had been a terrible year on the farm as it was. Commodity prices were low, retail prices and freight rates were high, the banks were restricting lending, and there were crop failures in many districts. Adding to these troubles was yet another invasion of grasshoppers, the third in as many years. At its peak, the plague of insects affected nearly 300,000 square miles in the Province. In June and July of 1921, Malyon drove throughout central Alberta, talking to farmers about how to mix and distribute poison baits that would control the pests. O.S.A. would undertake similar educational work during the scourge of the 1930s.

This grasshopper tour was only the latest in a long line of fieldwork that O.S.A. instructors undertook to increase the productivity of district farms. Weed control, for example, was a perennial topic of interest. Not only did every O.S.A. agricultural student receive instruction in the identification of weeds and weed seeds, but the School was an early leader in scientific research on herbicides. While the first Canadian trials of copper or iron sulphate, and of diluted sulphuric acid, had begun in 1899, it was not until 1911 that the Alberta Department of Agriculture began experiments with the application of iron and copper sulphates. Those experiments, done at the Olds Demonstration Farm, proved very expensive and not very effective.[40] Other trials, about which little is known, were conducted at Olds throughout the 1920s. When the Provincial Government hosted a major conference at Edmonton on the eradication of weeds in 1929, Olds School of Agriculture instructors were well represented. The most important early work in this area would come in the 1940s, when O.S.A. was on the forefront of research into the agricultural benefits of 2,4-D.

Enjoying a stroll along Art Kemp's beautiful flowerbeds behind the Main Building. The photograph probably dates from around 1948, when many buildings on campus received their first coat of stucco.

Hub of the District

The Olds School of Agriculture adroitly bridged the gap between the rarefied atmosphere of a post-secondary educational institution and the practical, everyday needs and concerns of the farming community.

The summer extension work of the instructors was the key to making this work. With their visits and their lectures, O.S.A. extension workers showed local farmers how they might benefit directly from the work being done at the School. As a result, O.S.A. became an indispensable part of the wider rural community.

In 1916-17 the Department of Agriculture began offering reduced fares on special excursion trains to farm families with an interest in seeing the Schools of Agriculture for themselves.[41] Thus began the annual Field Day at O.S.A., involving tours of the School and adjacent test plots, demonstrations and lectures. The overworked Domestic Science instructors provided a picnic lunch. These trips occurred in August before harvest began in earnest and while the School grounds and experimental plots were still at their finest.

The response to these excursions, as well as to other overtures made by the School and the Department, was tremendous. Often more than 500 people turned out for the one-day event. Principal Elliott and his colleagues were overjoyed. "It is very gratifying to see how the farmers of the district are visiting the schools and experimental plots during the summer," wrote H. A. Craig, the Superintendent of Demonstration Farms.

"From the very fact that more and more visitors are looking over the school and experimental work, we are led to believe that the school shares the confidence of the farmers of the Olds district."[42]

Craig was right. This was no fluke. Farmers from the Olds district and beyond were genuinely interested in the work of the School and the lessons they might derive from it. In a given year, some 4,500 visitors came to learn about the School and its practical experiments. The same degree of interest could be seen in the increasingly voluminous correspondence handled by Elliott and his secretary. In 1914, for example, the Principal responded to 3,184 letters. During the next half dozen years, he wrote back to nearly 2,700 people annually. As the letters dealt with every aspect of farming, he felt like he was offering an agricultural course by correspondence.[43]

Local farm organizations accepted the School quickly and whole-heartedly as well, seeing it as a welcome addition to the community. This happened, in part, because the Main Building was a rare, large structure with an Assembly Hall that could accommodate large gatherings of people. In 1914, for example, provincial weed inspectors and dairy producers from across Alberta met at O.S.A. In 1915, the first provincial convention of

the Alberta Women's Institutes was held at Olds. The Municipal Council and the United Farmers of Alberta met regularly at the School as well. Similar events and conferences were held at Vermilion and Claresholm around this time as well, causing H. A. Craig to remark that the schools "are now seen as the logical place to pursue such interests."[44] As the grounds of the campus were enhanced with flowers and shrubs under Art Kemp's watchful eye, organized picnics became common at the School during the summer months. In 1928, Grisdale estimated that 5,000 visitors had come to O.S.A. just to see the experimental plots, the farm and the beautified grounds.[45] The perennial borders were a favourite of the visitors.

A summertime tour of the gardens and orchards of the School. This tour was likely led by Art Kemp (in white shirt with back to the camera), who quickly became a favourite at the Farm Women's Week that was held at the School for more than 50 years.

That O.S.A. enjoyed the admiration of the farm community did not escape the notice of farm-related businesses and industries. Beginning in 1915, P. Burns & Co., the well-known meat-packing firm, donated $100 annually to the School to be awarded as four $25 scholarships to deserving first- and second-year students in agriculture and home economics. Others soon joined in: Swift Canadian, the Western Retail Lumbermen's Association, the Hayward Lumber Company, and the Atlas Lumber Company. By the mid-1920s O.S.A. was able to offer additional scholarships sponsored by the City of Edmonton (dairy prize) and the United Grain Growers (first year Domestic Science award), as well as smaller prizes for excellence in the meal-serving competition, for lingerie and millinery work, and for proficiency in stock judging. When the students

launched a publication called the *O.S.A. Magazine*, advertisements poured in from companies as diverse as Massey-Harris, International Harvester, T. Eaton and Co., line elevator companies, a jewelry store, a clothing store and a creamery. Clearly there were many business owners who felt it paid to be associated with the work of O.S.A.

In no small measure, the growing stature of O.S.A. was attributable to Frank Grisdale. Widely regarded as a born leader of men, he was a sincere and passionate advocate

As the School undertook more rural extension work in the 1920s, the campus began to attract thousands of farm visitors each summer. This 1928 photo shows the attendees at a British Settlers' picnic held on the grounds.

of the School and its contribution to the farming community. He had a knack for drawing out the best in his staff and students; they, in turn, offered him their support and friendship.[46]

As it turned out, Grisdale needed that backing late in 1927 when he was threatened with dismissal from the post of Principal on the advice of Premier John Brownlee's UFA Cabinet.[47] H. A. Craig, then Deputy Minister of Agriculture, turned up unexpectedly in Grisdale's office to tell him that he had 24 hours to resign or be fired. Theodore Moe, the O.S.A. janitor, stood quietly outside the closed office door while Craig put the ultimatum to Grisdale, and then quickly spread the news all over town.[48] The ostensible cause of Grisdale's dismissal was his personal involvement in the sale of registered Garnet wheat seed, which he had introduced into Alberta two years earlier.

Upon learning about the threat from Edmonton, Grisdale's colleagues and friends begged him not to resign. They then mounted an offensive of their own. The O.S.A. staff sent a telegram to Premier Brownlee to protest the dismissal, saying they supported Grisdale unequivocally. The O.S.A. Alumni Association did the same. Then a number of local men, led by Esper Espersen, who was particularly influential in the local Danish community, took the night train to Edmonton and demanded to see George Hoadley, the Minister of Agriculture. When Hoadley tried to defend the government's position, saying that O.S.A. would run just fine without Grisdale, the six foot, 200-pound Espersen shook his fist in Hoadley's face and said "Mr. Hoadley, we can do without you, too." The argument must have been effective, for Grisdale kept his position.

The Omnipresent Mr. Moe

Theodore Moe, whom Principal Elliott called his "pride and despair," served as O.S.A. janitor from 1913 to 1934. As he was also in charge of the School's steam boiler, many students jokingly claimed that he lived in the basement of the Main Building, venturing out only to clean rooms or trim the grass. Famous for both his temper and his Norwegian accent, Moe became no less of an institution than the School itself during his long reign in the boiler room. In fact, he was such a presence in the daily lives of staff and students that one graduate chose to honour him with a poem, entitled "The Omnipresent Mr. Moe".

Theodore Moe. O melodious name!
Is a long-suffering janitor of O.S.A. fame,
With 'vell, vell, by golly,' and 'vell, vell, allright,'
He seeks to impress a respect for his might.
Like a little tin god, he rules o'er the roost,
Till sometimes we long to give him a boost.
With shufflings and mumblings he appears to obey
The thousands of jobs that await him each day.
With 'Moe, fix the pressure,' and 'Moe, fix the light,'
His conflict of duties is a terrible sight.
With downstairs needing coal,
*   and upstairs wanting water,*
He says things that seem to make the air hotter.
But when Moe's feeling good—by golly, he's fine.
So three cheers for Theo, to fill in this line.

Traditions in the Making

Penhold native Frank Stevenett, who enrolled in the first
class at O.S.A. in 1913 and graduated two years later,
once remarked that, "a history could be written of the
celebrations on the top floor of the main building."[1]

4

Beyond the Classroom

In that spacious and well-lit Assembly Hall, students of every class between 1913 and 1927 danced to the school orchestra, put on skits, held musical recitals, listened to visiting lecturers, wrestled on floor mats, and received their diplomas each spring. Briefly, during the 1917-18 year, the Hall was converted into a temporary boys' dormitory when it proved impossible to find sufficient lodgings to rent in town. Until the first dormitory was constructed in 1927, the Assembly Hall was the indoor heart of the campus recreation. As Stevenett said, "Many of the graduates tell us that the social life at the O.S.A. was a most important part of the course, particularly in the formative years of the school."

This was exactly what Principal Elliott intended. He was as much concerned with the social and moral development of his students as he was with their intellectual growth. And in an era when most students remained on campus throughout the school year, with the possible exception of travelling home for a few days during the Christmas break, it was imperative that they keep busy in their off-hours. As a man of strong values, Elliott was convinced that idle hands are indeed the devil's workshop. He and his small band of instructors guided and shaped the lives of their charges inside the classroom and out.

As a result, disciplinary problems were few and far between in the early decades of the School. Elliott was proud of the students. Writing in 1914, he said, "We think that a word should be offered regarding the splendid discipline that was found among the students. During the two years [1913-14] not one serious case of discipline came before the principal."[2] When the customary orderliness did break down, the failure typically came after the Christmas break. In 1925, Principal Grisdale reported that during the first few weeks of the new term "many students let things slide" and "indulged in a good time generally." He remained confident, nonetheless, that this lapse of self-discipline would not be repeated.

The students acquired valuable social skills in the bargain, skills that would serve them well in life. As Morley Malyon observed, "You only had to see the difference in some cases of students arriving as freshmen and leaving as graduates. The girls improved in dress and deportment. The boys attained self confidence and an ability to take part in social affairs."[3]

Despite the demanding nature of the agricultural and home economics courses at O.S.A., the students also fit a host of leisure activities into their schedules. Many of these regular social events quickly became School customs that have endured to this day. As one student wrote as early as 1923, "The school has now reached the stage where traditions begin to gather about it."[4]

Above: The top-floor Assembly Hall of the Main Building was the social hub of the campus prior to 1927.

Left: The senior Domestic Science girls (1923-24) modelling their graduation gowns, which they designed and sewed themselves.

Customs of the Campus

Participation in social activities was not voluntary at O.S.A. Students had some say in the matter, of course, depending on their innate talents and their interests, but all were expected to take part in group activities of some kind.

In 1914-15, for example, all students were required to attend the functions of what was variously called the Literary Society or the Literary Committee. In later years, students usually referred to it as the Lit Society or Lit Committee. This group, run by about a half dozen students in any given year, organized events that usually spanned about an hour every Friday evening. Its activities might include singing, recitations and readings, instrumental performances, impromptu speeches, theatrical plays, orchestral performances or debates.

Plays, in particular, were always very popular, and several might be mounted in a given school year under the watchful direction of a staff member. The efforts of the actors seem to have been greatly appreciated by the other students. At the conclusion of a production of *The Dressing Gown*, in 1916-17, the lead performers received "a beautiful and costly bouquet of cabbage leaves, onion tops and tulips."[5]

Instructional staff were often involved directly in these theatrical productions. In 1925, for example, Animal Husbandry Instructor C. A. Weir inspired the students to put on a two-act play entitled *Mr. Bob*, and Art Kemp volunteered to serve as stage manager. This case of mistaken identity played to a packed Assembly Hall. The key role of the law clerk was played admirably by new Science Instructor Charlie Yauch, who "gave much opportunity for displays of nervousness, disgust and dignity, all of which Mr. Yauch carried off to the satisfaction of everyone." In later years, Yauch would act in the somewhat bigger role of Principal of O.S.A.

Members of the Literary Committee holding an event planning meeting in the Assembly Hall in 1920.

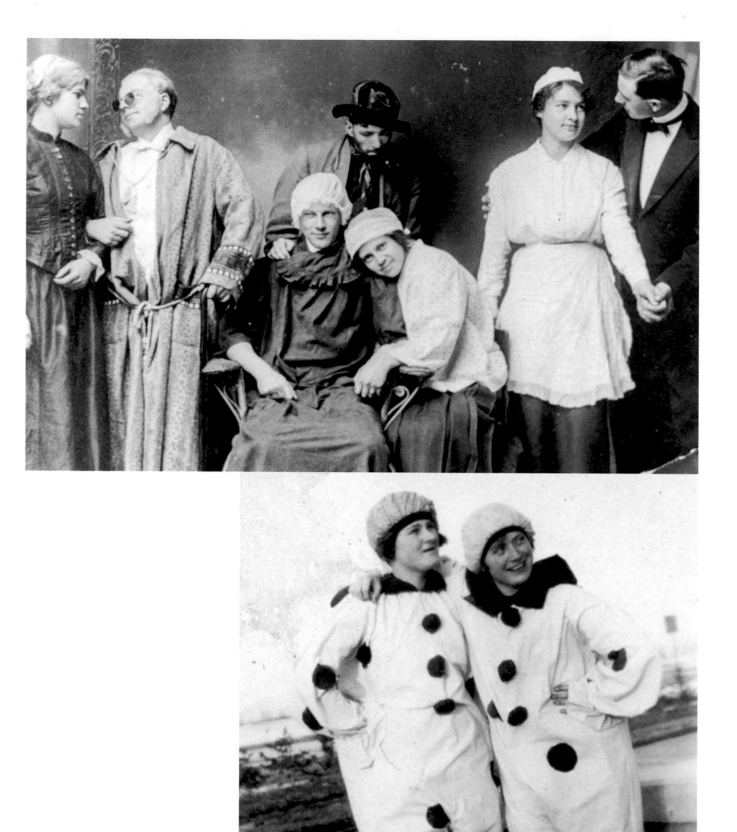

Debate was popular from the beginning. In 1914-15, O.S.A. entered 23 contestants in the regional High School Debating League, handily defeating both Olds High School and Red Deer High School before going up against the previous year's champions from Camrose. By 1921, the intercollegiate debate between teams from Claresholm and Olds was said to be the biggest literary event of the year. The debate judge gave the victory to Olds. In the next year this competition heated up as students from the Schools of Agriculture vied for a debating shield. In 1922, the O.S.A. teams (negative and affirmative) both proved victorious with their spirited arguments around the resolution, Be It Resolved that the Natural Resources of Alberta be Owned and Controlled Within the Province, a hot topic of the day.

Principal Elliott brought in outside speakers as well, such as Nellie McClung, the well-known novelist, women's rights advocate and temperance crusader, and Irene Parlby, who had helped to found the first women's local of the United Farmers of Alberta and later served as the first female Cabinet minister in Alberta.[8] With inspirational speakers like these, another O.S.A. tradition began.

One observer noted that in addition to "amusing us and letting us appreciate music...participation in the Committee frees us from that self-consciousness in public speaking that keeps many a capable man in his seat at a meeting."[6] That was exactly the outcome that Elliott and his staff were seeking as they tried to boost the self-confidence of the students so their leadership qualities might shine through. Not everyone took such a positive view. One young woman complained that, "life is not all pleasure, and we find ourselves on committees, which others claim are good training, but which we find exceedingly hard work."[7]

Although music was never a required subject at O.S.A., it filled many hours in the evenings and on the weekends. Individuals blessed with golden vocal cords or the ability to play an instrument frequently entertained their classmates. Following a debating event in February of 1921, for example, Jessie Redig performed on the violin and Elsie Harding sang for the audience. Sing-songs around the piano or a campfire were common, too.

The School had an orchestra from the beginning. In fact, it furnished the music at the first graduation exercises in

Above: The 1929 inter-class debate champions of the School. O.S.A. students also frequently debated regional high school teams. Left: O.S.A. was seldom without a school orchestra or two. The 1923 photograph shows the Olds Brass Band, featuring a slightly maniacal piano player.
Courtesy Glenbow Archives
ND-3-2210

April, 1915. George Holeton, Instructor in Farm Mechanics and clarinet and saxophone player extraordinaire, had taken the lead in organizing it. In addition to his instruments, the ensemble included violins, a lute, cornet, trombone, drums and a piano. Principal Elliott often contributed his horn playing to the group as well. Holeton wanted to encourage students with musical talent, as well as enliven School functions, but he also made it clear that his little band was available for town functions, too, and at a rate considerably lower than what was normally charged by local orchestras. Naturally enough, the make-up of the orchestra changed as students and staff came and went over the years, but there always seemed to be an instructor with an interest in leading a School band. When O.S.A. Physical and Musical Director Stanford Espedal was in charge in 1929-30, the band acquired its first formal name, the Aggie Collegians Orchestra.[9]

And then there were the dances! Eagerly anticipated by some and equally dreaded by others, School dances took place throughout the year. In the first years of the School, the second-year students usually hosted the freshmen at a dance very early in the term, with the freshman returning the favour a couple of weeks later. But almost any event justified a dance. In 1922-23, in addition to the first-term class dances, there was a Christmas tree dance, an alumni dance, a St. Valentine's Day dance, and a memorial dance. And in 1928-29, the customary second-year and first-year dances were followed by a hard-time dance, an Athletic Committee dance, a Junior UFA dance, a leap year dance and a Social Committee dance.

The girls always looked forward to the leap year dances when, for a change, it was the boys who had to line up and wait patiently to be chosen. On occasion, the boys,

perhaps laying claim to a moral rectitude on which they had only a slippery hold, insisted that their leap year partners escort them home after the dance.[10]

In the late 1920s, the students also danced to the music of the Brunswick Panatrope, a sensational new invention that used vacuum tubes and electricity to amplify the sound of phonograph records. Bill Swift, a Dean of Men who went on to become Alberta's Deputy Minister of Education, thought it was a "marvel of music" when he first heard it at an O.S.A. gymnasium dance in 1928-29.[11]

The sections of an O.S.A. orchestra changed annually to match the abilities of the students in attendance. This 1926-27 group featured the talents of (left to right): J. Niznic, A. Mark, H. Gervais, E. Evans, M. Craddock, G. Ferguson, W. Limpert, L. Loades, F. Loades, George Holeton, C. Doan, Marguerite Eikerman and Margaret Meyer. Courtesy Glenbow Archives PA-3496-15

Inevitably, youthful infatuation showed itself early in the fall term as 50 or 60 boys met 20 or 30 girls for the first time at close quarters. When this happened during a dance, it had the potential to disrupt the entire event. In 1915, "owing to the irresistible charms of some of the O.S.A. girls," enough members of the School orchestra deserted their posts that replacement musicians had to be recruited from the town.[12] More than one romance was sparked at a school dance, leaving many alumni to recall wistfully how unwelcome moonlight could be when a young couple was trying to evade the finger-wagging dance chaperones by hiding in the shadows. The chaperones, for their part, felt they had an obligation to preserve the virtue of the young women in their care; that had, in fact, been a condition laid down by many parents before they would allow their daughters to attend O.S.A. It is no wonder Principal Elliott focused so much of his attention on finding good homes in which the girls could board while at School.

Christmas, coming as it did near the middle of the term, was always one of the most eagerly anticipated occasions of the year. The students decorated the Assembly Hall in the Main Building with spruce branches, boughs tied with red ribbons, and a giant Christmas tree decorated with lights and 15-cent presents that the students contributed. They sang Yuletide carols until Santa arrived to distribute the presents, oranges, candies, popcorn and nuts, and then cleared the room for a dance. Even Santa got a present sometimes, but, as one student remembered, "he could not eat it on account of his whiskers interfering, although everyone enjoyed the fragrance of that lovely onion sandwich."[13] On at least one occasion, the students gathered up the unwrapped presents and donated them to a home for orphans in Calgary "to cheer and brighten the lives of some little tots who needed them more than we."[14]

If this roster of events were not enough to keep the students occupied, they had many others to choose from. Before 1930 O.S.A. also boasted a choral society, a Young Men's Christian Association (Y.M.C.A.), theatrical troupes, a weekly student newspaper called *The Scandalizer*, a Tuxis Square (similar to the Boy Scouts), a Students Christian Society Committee, a Mock Parliament, a Glee Club, and a campus local of the United Farmers of Alberta. Less formally, they regularly enjoyed skating and sleighing parties, sausage roasts over a campfire at Cloakey's Lake, "thimble teas" put on by the Principal's wife, and silent picture shows on the School's own Pathescope.

Top left: An undated photograph of another O.S.A. orchestra, again with George Holeton on clarinet. Great hats! Bottom left: A rare shot of Santa (probably George Holeton) arriving with his Oxford-shoed reindeer for the annual O.S.A. Christmas party.

Previous Spread: The students pose in their costumes in the streamer-filled Assembly Hall before the start of the Masquerade Ball, 1917.

Sports and School Spirit

Sports were popular from the start as well. As the fall term did not begin until November, it is not surprising that hockey was the sport of choice.

By early February, O.S.A. students were challenging the Olds High School team on the town rink. In the fall of 1915-16, the returning students took matters into their own hands and erected the first hockey rink on campus by borrowing a team of horses from the Demonstration Farm in exchange for agreeing to stook a 25-acre field of grain. Working with a grader and shovels, they levelled a piece of ground and then put up the boards. It was during the same fall that two steelworkers erected the water tower to provide the campus with fire protection. When the water tower was completed just before Christmas, the boys were able to flood their rink. It was used by both the boys' and the girls' hockey teams, as well as for general skating three nights a week.

A great regional rivalry soon developed. During the winter of 1914-15, for example, the O.S.A. hockey team not only played the Olds High School team but also rode the rails to play at Red Deer, Didsbury, and Claresholm. For a new team, they acquitted themselves well. Their schedule looked like this:

O.S.A. Hockey Team Schedule		
Dec 21	O.S.A. vs Olds High School	O.S.A. wins 8-4
Jan 18	O.S.A. vs Red Deer Rovers	Tied 3-3
Jan 20	O.S.A. vs Didsbury	Didsbury wins 3-0
Jan 28	O.S.A. vs Didsbury	O.S.A. wins 7-0
Feb 3	O.S.A. vs Didsbury	Tied 1-1
Feb 6	O.S.A. vs Claresholm	O.S.A. wins 7-2
Feb 8	O.S.A. vs Didsbury	O.S.A. wins 5-2
Feb 10	O.S.A. vs Red Deer Rovers	O.S.A. wins 8-5
Feb 12	O.S.A. vs Claresholm	O.S.A. wins 6-3

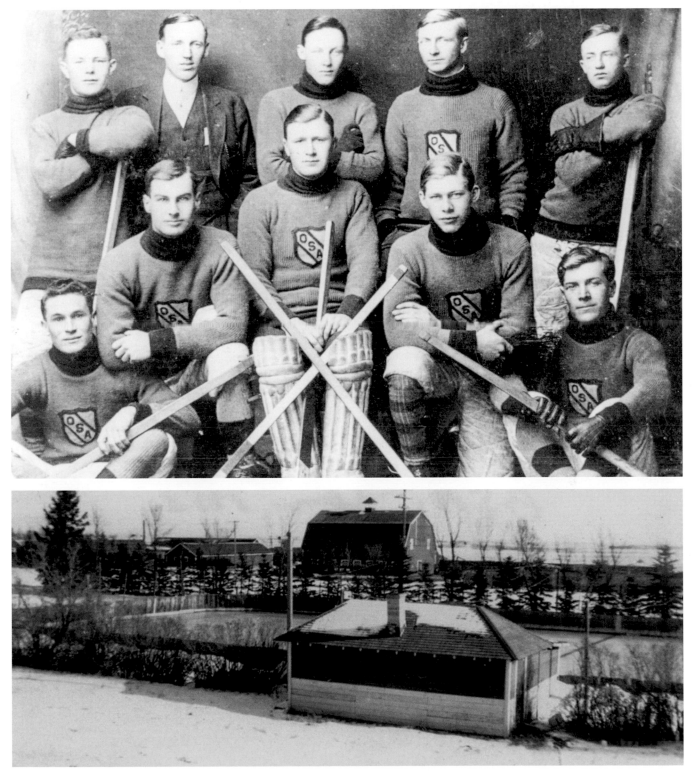

Top: The O.S.A. boys' hockey team rode the rails several times during the winter to play their rivals in Red Deer, Didsbury and Claresholm.

Bottom: The O.S.A. hockey rink, where so many hard-fought games were played over the years, was situated immediately east of the 1927 dormitory.

Top left: The 1913-14 O.S.A. girls' hockey team took to the ice in long skirts. Below: The 1928 O.S.A. rugby team. Top right: The 1929 girls' basketball team. Bottom right: Playing volleyball in the gymnasium that was part of the 1927 dormitory. This photo was taken in 1929.

140

Within just a few years, O.S.A. soccer, baseball, hockey and basketball teams were taking part in an active inter-collegiate league that pitted them against their peers at Claresholm and Vermilion and, for a brief time after 1922, at the new Schools at Gleichen and Raymond.

One of the most memorable early hockey games took place just before Christmas in 1926. To celebrate the re-modelling of the hockey rink, which saw it grow 20 feet longer and 10 feet wider, the "Flappers" challenged the "Ladies" to a game. The Flappers were members of the boys' hockey team, specially outfitted for the occasion in skirts and jazz garters. Flappers were allowed the use of only one hand while on the ice, resulting in a game of remarkably "brilliant shooting" that created "so many close calls and breathless moments that the spectators were chewing at the wood on the fence."[15] Despite their numerous handicaps, the Flappers won 5-3.

The fact that the O.S.A. students had little time to practise their skills together did nothing to dampen their enthusiasm for athletic contests. In fact, every fall term started with an athletic field day, usually in October. And each school year seemed to add a new sport or two to the roster. Throughout the teens and the 1920s, basketball, rugby, soccer, volleyball, badminton, curling, boxing, wrestling, gymnastics and baseball all vied for the attention of students.

Principal Elliott encouraged this, for he was a great advocate of sports as a way of building character and School spirit. Soon school yells were being written to cheer on the home team, and budding reporters were celebrating School victories with lines like these: "In two brilliant games against the townies, the girls' basket-ball team, covered themselves with mud and glory, by piling up umpteen to nought against the representatives of the burg."

An O.S.A. Yell

Chow, Chow, Catsup, hot and cold —
Bommeranga, Boomeranga, Blue and Gold —
Razoo, Bazoo, Zip, Boom, Bam —
Agriculture, Horticulture, Mathematexam,
Alpha, Gamma, Agricolayea,
O. S. — O. S. — O. S. A.

As early as 1914-15, School athletes were sporting blue and gold uniforms, while spectators waved pennants emblazoned with "O.S.A." By 1921, the students had formed an Athletic Association to oversee inter-class participation in sports and monitor playing schedules.

School staff frequently joined the students for impromptu sporting contests as well. In all likelihood, this was partly a result of their comparative youth (most were still in their twenties or early thirties) and partly a consequence of them having been raised in the golden era of "manly sports." The term, in common usage around the turn of the century when many of the instructors attended school, referred to the unquestioned ability of sports to turn boys into the right sort of men, men who were strong, courageous, co-operative and morally upstanding. It was also related to the notion of efficiency then in vogue. If the boys stayed in good shape through exercise, they would be better able to handle the physical demands of farming. Greater efficiency meant greater productivity. Stanford Espedal, the Physical and Musical Director of O.S.A., was still lecturing the boys on this topic as late as 1929.[16]

An O.S.A. Hockey Poem, 1924-25

Leo Halstead is our goalie,
And is of great renown,
The way he stops the puck
Is the wonder of the town.

Bill Cross is a lady chaser
He chases the rubber too,
The way he bores through their defence
Is a wonder to me and you.

Neilsen is our centre
And has a wicked shot,

He always plays very well
And gives the best he's got.

Patriquin is a hockey player
And a regular jazz hound,
He always plays a little com,
And shoots on the rebound.

McDermid is our star defence,
And checks with skill and force,
Many of our goals,
Are traced to his source.

Kirkwold is Mac's chief aid,
He has a wicked check,
He plays with great consistency,
And does their forwards get.

And so here's to our hockey team,
They've licked several local teams brown,
We hope the future O.S.A. boys,
Will uphold their renown.

Documenting Their Doings

If students captured O.S.A.'s sporting triumphs in enthusiastic doggerel a little too often, they redeemed themselves by adopting an attitude of remarkable maturity and restraint in their contributions to School newspapers and magazines.

The first of these — *The O.S.A. Magazine* – came out in March, 1914, at the conclusion of the 1913-14 school year. The next year's issue, renamed *The A.S.A. Magazine*, included stories and student information from all three Schools, although O.S.A. took the lead and did most of the work. Duncan Marshall's *Gazette* press printed the magazine. Thanks to the sale of advertisements — probably handled by *Gazette* staff rather than O.S.A. — the three Schools were able to print 1,550 copies. These were mailed directly to the families of students and other interested individuals. By 1916, the circulation had risen to 2,000 copies. *The Magazine* continued as a joint venture of the three Schools of Agriculture through 1918.

The Magazine was the School's first yearbook. It was more appropriate to call it a magazine, however, for it not only included the usual tongue-in-cheek comments about students but also many serious articles written by School staff and Department of Agriculture personnel. Representatives of the Dominion Experimental Farms sometimes provided articles as well. Duncan Marshall contributed the lead piece as long as he remained Minister of Agriculture. In it, he never failed to extol the virtues of a scientific agricultural education. Readers could also browse articles like Claresholm Principal W. J. Stephen's "The Farming Profession," Miss E. Cumings's "Housekeeping: A Profession," and A. E. Qually's "The Small Tractor." Students might report on the success of the School teams, reflect on the value of their O.S.A. education, or relate the more notable events of the school year. While the A.S.A. magazines were dense with text, a handful of photographs were included in each annual issue along with advertisements for everything from tailoring shops to the Calgary Exhibition and Stampede.

The table of contents for the first O.S.A. yearbook, published as *The O.S.A. Magazine* in March of 1914.

144

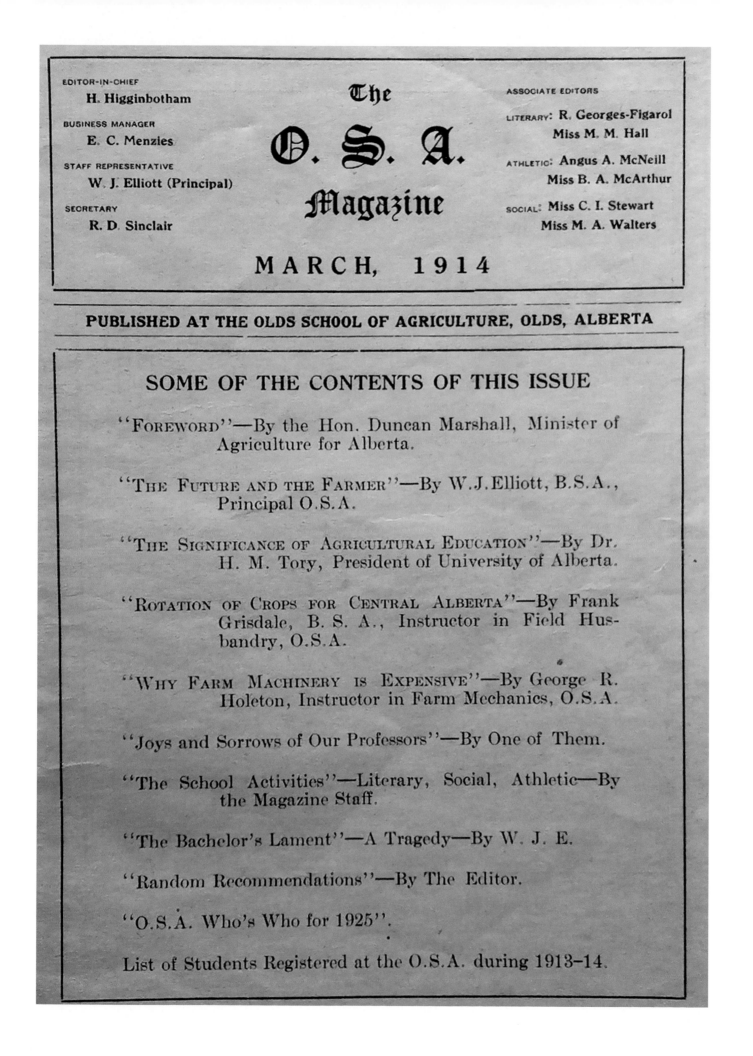

EDITOR-IN-CHIEF
H. Higginbotham

BUSINESS MANAGER
E. C. Menzies

STAFF REPRESENTATIVE
W. J. Elliott (Principal)

SECRETARY
R. D. Sinclair

The O. S. A. Magazine

ASSOCIATE EDITORS

LITERARY: **R. Georges-Figarol**
Miss M. M. Hall

ATHLETIC: **Angus A. McNeill**
Miss B. A. McArthur

SOCIAL: **Miss C. I. Stewart**
Miss M. A. Walters

MARCH, 1914

PUBLISHED AT THE OLDS SCHOOL OF AGRICULTURE, OLDS, ALBERTA

SOME OF THE CONTENTS OF THIS ISSUE

"FOREWORD"—By the Hon. Duncan Marshall, Minister of Agriculture for Alberta.

"THE FUTURE AND THE FARMER"—By W. J. Elliott, B.S.A., Principal O.S.A.

"THE SIGNIFICANCE OF AGRICULTURAL EDUCATION"—By Dr. H. M. Tory, President of University of Alberta.

"ROTATION OF CROPS FOR CENTRAL ALBERTA"—By Frank Grisdale, B. S. A., Instructor in Field Husbandry, O.S.A.

"WHY FARM MACHINERY IS EXPENSIVE"—By George R. Holeton, Instructor in Farm Mechanics, O.S.A.

"Joys and Sorrows of Our Professors"—By One of Them.

"The School Activities"—Literary, Social, Athletic—By the Magazine Staff.

"The Bachelor's Lament"—A Tragedy—By W. J. E.

"Random Recommendations"—By The Editor.

"O.S.A. Who's Who for 1925".

List of Students Registered at the O.S.A. during 1913-14.

Sometimes, the magazine gave considerable space to student musings. In 1917, for example, former student Arnold Baker wrote a piece he called "The Value of My Agricultural Training." It read, in part,

To pick out the steer that will make a good feeder, to doctor a lame horse, to cut rafters, or to sharpen ploughshares. Such things appeal most to the average farmer who generally has somewhat of a lurking contempt for 'book farming'. This same despised 'book farming,' however, has a tremendously practical value when you come to the point. To work out a 'balanced ration' for your stock, which shall be at once most economical and most nourishing, to plan a crop rotation in which one crop restores to the soil the constituents upon which a previous crop has drawn. What could be more practical?

And then there was Earna Roedler, who graduated from the agricultural program in 1918, perhaps the first woman to do so at O.S.A. She took the course because she believed it was very important for a woman to understand all facets of farm life, including blacksmithing. Not only did the knowledge come in handy when a small repair needed to be done or a sick calf needed tending, she wrote, but "unless both husband and wife understand and know their business, they cannot succeed." She added, for good measure, that the boys "were princes...The West makes such boys and any parents may safely send their daughters to study with them."[17]

Publication of the magazine seems to have lapsed for a year following the Spanish flu outbreak of 1918-19. When it returned during the following school year, it was reincarnated as *The O.S.A. Magazine*. Co-ordinating the editorial work among the three schools had proved unworkable. The new magazine, which was usually kept to fewer than 50 pages in the early years, was a handsome dark blue or grey soft cover publication, roughly nine inches square, that featured the O.S.A. crest on the cover and the motto "Opportunity, Service, Advancement" beneath. It would continue to be known as *O.S.A. Magazine* until the 1936-37 year, when it was renamed *Echoes*.

While the elaborate *O.S.A. Magazine* was the "official" School publication, the students put out several less formal publications of their own. The chief purpose behind all of these was, as one student put it, to "record the deeds and misdeeds, the comings and goings, the behavior and misbehavior of the students down the years."[18]

We can't be certain when the first student newspaper was published, but as early as 1917-18 there was a so-called weekly with *The Scandalizer* on its masthead. It was edited by Wilbur Ray Wood, "whenever he has an inspiration, which is generally about once or twice a month."[19] It contained various sections, such as Society Notes, Wit and Humor, Obituary, Police Court News, Poet's Corner, and Dippy Doughty's Diary.

During the following school year — 1918-19 — the first issue of *The Chinook* appeared. Reading the latest news provided everyone with a great deal of entertainment. Unlike *The Scandalizer*, this was truly a weekly paper. Editing *The Chinook* fell to each class in turn, which must have made it easier to get each issue out on time. In the 1940s it went to a biweekly publishing schedule. It seemed to have been published continuously until at least 1967.

The O.S.A. Magazine staff, 1915-16, hard at work under the
watchful eye of Principal Elliott. Art Kemp, who was then a student
at O.S.A., is standing at the extreme left.

Clearness of Vision and Loftiness of Purpose

Not only did O.S.A. students participate in a wide range of organized activities, they also organized themselves. Their most important and enduring creation was the Alumni Association.

Launched at an O.S.A. class reunion in December, 1917, the Alumni Association declared its purpose to be the promotion of agriculture in Alberta through the exchange of knowledge and views among alumni of the School. Its members hoped to bolster the farming sector by encouraging enrolment at O.S.A., supporting faculty members and speaking out about the need for education in agriculture and home economics at all levels of schooling. Membership was open to anyone who had attended the initial short course prior to the School opening formally in 1913, had attended for at least one full winter session, or was currently serving in the armed forces. An annual membership fee of 25 cents was levied. Bob Sinclair, Class of '15, served as the first President.

Little is known about the first years of the Alumni Association, although a reunion did take place annually. The Association's most important work between 1917 and 1921 may well have been its steadfast support for the Experimental Union that encouraged the use of superior seed and plantings throughout the Province. Unfortunately Frank Grisdale, the moving force behind the Experimental Union, relocated to Vermilion in 1915, leaving that organization rudderless. With Grisdale's return as Principal of Olds in 1919, the bond between the Alumni Association and the Experimental Union was not only renewed but greatly strengthened.

In 1920, Bill Jacobson, the incoming Alumni Association President, decided to launch a regular newsletter for the membership. Called the *O.S.A. Newsletter*, this periodical was to be published on the first day of each month. Jacobson thought it best to send all O.S.A. alumni the first three issues without cost before limiting its distribution to paid-up members of the Alumni Association.[20] By March of 1921, the cost of membership had risen to one dollar per year for full members (alumni who had graduated) and fifty cents for associate members (those who had attended without graduating). The first newsletter, a one-page affair that was printed in Calgary, went out to 771 alumni.[21] Jacobson invited all readers to submit news about their own activities or about events that might be of interest to other alumni.

Even at this early date, a basic format for yearly alumni get-togethers emerged. The reunion was held in winter, usually in January. Those in attendance (some 200 in 1922) would listen to a round of speeches by distinguished guests such as the Minister of Agriculture, Principals from the other Schools of Agriculture, representatives of the Faculty of Agriculture at the University of Alberta, and regional Members of the Legislative Assembly. A banquet would follow in the large classroom of the Domestic Science department, and a dance in the Assembly Hall would conclude the day's events. In 1923, the Association chose to organize a second annual meeting, this time in the form of a one-and-a-half day picnic event during the third week of July. The organizers felt this presented a better opportunity for thorough discussion of rural issues and offered visitors more time to inspect the School and its experimental plots.[22]

Arthur Kemp, elected President of the Alumni Association in 1923, was the driving force behind many of these changes. Almost from the date of his engagement as Instructor in Horticulture in 1922, "Skipper" became known as "Mr. Alumni." He was forever chasing down graduates in order to sign them up as Association members. And although he held the presidency for only one year, he remained intimately involved in Alumni matters from 1923 until his death in 1948. From 1924 to 1937, he served as secretary-treasurer of the organization.

To Kemp, participation in the Alumni Association was an act of responsible citizenship. "The individual members," he wrote,

> have each enjoyed the advantages which arise from education. They have caught a glimpse of the ideals held by those who directed that education. They have broadened their viewpoint on many things by contact with others from varied walks of life. And in acquiring their education they have fallen heir to a responsibility – the responsibility of paying back in some form or other, the debt incurred by others in making that education possible.[23]

As participants in Canada's great agricultural industry, members of the Alumni Association had an obligation to seek better approaches to farming and a higher standard of homemaking. Kemp believed that the Association reunions generated fresh ideas and renewed enthusiasm for the pursuit of a better rural life. With the alumni lay the responsibility for ensuring a "clearness of vision and a loftiness of purpose" in addressing the important rural issues of the day.

In 1922, the Alumni Association thought something needed to be done to honour those O.S.A. students who had died while serving with the armed forces during the Great War. Communities everywhere were erecting cenotaphs and other symbols of remembrance, and the Alumni Association was "assailed from within by the question of whether or not we have done our part in preserving from oblivion the record of our fellows...The outstanding fact is that they and we at one time wore the blue and gold."[24]

The initial goal of the Association was to raise funds sufficient to construct a "Memorial Gymnasium Hall" on the School grounds.[25] The promoters of this idea quickly realized that they would never be able to solicit contributions equal to the cost of construction, so they changed tack. Instead of a gymnasium, they focused on the more realistic purchase of a memorial clock, to be accompanied by a bronze slab engraved with the names of the war dead. The cost of this was $350. Most of the needed funds came from the operation of a snack booth at Alumni dances.[26] Principal Grisdale unveiled the memorial at a public ceremony on July 15th, 1926, during the summertime reunion, while George Holeton played *The Last Post*.

> *Surely if these men were inspired to give up all, there will be a constant succession of the youth of this Province who will pass through these halls and who will also be inspired by the glorious example here dedicated, to give a fuller measure of their energies and life's opportunities to the advancement of the aims for which men died. Then our humble offering in the erection of this memorial will not have been in vain and the inscription remind us by our actions that Their Names Liveth For Evermore.*

It fell to Art Kemp to reflect on the ceremony and memorialize the fallen men in *The O.S.A. Magazine* that year. He wrote:

The annual reunions, with occasional special events like the dedication of the memorial clock and the establishment of scholarships, brought and kept O.S.A. graduates together "as one big family."[27] In fact, by 1926-27 the Association was able to report its best year ever and declare that it had the most active members in the Province. The newsletter, now sporting the shorter name, *O.S.A. News*, had doubled in size and was being received by more than 7,000 former students. The Experimental Union was responsible for the most successful annual seed fair in the Province. The Association's latest cause, development of the Extension Library, was proving a tremendous success with the wider rural community. In July of 1927, close to 400 alumni would attend the summer reunion.

The first annual summer reunion, which the School hosted in 1923, was organized by the Alumni Association. It was a well-attended affair and would grow in popularity over the years.

The Fallen, 1914-1918

W. A. Bicknell	Horace Gallagher
John Hutchinson	Robert Lougheed
Arthur McAllister	John McRae
Jack Peckham	J. Doan Quantz
William Rogers	Alvin Seymour
Raoul Simon	

The Alumni Association Poem

If you think your Alumni is best,
Tell 'em so.
If you'd have it lead all the rest,
Help it grow.

If you're used to giving knocks,
Change your style;
Throw bouquets instead of rocks,
For a while.

When a member from afar,
Comes along,
Tell him who and what you are,
Make it strong.

When there's anything to do,
Let the others count on you;
You'll feel good when it is through,
Don't you know.

Let the other fellow roast,
Shun him as you would a ghost,
Meet his banter with a boast,
And a smile.

Never flatter, never bluff.
Tell the truth, for that's enough.
Be a booster, that's the stuff;
Don't just belong.

The Crisis in Accommodation

The growth of the Alumni Association during the 1920s reflected the fact that O.S.A. was a tremendous success. It had not only succeeded as an educational institution, but also had begun to create a genuine sense of community among its graduates.

They, in turn, became enthusiastic promoters of the School and everything it had to offer. With this kind of support, the School was soon bursting at the seams.

It was never easy to find accommodation for students. That much is clear from Principal Elliott's plaintive call to the townspeople for billets in 1913. But as the size of the student population grew, the housing problem grew along with it. While 104 youth attended O.S.A. in 1913-14, by 1924-25 that figure had nearly doubled to 191.

Housing became a particularly vexing problem because of the increasing presence of young women at the School. Fifty-nine were attending by the 1924-25 school year, compared to 39 in 1913-14. While the figure does not seem very high, it was practically impossible to secure appropriate lodgings for both them and the boys in town. The girls and boys were, in essence, competing for the few available rooms. As if that were not enough of a challenge, parents continued to express misgivings about the level of supervision of their daughters at the School.

Throughout the early 1920s, the School administration responded in a makeshift manner. It did so by supplementing private, in-town lodgings through its own operation of three nearby houses (Craig House, Farm Dorm, and Hall House) and through conversion of the former Demonstration Farm manager's house into a fourth School-operated dormitory for women.

The best known of the private dormitories was the Brown house. Located at 4809 – 49 Avenue, facing the railway tracks near the creamery, this residence was constructed by a well-known Olds storekeeper and milliner, Mrs. Brown, in about 1903. "Brownie," as her female charges knew her, took great pride in running a boarding house for respectable young women. Gentlemen might call, but at 10 pm sharp a curfew bell rung loudly and they were instructed to leave without delay. It is believed that O.S.A. girls continued to board with Brownie until 1925, when the house was converted into a private residence.

Life in the four School-run women's dormitories was regimented. Each house was supervised by a female staff member, usually referred to as the "house mother." Dorothy Houston, who came to Olds in 1922 to teach Domestic Science and later married Art Kemp, was one of them. The house mothers enforced study hours and allowed boys to visit only on Sundays. They also distributed housekeeping duties among the girls who usually took turns with the cleaning and the cooking. If a girl was working for her board because money was tight at home, she might do extra chores around the house. Regardless of where they were billeted, the girls all ate their meals in

the large Craig House.[28] They said grace before each meal. Dorothy Raham, who attended O.S.A. from 1923 to 1925, recalled that,

Saturday's supper was baked beans and Boston brown bread. Sunday's supper of sandwiches, cake and tea, was served around the living room fireplace followed by a singsong at the piano, then evening church.[29]

Toilet facilities were located either in the attic or the basement. According to Lottie Leader (Class of '25), "It was a long trip to the attic in an emergency." A male student,

working for his board, would come over every morning to empty the honey bucket before the girls arose. The same lad often hauled in fresh water for washing and cooking. Baths were scheduled once each week. Between 1918 and 1921 the Alumni Association operated one dormitory at a monthly charge to students of $20. By 1924, as Inger Hale recalled, the cost of such accommodation had risen to $23.[30]

This 1921 snapshot shows female students on the steps of one of the crowded girls' dormitories operated by the School before 1927.

153

The Student's 23rd Psalm

The Professor is my Shepherd, and I am in dire need. He preventeth me from lying down in the bed which I owneth. He leadeth me to distraction with his exam questions.

He shaketh my senses to get a College Degree. He leadeth me to make a fool of myself before my class-mates.

Yea, though I burn my light until my landlady complains, I fear much evil for he is against me.

His threatenings frighten the wits from me, he assigneth me extra work as a punishment in the presence of mine enemies.

He anointeth my paper with low pencil marks, and my errors fill a whole column. Surely work, worry, and exams, will follow me all the days of my college life, and I will dwell in a boarding house for ever.

Ironically, the administration succeeded in addressing the growing need for female accommodation while failing to do the same for the rapidly rising number of young men coming to School. In 1925, Principal Grisdale said that it had been "very difficult" to house all the students for the previous three years. Moreover, the School now lacked classroom, laboratory and dining space sufficient to meet the enrolment numbers.

Fed up with the lack of a government response to his repeated requests for help, Grisdale struck his own committee to find a solution. After soliciting the advice of colleagues and students, his committee submitted a detailed plan to the Provincial Government for a large, three-storey, E-shaped brick-and-stucco veneer structure that would include men's and women's dormitories (95 and 75 spaces, respectively) with toilet facilities, a combined auditorium and gymnasium (42' x 72'), a library (44' x 54'), two classrooms (each 40' x 36'), four staff offices, and a dining hall (70' x 36') with associated kitchen. Two of the three floors also had small sitting rooms where the students could meet and mingle. Perhaps to calm parental concerns, the committee stressed that, "Each of the residences and the main section of the building will be distinctly separate units in that they will each have their own entrance and the only means of communication [between boys and girls] will be through the dining room."[31] Or so they hoped.

This offensive did the trick. In late May, Grisdale was able to meet with representatives of the Department of Public Works to select the site for the new dormitory. They staked out a large open area south of the existing campus buildings, about 100 feet from the Principal's residence, and made plans for a six-foot cement sidewalk that would connect the dormitory to the existing Main Building with its classrooms. Once the new building was ready, the old Assembly Hall would be converted into two new classrooms, ensuring that there would be lots of foot traffic between the Main Building and the new dormitory.

Construction tenders were soon issued and building began during the first week of June. On July 27, George Hoadley, the Minister of Agriculture, came from Edmonton to lay the dormitory cornerstone during the summer reunion.

Some 300-400 Alumni Association members listened to him speak. The cornerstone contained Canadian 60th Jubilee anniversary and other stamps, a 2,000-word survey of the School's history, the membership card of the first life member of the Alumni Association and a copy of the Jubilee issue of the *O.S.A. News*.[32]

The cost of the dormitory, when all was said and done, ran to $164,130 for construction and another $32,000 for furnishings.[33] Some small portion of this was covered by grants applied to the costs of the library and gymna-

sium. Because construction ran longer than anticipated, the 1927-28 school year was delayed until November 15th. The official opening of the dormitory occurred on January 4th, 1928.

The spacious new dormitory under construction in the summer of 1927. The view is to the southwest.

Learning the Game of Life

The opening of the dormitory to students in January of 1928 was a watershed event on campus, one that would influence the lives of O.S.A. students for the next 40 years.

With remarkable insight, the Student Council called 1927-28 "the year of greatest change in the history of O.S.A.", and singled out the new dormitory's true value as the opportunities "it offers to learn the game of life."[34]

The comments were astute, for life studies would always trump academic studies in the dorm. Those lessons began with the accommodations themselves.

In comparison with many of the farm houses in which O.S.A. youth were raised, the dormitory offered a lick of luxury. The building was heated by steam radiators, and so long as Theo Moe was manning the boiler room, shivering in bed on a cold winter's night was a thing of the past. Showers and tub baths with hot water lay just down the hall. Communal laundry facilities were provided. There was electrical lighting throughout the building, and students even enjoyed the shared use of a telephone.

True, the student rooms were small, but each had two single beds with proper mattresses (from Simmons®), dressers, a clothes closet, a combination study table and book shelf, and armchairs.[35] The large windows let in plenty of light, and many students revelled in the fact that they now had (at least temporarily) a sunny room they could call their own. All of this, and three square meals a day, was available for $30 a month.

The dormitory, shown here in the late 1950s, was home-away-

from-home for thousands of O.S.A. students over four decades.

Accommodating the students in one building meant that the administration could monitor their behaviour as never before. Ensuring that the students learned and observed proper behaviour fell to a Dean of Men in the north wing and a Dean of Women in the south wing. They were typically unmarried individuals who did not mind living in residence as much as married staff might. The Deans dictated that everyone should rise by 6:45 am so that they might wash and dress appropriately for breakfast in the 250-seat dining room at 8 am sharp. Some arrived looking more than ready to face the day; others, particularly among the boys, were often dishevelled with hair unbrushed, missing collars or ties or both. No one got to tuck into their eggs and jam and toast until a Dean rang the bell and said grace. On occasion, a daring student would put a piece of gum on the bell clapper to the amusement of everyone but the Dean. With breakfast done, the students returned briefly to their rooms to sweep the floor and make beds before the janitor's inspection. They then grabbed their books and headed to class.

Weekdays followed a familiar pattern. Morning classes usually began at 8:45 or 9. Usually, the first half of the day was given over to academic lectures in subjects like Constitutional History, English Literature, and Mathematics. The students broke for lunch in the dining room at noon and then gabbed in the hallways or snuck around the corner for a prohibited cigarette. When the bell rang again at 1 pm, they marched off to laboratory classes, which lasted until around 4 or 4:30 pm. On a given day these labs might include anything from farm mechanics and seed grading to cheese making and chicken plucking.

Then everyone piled back into the dining room for supper. The seating arrangements for supper were more formal, with a list of table companions being posted on the bulletin board every Thursday. The idea was to get the young people to mingle, especially the shy ones, and everyone hoped that someone interesting of the opposite sex might end up at their table. The meals were very much of the meat-and-potatoes variety, with almost everything coming to the table from the School farm itself.

Following supper, the students might enjoy a game of baseball on a nice fall day or basketball in the gymnasium if the weather was less clement. Around 8 pm, everyone headed for their rooms, supposedly to study for a couple of hours before it was lights out at 10 pm. One exception to this routine occurred on Monday nights when the Dean called everyone into the sitting room for an hour to share the latest School news and listen to student grievances for an hour or so. On Friday nights, when many social events took place, the students were allowed to stay up until 11. Saturday dances extended the evening to 11:45, but on Sunday nights only an extra 15 minutes were added to the usual 10 pm curfew.

On most nights, quiet talking and muted giggling could easily be heard through the thin walls of the dormitory. This lasted until a Dean poked his or her head into the offending room. Then silence reigned. At least for a while. Some nights, things got more boisterous. Pillow fights seem to have been common over the years, and on more than one occasion metal chairs or garbage cans mysteriously fell down three flights of stairs in the middle of the night.

Top right: Shared rooms in the new dormitory were cozy and, with meals, cost $30 per month in the late 1920s. The rare shot was taken in the early 1950s. Bottom right: The dining room in the 1927 dormitory, untrammelled by students.

Feeding several hundred students each day required plenty of kitchen staff. Students often worked part time as servers and washing-up staff to help pay for their schooling.

Not everyone who attended O.S.A. lollygagged about during the late afternoon and the evening breaks. Some worked to earn a part of their boarding costs. There was plenty of help needed in the basement kitchen of the dormitory, although that work was made a bit more palatable by the 12-foot kitchen range for making meals, the *Fearless* dishwasher, steam ovens, gigantic coffee urns and even a mechanized potato peeler. If there was no room left on the kitchen detail, then students might find themselves serving in the dining hall or cleaning the floors of the dormitory. There was always plenty to do.

With more than 200 students customarily present in a single building at once, the incidence of communicable diseases grew markedly. Every year, there were outbreaks — some serious, many less so — of influenza, chicken pox, measles, mumps, scarlet fever and diphtheria. Sometimes enough students were infected to curtail classes for a while or to cancel a special event. On rare occasions a student died, as was the case with Wilbert Murray Caskey of Oyen, who passed away in hospital in 1929 after contracting measles on campus. The School, which had only a small infirmary room in the basement near the kitchen and food storage lockers, was poorly equipped to deal with outbreaks of any kind.

To reduce the incidence of disease, the School insisted that all incoming students be subjected to a complete medical examination. The earliest record of such exams dates from 1925.[36] These were quite thorough and led to the discovery of all manner of malady. In 1929-30, for example, testing of 227 students turned up 62 with enlarged tonsils, seven with unhealthy gums, 19 who needed dental work, three cases of impetigo, one pronounced hernia, 28 with half normal vision, 14 with

heart conditions and one with tuberculosis.[37] The last was not permitted to attend classes.

While these examinations said much about the contemporary state of rural health care, they likely did next to nothing to curtail the spread of communicable diseases. Despite nearly annual calls from School administrators for a proper, separate infirmary on campus, no action seems to have been taken by the Department of Agriculture. Presumably, some afflicted students were accommodated at the nine-bed Olds General Hospital, established in 1923. More serious cases were taken to Calgary for treatment.

The rigor with which annual medical examinations were administered said much about the general attitude of the school administration. A kindly sternness prevailed. While many instructors got on famously with their classes, they were always aware that an important part of their function was to act as what we now call role models. Their own behaviour was to serve as an example of the virtuous life to the impressionable youth of O.S.A.

Instructors dressed formally, even when coaching basketball or judging livestock. Like upstanding citizens, they were not allowed to smoke or drink on campus. They were expected to participate in everything from sporting matches to theatrical productions. They were to say grace before meals and to attend Sunday services. Some served on town council, on school council and in benevolent fraternal organizations that assisted the needy.

Most of all, they encouraged every student to take an active part in the daunting round of social activities on campus. Those who could not dance were given lessons.

Those afraid of public speaking were coached and then given new opportunities. Those with musical, literary or acting talent were given a stage on which to perform. In the new dormitory, which quickly became the venue for almost every activity of this sort, the Deans did their best to curb the natural instincts of youth in an effort to show them what would be expected of them in life after graduation.

Through their example, the instructors worked to impart elevated moral values, a sense of responsibility and a dedication to community service. To a certain degree, they succeeded. Art Kemp said it succinctly: "We not only gained in knowledge but we had many rough corners chipped off and made smooth."[38] These lessons in the game of life, learned in the new dormitory, served generations of O.S.A. graduates very well.

While most photographs of the School were taken during the summer months, this candid shot of students returning to the dormitory shows the usual experience of those who attended O.S.A.

Depression and War

The collapse of world financial markets on October 29th, 1929, went largely unnoticed in Olds. In the weeks and months leading up to Christmas, the editor of The Olds Gazette turned his front-page attention to items like the progress being made on the Town's new covered skating rink, the ambitious drilling plans of the Didsbury investors who had optimistically formed the Olds Dome Oil Company Limited, and the excellent showing of an O.S.A. steer at the Royal Agricultural Winter Fair in Toronto, but said nothing about the stock market crash that was already affecting the United States and would soon change many local lives for the worse.

The Years of Challenge

On November 1st, just three days after the Wall Street markets had sunk to an all-time low and set off a global financial panic, the editor chose to devote part of a front-page column to the arrival of the new crop of O.S.A. students. "Registration compares favourably with the big attendance of past years," he noted with satisfaction, "which is well over the 200 mark."

The actual figure was 227. This was good news for the School and for the Town, even if the near-record turnout meant that the capacity of the dormitory would be over-taxed and male students would once again be looking for private accommodation in town.

Calamity was not yet in the air. In fact, the opposite was true. With no sense of the impending economic depression that would hurt farmers and farming communities everywhere, the residents of Olds and district continued to see good times ahead. They had good reason to believe in a bright future. After the terrible storms, drought, grasshopper invasions and widespread crop failures of the early 1920s, which had been accompanied by a short but serious economic recession that pushed down farm commodity prices, agricultural conditions improved markedly from 1923 to 1928. Local farmland remained inexpensive, as did farm machinery. New settlers continued to arrive in the district from Great Britain and Europe, adding to the post-war influx of Soldier Settlement Board farmers. Crop yields were up, prices were good, and demand for livestock and hogs and poultry was rising steadily. When the 1929 crop year brought drought and low yields, it was seen as nothing more than an aberration, a temporary setback.

The experience of William Birdsall during the 1920s was typical of the times in the Olds district.[1] After serving with the Canadian Army Medical Corps in England during the war, Birdsall brought his wife and five children (soon to be six) to the Coburn district southeast of Olds. This was in 1920. With credit from the Soldier Settlement Board, he bought a quarter section, four horses, a wagon and a democrat, a two-bottom sulky plough, a disc harrow and a spike-toothed harrow. He broke some land, used a neighbour's seed drill to put in the crop, and then borrowed haying equipment to put up winter feed. When an adjacent half section became available, Birsdall quickly obtained a three-year lease on it. Before that lease expired, he had saved enough to purchase a nearby quarter section. Then he rented more land to the west of his farm. Meanwhile, he increased both his dairy herd and his drift of hogs.

By the end of his first decade on the land, Birdsall owned a Model T Ford touring car, a Wallis tractor, a threshing machine and a power binder, among other equipment. His home, with its gasoline-powered washing machine, radio and gasoline lamps, also reflected the growing prosperity of his family. If that were not enough evidence of moving up in the world, in the fall of 1931 he had the pleasure of seeing one of his sons, Everett, enrol at the Olds School of Agriculture and serve as Class President in his first year. The ability to pay even a part of the costs of attendance at O.S.A., especially after the Depression

began in earnest, was yet another sign of comparative success in the district.

Despite the hard times that would soon befall him and his neighbours, Bill Birdsall had little reason to regret the choices he had made during the previous decade. Farmers like him, who owned their farms and ran them as businesses, were usually able to hold on to what they had during the Depression. They made do with less, as did everyone, but they kept their farms. Farmers who rented from others or had borrowed heavily to purchase their farms, often lost everything when they were unable to pay their bills.

One thing that farm owners and farm renters had in common, however, was their declining importance to the Canadian economy as a whole. By 1921, Canada was more urban than rural. Industry, not farming, was in the ascent, with mineral extraction and newsprint constantly stealing the headlines from agricultural production. Support for institutions offering agricultural education became harder for governments to justify. It would take nothing less than another world war to return some of the lustre to the occupation of farming, as the world once again recalled the importance of food production. But that was nearly a generation away. Meanwhile, farmers in the Olds district and the staff at the O.S.A. had no choice but to tighten their belts and hope for the best.

Building on the Grisdale Legacy

In 1930, Frank Grisdale resigned his position at Olds. He had never made a secret of his deep interest in politics and, with the encouragement of those who were still angry at his "firing," he decided to run for provincial office in the upcoming general election.

Well known and popular, he took the seat for the United Farmers in a narrow victory. In the years to come, he would be appointed Alberta's Minister of Agriculture. As Minister, he is best remembered for promoting the District Agriculturalist Service and the school fair program, as well as for reopening the Vermilion School of Agriculture that was closed in 1933 for economic reasons.

But Grisdale's true and more lasting legacy in Alberta was O.S.A. His clear vision of the School's future, together with his strong administrative capacity, had given O.S.A. a leading role in provincial education and extension work. On his watch, both student enrolments and instructional staff doubled. His ability to attract instructors like Morley Malyon, E. W. Churchill, Christine McIntyre and Arthur Kemp, and his confidence in turning them loose to exercise their talents, resulted in top-notch teaching with little staff turn-over.

While instructors like Malyon and McIntyre took education on the road each summer, other teachers, notably Art Kemp, usually remained behind to transform the campus into a farming showcase that attracted more visitors every year. Churchill's bold lending library initiative, which put books into the hands of appreciative isolated rural residents across the central part of the Province, was yet another reason for Albertans to sit up and take notice of O.S.A.

This public support stood the School in good stead during the 1920s and especially during the Depression. When the Provincial Government deemed it necessary to close some Schools of Agriculture during the sharp recession of the early 1920s, it consolidated agricultural and domestic science teaching at Olds, Claresholm and Vermilion. With that aggregation of students came greater responsibility for extension work as well, and soon Olds instructors were travelling most of Alberta's roads each summer. By 1931, O.S.A. would be the only remaining School of Agriculture in Alberta. If there was one School that seemed to be well run and worth retaining, it was Olds.

James Murray, who took Grisdale's place at Olds in 1930, had big shoes to fill. However he may have seen his new challenge, he was undeniably well suited to the job. As a member of the original 1912-13 Board of Agricultural Education, he had been present at the birth of the first three Schools and helped to develop their original curricula. He came to his new job with a solid understanding of Alberta's system of agricultural education. It also helped that he himself was an agricultural school graduate.

But he was also a man of practical farming experience and knowledge. He did both experimental and extension work with government agencies in Western Canada prior to becoming manager of the 56,000-acre Canadian Wheat Lands Company at Suffield. When that audacious enterprise folded in 1914, Murray returned to eastern Canada and spent four years as Professor of Field Husbandry at Macdonald College.

In 1919 he came west again, as though drawn inexorably to the prairies. This time he managed the activities of the Noble Foundation Ltd. The Foundation was an extraordinary 30,000-acre farm owned by Charles S. Noble, the 1915 "World Oats King," noted soil conservationist and subsequently inventor of the revolutionary Noble Blade that cut weeds off at the roots without disturbing the surface soil. Unfortunately for Murray, Noble went bankrupt in 1922 during the post-war recession. As a result, Murray found himself obliged to earn a living as District Agriculturalist at Medicine Hat

from 1922 to 1930. Murray's personal roller-coaster of experience in Alberta taught him about the ups and downs of farming as nothing else could.

The 48-year-old Murray would remain at the helm for the next 16 years. During his tenure, and under the heavy weight of the Depression and the war, he added substantially to Grisdale's good work. If anything, he transformed O.S.A. into even more of a hub for scientific research, extension work and community leadership.

James Murray, Principal from 1930 to 1946, kept O.S.A. on an even keel during the Great Depression and the Second World War. He is best remembered for his pioneering work with Creeping Red Fescue.

Adjusting to a Changing World

The first years of the Great Depression piled disaster upon disaster. The collapse of world markets for farm commodities was bad enough, but then drought, frost, hail, drifting soil and grasshopper infestations made the situation for farmers even more precarious.

Those who had turned away from cereal production in the hope that feeder livestock might prove a better investment found themselves stymied first by a feed shortage and then by new American tariffs that stifled cross-border trade in cattle and poultry.

To keep food on the table, people in the district planted larger gardens and raised more poultry, milk cows and hogs. This made sense for reasons of self-sufficiency of course, but with beef and hog selling for five dollars a hundredweight and eggs at five cents a dozen, selling these products brought little income. Beekeeping took on a new importance, too, as honey substituted for expensive sugar. Some residents, like the Kemps, traded their honey for farm-made butter.[2] Unwilling, and in some cases unable, to purchase expensive gasoline for tractors bought in better times, farmers harnessed up their teams once again. Everyone economized.

James Murray and his staff swiftly learned to economize and change direction, too. The first sign that they would need to do so was not long in arriving. In the fall of 1930, enrolment dropped by almost one-third compared to the previous year — from 226 to 145. This was particularly troubling because many of those students had transferred to Olds from Claresholm and Raymond, which had been closed by the Provincial Government as an austerity measure. The O.S.A. student population would hover around the 150 mark for several years before beginning to recover slowly.

Following the 1934-35 school year, the School would also choose to discontinue the Third Year Matriculation class it had offered for a decade. Demand had dropped to an unsustainable level, partly because more rural students were obtaining their Grade 12 standing and partly because the Depression was making it difficult for many to afford to continue their education at a university.

The Last Day of Matric

With haunting lure this place once filled with cheer.
Two weeks have passed—to us it seems a year.
These corridors, where sunlight seemed to beam
Are barren, bare and dull to the extreme.
No more we see the Freshman's eager look,
Or intelligent "Two in One's" thoughts buried in a book,
Nor hear the bold Sophomores say ere they go to bed
"Let's fill the bath with cold water and
duck in someone's head!"
Alas! they've packed their trunks and gone
With their Diplomas they've just won,
And now are strewn along the shore
In their respective homes which they adore.
New hope is born in them to conquer strife
No matter which course they take in life,
And may they all successful be
In life and in eternity.
To us whom they have left behind
We find it mighty hard to find
A place where we our time may spend
To take our thoughts from such dear friends.

The Dorm seems like a hollow cave.
And we within its walls do crave
For those we loved and friends we made,
But all our wants are not repaid.
Instead, from the still shade we hear
Echoes resound which fill us with fear
And when we hear these sounds we stare
As though someone had said "Beware!"
Of course the time is drawing nigh
When we ourselves will say good-bye
For only five more weeks remain
Until we leave this great domain.
Some may to pastures greener go,
And for themselves and others gain
A peaceful place on earth to reign.
Come! Let's forget these parting days
And think of when the sunshine's rays
Will shine upon us all once more.
Perhaps that will be on the further shore.
But could we wish for a better place
In which to gather face to face?

While undoubtedly relieved to be spared the indignity of outright closure that had affected Claresholm and Raymond, O.S.A. still had to cope with many trials. Murray became particularly concerned about the well-being of his staff once him learned that the Government intended to keep only him and the farm manager, Freeman (Fred) Parkinson, on salary during the summer of 1933. This would not only mean an end to the normal summer extension work, but more importantly might well prove ruinous to many instructors and their families. As teachers, and often young teachers at that, most would have had little to fall back on. You could sense this concern in the request of Art Kemp, who was raising three young sons with his wife Dorothy, a former instructor herself, to be kept on at a reduced salary over the summer. His request was denied, and the School caretakers handled most of his groundskeeping duties that summer.[3]

Fortunately, the layoffs do not seem to have extended beyond the summer months. It is certainly suggestive that the names of the staff members between 1929 and 1940 are almost the same. Perhaps the Government found sufficient funds from the closure of the Vermilion School in that same year to retain the O.S.A. instructors. We don't know, but the rate of turn-over that you might expect in an era of sharp retrenchment did not occur at O.S.A. during the Depression years.

Regardless, staff did make concessions in order to stay on. In the autumn of 1933 Dave Andrew, who had just transferred to O.S.A. from Vermilion, received a personal request from the Deputy Minister of Agriculture, H. A. Craig, to act as Dean of the Men's Residence as well as teach both Animal Husbandry and Farm Management. Craig asked this "in the interests of economy."[4] Andrew readily agreed, notwithstanding the fact this meant he could only spend about an hour a day with his wife and children who lived in an apartment in town.

Even with such "economies," there was less money to go around. The Alumni Association noticed this soon after the Depression struck. While 6,000 copies of the Alumni newsletter were mailed out in 1929-30, by the following November Secretary-Treasurer Art Kemp informed the membership that he had thought it

advisable to curtail expenditures. This seems to be a year of economy, and our membership has not kept up to the standard. It cannot be helped, people just have not got the money and the Alumni Association is in the same predicament as other organizations. With this in mind, the News for the months of November, December and January will be cut down to a two-page issue...[5]

For a time, the Experimental Union remained nearly as active as it had been before the onset of the Depression. This was perhaps because its members received more than the value of their membership in each yearly package of seeds and seedlings. The January seed fair continued as well. But as the years went by and the Depression deepened, more and more alumni discontinued their membership in the Association. Participation in events by those who remained fell as well. Everett Birdsall later remarked that, in the 1930s, "Even the weather seemed to be working against the association as several functions had few in attendance because of stormy weather."[6]

Coming of Age

Even in the worst of times, people seem to find something to celebrate. The turning point for Depression-era alumni and students at O.S.A. came in 1934 when they joined forces to organize what they called The Big Birthday Party.

The idea originated with Angus McKinnon. A member of the first graduating class (1915), McKinnon felt it was high time O.S.A. celebrated the achievements of its students. To the sceptical, he pointed out that the School was linked closely to three Ministers of Agriculture: Duncan Marshall in Ontario, J. Gordon Taggart in Saskatchewan, and Frank Grisdale in Alberta, in addition to dozens of other successful graduates. Clearly O.S.A. was, after only 21 years of operation, reshaping the agricultural policies of the country.

Working closely with other members of the Alumni Association, McKinnon invited the three Ministers to attend the festivities. These were planned to coincide with the actual 21st anniversary on November 13th and 14th, 1934. All agreed to come. As the date approached, the Association published a series of articles and photographs in *The O.S.A. News* that showcased various milestones in the evolution of the School. This was a fine addition to the small collection of artifacts in a museum that the Alumni Association had started in 1931.[7] Soon everyone was talking about attending what was to be the first of several notable School anniversary celebrations.

The temperature was near freezing as former students and staff began arriving on Monday, November 12th, a full day before the official festivities were to start. Every class since 1913 had a former student or two in attendance, with the first class being represented best. Providentially, as soon as the guests checked into their hotel rooms or bunked with friends or relatives, the sun came out in all its glory. The temperature peaked at 55° F that first day. The sun continued to warm the entire event; in fact, the temperature did not return to the freezing mark until the party was over. It provided one more reason for the *Gazette* to call the 21st anniversary celebrations "the biggest and best and the happiest birthday party ever experienced in the history of Olds."[8]

The sun and the setting put everyone in the mood to reminisce. To help matters along even more, the School administration decided to conduct regular classes on the 13th. This not only allowed everyone in attendance to see the School in operation, but also prompted former students to "more vividly recall their student days." If alumni were not in the classroom, they could almost certainly be found near the livestock pens or among the test plots north of the campus.

Among those in attendance, no one was in a better frame of mind than Duncan Marshall. Now 62, he looked back on his proudest political achievement with delight, calling Alberta's system of Schools of Agriculture a "dream fulfilled." In his address to the crowd of about 350,

174

Twenty-first Anniversary

of the

Provincial Schools of Agriculture

1913 - 1934

November thirteenth and fourteenth
nineteen thirty-four

AT OLDS, ALBERTA

Sponsored by O.S.A. Alumni Association

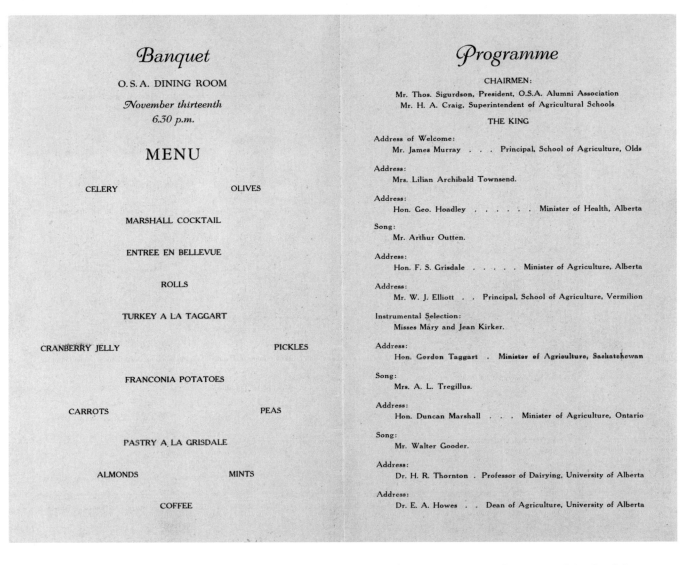

Banquet

O. S. A. DINING ROOM

November thirteenth
6.30 p.m.

MENU

CELERY   OLIVES

MARSHALL COCKTAIL

ENTREE EN BELLEVUE

ROLLS

TURKEY A LA TAGGART

CRANBERRY JELLY   PICKLES

FRANCONIA POTATOES

CARROTS   PEAS

PASTRY A LA GRISDALE

ALMONDS   MINTS

COFFEE

Programme

CHAIRMEN:
Mr. Thos. Sigurdson, President, O.S.A. Alumni Association
Mr. H. A. Craig, Superintendent of Agricultural Schools

THE KING

Address of Welcome:
Mr. James Murray . . . Principal, School of Agriculture, Olds

Address:
Mrs. Lilian Archibald Townsend.

Address:
Hon. Geo. Hoadley . . . . Minister of Health, Alberta

Song:
Mr. Arthur Outten.

Address:
Hon. F. S. Grisdale . . . . . Minister of Agriculture, Alberta

Address:
Mr. W. J. Elliott . . Principal, School of Agriculture, Vermilion

Instrumental Selection:
Misses Mary and Jean Kirker.

Address:
Hon. Gordon Taggart . Minister of Agriculture, Saskatchewan

Song:
Mrs. A. L. Tregillus.

Address:
Hon. Duncan Marshall . . . Minister of Agriculture, Ontario

Song:
Mr. Walter Gooder.

Address:
Dr. H. R. Thornton . Professor of Dairying, University of Alberta

Address:
Dr. E. A. Howes . . Dean of Agriculture, University of Alberta

Marshall spoke at length about the early days at the School, noting the initial reluctance of his Cabinet colleagues to support his lofty proposal. Given the success of O.S.A. over the years, that reluctance now seemed misplaced. He also expressed his heartfelt appreciation of the spirit of Western farmers as they confronted the daunting challenges of the last few years, and called Olds "one of the finest farming districts, not only in Canada, but in the world."[9] The master orator still knew how to play a crowd.

The speeches went on interminably during much of Tuesday and Wednesday, as they often did at formal O.S.A. functions. By the afternoon of the final day, every one was ready to relax and enjoy a splendid screening of old photographs narrated by H. A. Craig, the Deputy Minister of Agriculture. To many in the crowd, including Duncan Marshall, the most touching photograph was of Christena Marshall as she stood tall and proud behind the walking plough that had turned the first sod on another sunny day, many years before, when everyone was somewhat younger and brimming with hope for the future.

As the Great Depression wore on, Angus McKinnon (class of '15) lifted everyone's spirits by organizing a very successful O.S.A. 21st birthday celebration.

Like those who went before them, O.S.A. students in the 1930s quickly fell into a pattern of behaviour that included participation in Lit nights, weekly dances, evening excursions to Cloakey's Lake for skating parties and sausage roasts over an open fire, the Little Royal, public speaking contests, newsletter and yearbook editing, the fall field day, and sports events that ranged from hockey to boxing to basketball. There were even those who, like Leeson, followed the example of many of his predecessors in climbing to the very top of the campus water tower. "Our Everest," he called it. "A forbidden challenge to be climbed, just because it was there. I remember standing on that little post on top, my supreme accomplishment."[13]

The students' introduction to many of these O.S.A. rituals followed a well-established routine. Just days after they had settled into their rooms in the dorm or in private houses in town, they were expected to turn out *en masse* for the Staff Reception that was held in the gymnasium. This usually took place on the first Friday of the term and often followed the traditional athletic field day. Many found the formal Reception a daunting experience, as coming to O.S.A. was their first real experience away from home. One 1935-36 student saw the ordeal this way:

We came rather timidly into the gym, wondering what was before us, advancing gingerly along the receiving line, shook hands in our most dignified manner with Miss Rogers, Mr. Phillips, Mr. and Mrs. Murray and breathed a sigh of relief...Then we went to our respective color group, wishing we knew someone in it, and wondering if we should ever make friends and if everyone else felt as miserable as we did.[14]

Concern quickly gave way to relief, however, as the instructors involved everyone in a series of stunts and contests that made everyone forget their shyness. Often there was a Get Acquainted Circle, where an instructor gave each student a topic and "encouraged" them to discuss it with the student opposite. Soon the gym, which had been nearly silent just moments before, boomed with a cacophony of young voices. Sometimes there was a pie-eating contest. On occasion — much to the surprise of the freshies in the room — the staff even turned everyone loose for a good, old fashioned pillow fight, the kind that had often taken place since the new dormitory had opened in 1927.

When these shenanigans concluded, another instructor presented the ribbons and medals won at the track-and-field events earlier in the day. Everyone then adjourned to the adjacent dining room for supper. This offered yet another chance for the students to get acquainted, as boys and girls were paired up randomly at the tables. Then the members of the school orchestra took up their places and the dance began. The staff managed to get in a dance or two of their own while playing chaperone, and then served a late snack to the students. As midnight approached, the music ended and everyone retired to their rooms, feeling tired but thinking that perhaps O.S.A. might not be so bad after all. Looking back on these events, one student recalled that it was "a nice start to what seemed like a lonely first week."

School of Agriculture
Olds, Alberta,
January 13, 1959.

Dear Jim:

Breakfast is being served in the Apartment on Thursday, January twenty second at 7:30. o'clock.

We would like to have you join us.

Yours Sincerely,
Marilyn Rasmuson

The Apartment
"Our greatest ordeal was that of being waitress and hostess in the Apartment."[15]

So said many of the young women in the care of formidable Miss Christine McIntyre. The Apartment (always capitalized) was a special room in the Main Building that had been outfitted with a kitchen and small dining room. This was where Home Economics students learned the finer points of being a gracious hostess. Each of the Two-in-one and second-year girls spent four days in The Apartment, two as intermittent maids (usually only to wait on table at breakfast, set the places at noon, and then assist with the dinner) and two as all-day hostesses.

The hard work fell on the hostess. With a limited budget, she had to plan menus for six meals (two breakfasts, two lunches, and two dinners), shop for groceries, extend formal invitations to all meals but the breakfasts, cook the meals, set the table, say grace before dinner, play the part of hostess and clean up. She was usually in The Apartment from 6:30 a.m. until 9 p.m. or later. Miss McIntyre was always one invited guest, and another staff member (usually a man) would be invited to the second dinner. Of course formal dress was required.

If anything could go wrong, it did. Soufflés refused to rise. Never-fail cakes failed. Once the nervous hostess used a heavy hand to dust her dish of cottage cheese with cayenne instead of paprika. On another occasion the gas oven exploded and blew out two windows. All too often, the hostess and the maid got the giggles during the formal dinner and mayhem reigned until Miss McIntyre found an appropriately polite way to restore decorum.

Where, except at O.S.A., could Depression-raised farm girls get such an unforgettable experience?

Top: Formality was the order of the day as the senior Home Economics students practised their domestic skills before the staff and their peers in The Apartment. This image is from the early 1950s. Left: Miss Christine Mcintyre taught the domestic sciences to hundreds of young women between 1930 and 1951. She was a tireless in her devotion to her profession. Opposite page: Extending hand-written, personalized invitations to guests was part of The Apartment ritual. This breakfast invitation from 1959 was sent by Marilyn Rasmuson to Jim Stone, who later became an instructor at Olds. Courtesy Jim Stone

Within a month or so, new students became the unwilling subjects of a somewhat less genteel rite of passage. Initiation of the freshies and freshettes (as the first-year girls were known) usually took place around November 1st. Responsibility for this 'welcoming' tradition fell, of course, to the second-year students. It was the much more mature male sophomores who, on at least one occasion, herded the blindfolded and man-acled first-year boys into the stock pavilion and painted moustaches, sideburns, and goatees on their faces with molasses and lampblack before crowning them with a bucket of sawdust or oat chop.

The second-year girls got their hazing licks in, too. Each year they managed to concoct some new form of humiliation to inflict upon the latest crop of freshettes. As domestic science professionals, they seemed more than a little attracted to matters of food and clothing. Once they cooked what they called a "sumptuous banquet" that they obliged the younger girls to eat — it consisted of cooked porridge and macaroni, topped with a good dollop of castor oil. They then made each freshette don a

> ponderous chain of earrings composed of peanuts, suspended from each ear to the waist tied at the ends with green ribbons adorned with carrots. Also had to don clothes front to back, wear odd stockings trimmed with green ribbon at the ankles, part hair in middle and plaster it down behind the ears. Those with long locks had to braid them and tie each braid with green ribbons.[16]

This kind of thing often went on for days. In addition, both first-year boys and girls were expected to bow down before any approaching sophomore, address them as "Sir" or "Madam" (or risk a ten cent fine that always went to a good cause), polish their shoes and open doors for them. As Principal Murray said of the students, "They could not afford to buy their fun; they had to make it. And make it they did."

On occasion, the staff made it for them. On one memorable day in 1944, everyone turned out in the gym to watch the "game of the year" between the O.S.A. Girls basketball team and the Staff Glamour Girls. While we don't know the identities of all the Staff Glamour Girls, the crowd couldn't help but notice that Mr. Hawker and Mr. Malyon "looked like twins in their swing skirts and stockings." The boys in attendance were nearly unanimous in voting Hawker the "most chic" Glamour Girl on the court. If anyone present expressed a concern about the rough-and-tumble game, which resembled hockey more than basketball, their sympathies went first to Dr. Ross Walton, who taught veterinary science. By the end of the game most spectators were convinced that Walton had a heart condition, "judging from the number of times he was carried off on a stretcher."[17] Skirts notwithstanding, the Glamour Girls carried the day 30 to 13.

Top right: The first-year girls of 1921. Like many before and after them, these "freshettes" as they were called, underwent bizarre hazing experiences during the first weeks on campus. The initiation rites inflicted on first-year students were guaranteed to be funny and humiliating. Bottom right: This rare shot of young men showing more than enough leg beneath their skirts shows the tamer side of the annual hazing practices. Others included being painted with molasses and then dusted with oat chop.

New Directions in Experimental Work

Like so many other aspects of life at O.S.A., the character of experimental work changed during the Depression. Reporting in 1932-33, Principal Murray said,

> *It has been necessary to curtail our experimental work with farm crops, but it has been possible still to carry on some useful and valuable work. Cereal varieties are no longer carried in large numbers. We grow only a few of the more important ones to gather additional data on their behaviour and to serve as demonstrations for those who visit our trial plots.[18]*

With a noticeable nod toward declining local interest in cereal production and growing interest in livestock, the School would begin to shift its experimental work to hay and forage crops. In addition, the staff seeded 25 test plots to lawns, trying out different mixes of grasses that might be suitable for home lawns, bowling greens and putting greens.

More land was given over to experiments with fruit crops as well. The beautiful flowering trees and bushes not only offered a spot of beauty amid the gloom affecting everyday life, but also opened the possibility of home-grown canning fruits for winter consumption. Art Kemp had begun this work in the late 1920s, but his experiments really took off after the Department of Agriculture acquired the Brooks Experimental Station from the Canadian Pacific Railway in 1935. This meant that Kemp had ready access to a greatly expanded stock of fruit trees, shrubs and perennial flowers.

By 1942, he was experimenting with 450 varieties of crab-apple and apple trees and more than 50 other fruits, including 40 strawberry varieties. The School's plum, pear and apricot trees were producing heavily that year, to the astonishment of many visitors. Principal Murray was pleased to say that,

> *No small amount of time is required during the summer to show visitors over the orchards and fruit plantations. This is well spent energy, as 'seeing is believing'.*

Many visitors have never seen heavily laden fruit trees in this Province, and they thus get a new conception of its fruit growing possibilities.[19]

A greater focus on beekeeping went hand-in-hand with the developing orchards, not just to assist pollination but also because home canning of fruit demanded bought sugar that was simply too expensive for many families. Syrup made with watered-down honey was one answer. O.S.A. had been involved in beekeeping since 1922-23, when it acquired two bee colonies. By 1938, O.S.A. bees were producing 580 pounds of honey annually, and instructors provided both talks and demonstrations to local farmers throughout central Alberta.

Under Art Kemp's guidance, the O.S.A. orchard produced an abundance of apples and other fruits to the disbelief of many district farmers.

Charles Yauch and Chemical Farming

The most significant changes in O.S.A. experimental work were a new emphasis

on longer term projects related closely to district soil issues and greater co-operation

with other agencies on herbicide and pesticide research.

Charles Yauch, who would serve briefly as Principal from 1949 to 1952, was responsible for most of this work. A native of Lafayette, Indiana, Yauch graduated from the Claresholm School of Agriculture in 1921 and then continued on to the University of Alberta where he received his Bachelor of Science in Agriculture degree in 1924. He then did post-graduate work at Macdonald College in Quebec for his Master's degree. In 1925, at the behest of Frank Grisdale, Yauch joined the Olds teaching staff as Instructor in Chemistry and Soils.

When not teaching his classes or serving as the district apiarist or performing with the O.S.A. Dramatic Club or acting as Secretary-Treasurer of the Alumni Association (he followed Kemp in this position), the busy Yauch was out in the field, counselling farmers as to the most effective kinds of poison bait to use against the hordes of grasshoppers that plagued central Alberta throughout the 1920s.

In the early 1930s, he began to receive requests from farmers around Sundre for more information about how best to farm their land. This area, which was settled during the 1920s, was not as productive of grain and forage crops as the farmers had hoped it would be. The grey-wooded soils in particular were producing poor yields. With their co-operation, Yauch designed and implemented a detailed fertilizer-testing program using super-phosphates. These were obtained at no cost from the Consolidated Mining and Smelting Company smelter at Trail, British Columbia. One hundred pounds of super-phosphate per acre were applied to wheat and oats crops on both summerfallow and spring ploughing. This was soon followed by other experiments involving clovers, crop rotation, and soil conservation. The work stretched over the next decade and, at its peak, Yauch was in regular contact with 100 farmers every summer. As the years went on, he extended this research to Didsbury in the south and Innisfail in the north.

Working closely with between 20 and 30 farmers, Yauch determined that the soils suffered from too little sulphur. Some farmers, like H. A. Plumb of Bearberry and George Botham of Sundre, offered their experimental plots as venues for field days that were attended by many of their neighbours. Their fields showed the extraordinary effects to be obtained by the regular application of fertilizer. Plumb, for instance, saw increases of 46 per cent and 60 per cent, respectively, in the yields from two fields of clover that he harvested in 1936. Yauch was soon able to tell many stories about local farmers who had embraced fertilizers: where some had previously harvested little forage, they now enjoyed routine surpluses.

His influence on the district went further as the chemical eradication of weeds and insects began in earnest. In 1929, when the first large Canadian conference on herbicides took place in Edmonton, O.S.A. representatives were there along with representatives of experimental facilities in Manitoba and Saskatchewan. The conference organizer was none other than Henry Marshall Tory, who was then President of the National Research Council. These discussions, which referred to the ongoing "war" on weeds, focussed mainly on the eradication of wild oats, sow thistle, Canada thistle, and quack grass. Conference speakers stressed the use of chlorate-based chemicals as the potential answer to weed control, together with proper crop rotation and summerfallowing.[20]

The National Research Council subsequently spearheaded formation of an Associate Committee on Weed Control, comprising experts from across Canada, that began tests of sodium chlorate, sodium chloride, sulphuric acid, iron sulfate, calcium cyanmide and creosote. Weed maps were drawn up showing the distribution of the "seven worst weeds" — perennial sow thistle, Canada thistle, wild oats, wild mustard, stinkweed, couch grass, and povertyweed — and the battle was joined.

O.S.A. was one of the combatants in the war on weeds, with Yauch leading the local charge. He, along with his colleagues in the other Western provinces, soon found that the chlorates in which everyone had placed so much hope, eliminated not only weeds but nearly everything else. The problem was that chlorates sterilized the soil, making them useless for the control of weeds in growing crops.

Yauch's attention soon turned to a new prospect called

2,4-D. Discovered in the early 1940s, 2,4-D was highly effective even when used in low concentrations. At Olds, the new panacea was tested on wild mustard, dandelion, plantain, Canada thistle and sow thistle. Yauch reported that it looked promising. Released commercially in 1945, 2,4-D was in use on half a million acres of prairie farmland within two years. By 1950, that figure would rise to more than 13 million acres.

O.S.A. was also involved in trials of Sinox (sodium dinitro-cresylate), which was introduced in 1944 with the assistance of the Field Crops Branch and the National Elevator Company. Yauch reported that Sinox, when used on a field of oats infested with wild mustard, produced reasonably good results with minimal crop damage. These pioneering trials at Olds marked the beginning of another phase of scientific agriculture, the use of chemical herbicides, that would transform farming completely in the years ahead.

Charles Yauch, who joined the staff as Instructor in Chemistry and Soils in 1925, undertook the first long range studies of district soils and introduced chemical farming to the Olds area. Courtesy Barbara Lees

189

The Miracle of Creeping Red Fescue

Perhaps Principal Murray was drawn to the propagation of grass seed by his love of golf;[21] we may never be sure, but when he had the chance to secure a sample of Creeping Red Fescue seed from Czechoslovakia in 1931, he jumped at the chance.

With the help of L. P. (Pete) Erickson, the O.S.A. plot-man, Murray sowed the first half-acre plots in the spring of 1932. O.S.A. was trying many other potential pasture grasses at the time: Western Rye Grass, Crested Wheat Grass, Westerwolth, Brome, Wheat Grass, Timothy, Meadow Fescue, Kentucky Blue, Arctic, Alsike Clover, Alfalfa, White Dutch Clover and Yellow Sweet Clover.[22] For a time White Dutch seemed most promising. It grew well, kept weeds down, and combatted soil drifting quite effectively. Within two years, however, Creeping Red Fescue had become the darling of the test plots. O.S.A. staff were also pleased to discover that it provided superb sheep grazing once the seed was harvested.

By 1936, word of the miraculous grass had spread far and wide. As the number of livestock rose on farms across Alberta during the Depression, so too did demand for good pasture seed. The plant's extensive root system also held the soil very well. Soon the School was inundated with requests for seed. To convert even more farmers, Erickson began adding a pound of the seed to each Experimental Union parcel that he dropped into the mail. Within four years of planting the first plots, O.S.A. could report that some local farmers were already growing fescue on a commercial scale for sale in the United States. Andrew Anderson, who farmed near Innisfail, was among the earliest commercial producers.

The seed proved itself year after year in pastures, lawns and golf courses. In 1935, two pounds of it were sent to the Beaverlodge Experimental Station in Alberta's northern Peace River district. Those trials proved extremely successful and resulted in new varieties that would transform the regional economy and eventually give the Peace Country the moniker of "Creeper Capital of the World." During the war, the resilient, fast-growing Olds grass also became the tough turf of many Canadian airfields and

army bases. Following the war, fescue seed became the foundation of lawns and fairways across Canada and beyond.

Murray's careful program of selection and testing at O.S.A. led to recognition of what is now known as the Olds cultivar of Creeping Red Fescue. In 1944, the Olds variety was accepted for registration by the Canadian Seed Growers' Association. By 1948, Alberta's fescue seed production reached one and a half million pounds; five years later, the figure was six million. From then until 1966, O.S.A. was responsible for production of the foundation seed of the variety. Its contribution to the success of agriculture here and abroad has been extraordinary.

Charlie Yauch, on the left, worked closely with district farmers like H. A. Plumb of Bearberry to demonstrate the wonders of synthetic fertilizers. James Murray, an expert in field husbandry and avid golfer, is renowned for the experimental work with Creeping Red Fescue that occurred during his tenure as O.S.A. Principal. This is one of his own photographs of the seed trials that eventually put the School on the map.

CREEPING RED FESCUE SEEDED 1935 ½Lb pr ACRE ROWS 2' ApART

Short Course Rendezvous

During the 1930s, the Olds School of Agriculture became even more of a meeting place for members of the farming community.

Where once O.S.A.'s field day in July had brought hundreds of families to the campus for neighbourly visits, a picnic on the lawn and a tour of the test plots and the students' displays of baking, dressmaking, woodworking and blacksmithing, now that annual event took a back seat to those organized by groups unaffiliated with the School. With each passing year, more farm organizations convened at O.S.A. for summertime short courses, discussed the problems they had in common, and formulated plans for a better future.

The United Farm Women of Alberta (UFWA) was one of the first organizations to seize upon the potential of O.S.A. as a centralized meeting place when it put together the first Farm Women's Week. In 1930, UFWA representative Isobel Townsend conceived the idea of what she initially called Farm Women's Rest Week. A compassionate woman, Townsend thought it high time that hard-working farm women got a break from the rigors and isolation of their home life. She approached the leaders of several farm organizations and the Minister of Agriculture for support, received it, and then worked closely with the new Principal to put together a special program.

James Murray remembered the inaugural event vividly, as Townsend struck during the first month of his tenure at O.S.A. Together, they devised a week-long program that mixed education with relaxation. At Murray's behest, Miss McIntyre, Miss Switzer, Miss Moseson and Mr. Kemp "volunteered" to lecture about sewing, handicrafts, cooking and horticulture. Special lecturers were brought in as well, including Dr. Hartman from Olds and former Principal Frank Grisdale. Lilian Rogers, the newly arrived Dietitian and Dean of the Women's Residence, arranged accommodations and meals in the dormitory. The week concluded with a banquet put on by the School, an amateur hour in which the attending women got to display their talents, and a dance featuring the O.S.A. orchestra. Everything was free, including transportation to Olds. Attendees paid only for their room-and-board in the dormitory.

That was available for a nominal $1.50 per day. Even at that, many farm women who wished to attend could not do so because of the cost. As it was, 34 women attended that first year. Much later, Townsend recalled that,

> *We always feel we are welcome guests since our every need is foreseen and our meals [are] so good. The Week stays with us too. We gain new ideas, new friends and a new outlook. There are no meals to prepare, no dishes to wash, and we need not even attend lectures unless we want to.*[23]

Top: Beginning in 1930, O.S.A. became the venue for many annual summer conventions. The first of note was Farm Women's Week, organized by the United Farm Women of Alberta. This event was held at Olds for the next 56 years. The Alberta Women's Institute Girls' Club, dedicated to providing guidance to young rural women, made O.S.A. its permanent summer home in 1932.

The event proved very successful over the years, and in 1935 it was opened up to all Alberta women, not just to those living on farms. As the years passed, the lecture series was extended as well, offering discussions of proper diet, labour-saving devices, how to dry fruits and vegetables, sewing machine attachments, landscaping, flower arranging, historical talks, home first aid and much more. Sorely needed and greatly appreciated, Farm Women's Week would continue to be hosted by the school at Olds for the next 56 years. As one woman said when referring to the benefits of the movement, "We had dairy for 26 years, 365 days a year, 100 cows and never a holiday, and I always said it was the only thing that kept me sane."[24]

The Alberta Women's Institute Girls' Club (A.W.I.G.C.), which had been in existence since 1921, found a new, permanent home at Olds beginning in 1932. Many of the women who took part in the annual Farm Women's Week saw O.S.A. as the perfect place to send their daughters as well. "Life means service," declared A.W.I.G.C. President Betty Thompson, and the Olds School of Agriculture became the venue of choice for an annual training session for young rural women. There they received instruction not just in the domestic arts and recreation, but also in community leadership.

Representatives of various Girls' Clubs from around the Province would convene at O.S.A. for a week in July. Under close supervision, they participated in sports competitions, public speaking contests, exhibitions of the manual arts and a variety of demonstration classes put on by O.S.A. instructors and other lecturers.

In 1936, for example, Miss McIntyre presented a talk entitled "The Magic That Comes From Bottles and Jars," which taught the girls how to make moisturizers and astringents and, more generally, how to "care for the body." She later gave a second, even more sobering talk covering everything from career choices to conduct with boys to preparation for marriage. A Miss Current talked to them about beautifying with crepe paper and salt paste, a talent that would stand them in good stead as they organized rural dances later in life. A bit more engaging, perhaps, was the talk given by Mr. W. H. Fisher, who had been the O.S.A. bookkeeper for the previous eight years. He often entertained O.S.A. staff with his stories of the Klondike gold rush, and on this special occasion he regaled the wide-eyed girls with tales of bandits and robbers in a lawless land, as well as his own harrowing experience as he staved off starvation one winter while snowed in at an isolated Yukon cabin.

A Women's Institute Girls' Club Poem, 1937

You are the girl who has to decide
Whether you'll do it or toss it aside.
You are the girl who makes up your mind
Whether you'll lead, or linger behind,
Whether you'll try for the goal that's afar.
Or be contented to stay where you are.
Take it or leave it, there's something to do
Just think it over, it's all up to you.

The A.W.I.G.C. Magazine, 1937

"Learn to Do by Doing"

The Schools of Agriculture emphasized hands-on learning from the outset. Nowhere was this more evident than in the time instructors gave to the organization of school fairs and boys and girls clubs throughout the Province.

By 1924, interest in livestock, dairy and grain clubs had grown to the point where the Department of Agriculture thought it worthwhile to strike a deal with the two transcontinental railways to provide free passage to the Royal Agricultural Winter Fair in Toronto to the winning provincial Junior Club teams. Four O.S.A. students took top honours that year in the competition among post-secondary students.

As the Depression took hold, however, participation in Alberta's school fair program peaked in 1931 with more than 35,000 students preparing 160,000 exhibits.[25] Staff from the School of Agriculture could no longer handle the load and responsibility shifted to Edmonton, where G. S. Black became Supervisor of Boys and Girls Livestock Clubs and School Fairs. Within a few years, the Livestock Branch assumed control of the junior livestock clubs, while the Field Crops Branch oversaw the work of the field crop clubs. It was also in 1931 that the Canadian Council on Boys and Girls Club Work was established to foster the adoption of countrywide policies, develop leadership programs, and encourage business sponsorship of the clubs. This organization would later become the Canadian Council on 4-H Clubs.

In the fall of 1933, the new Animal Husbandry and Farm Management Instructor, Dave Andrew, introduced a novel concept that he called the "Little Royal." Rather than emphasizing the customary competition in livestock on the hoof, Andrew thought it would be better to give O.S.A. students experience in preparing for such contests. He worked closely with the students in grooming animals for shows, handling them appropriately, and showing them. Soon hundreds of spectators came to the School each February or March to see how much the students had improved in their show ring skills. For many years, the Little Royal was held in conjunction with the Provincial Junior Seed Fair at Olds. In 1951, Andrew's creation and the annual Achievement Day were combined into a single event.

If there was one O.S.A. name associated with the ongoing success of the junior clubs in the Olds district, it was that of Hugh McPhail. Born in Paisley, Ontario, he was educated at the universities of Manitoba and British Columbia. He served overseas during the Great War, worked with the Soldier Settlement Board and the Saskatchewan Livestock Pool and then homesteaded in Saskatchewan.[26] He joined O.S.A. in 1930 as Instructor in English, Mathematics and Economics. During the summer months, when he served as a District Agriculturalist, McPhail was widely recognized as devoted to the cause of junior clubs. He worked with them day and night. It was said that he "loved people and came to know each club member and his or her family so well that he thought of them all as friends and they reciprocated."[27] In 1946, McPhail became the first full-time district agriculturalist at Olds.

During Junior Club Week, O.S.A. was the temporary home of dozens of young people from across Alberta.

The 4-H Pledge

I pledge:
My head to clearer thinking,
My heart to greater loyalty,
My hands to larger service,
And my health to better living,
For my club, my community, and my country.

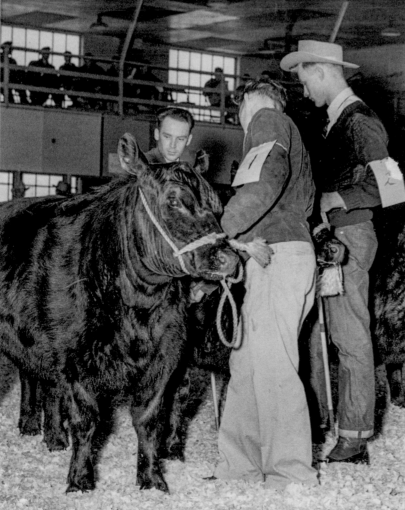

The Little Royal, introduced by Instructor Dave Andrew in 1933, helped students to prepare for show ring exhibitions. These photographs are from the early 1950s. Hugh McPhail, who joined the O.S.A. staff in 1930, was instrumental in organizing the junior clubs as part of his summer work as district agriculturalist.

199

The School of Community Life

While most of the public gatherings at O.S.A. were agricultural in nature, the School also hosted many non-farm events such as conventions of teachers and school trustees from Calgary, meetings of the United Farmers of Alberta political party, the Alberta Home and School Association, the Crossfield Board of Trade, and the annual picnics of many district organizations. Without a doubt, the revenues from facility rentals by various organizations boosted the School's bottom line. More importantly, with each passing year, visits like these wove O.S.A. more tightly into the fabric of Alberta society.

One of the most unusual recurring events at O.S.A. during the Depression was called The School of Community Life. This began in 1937. Organized and run by the Extension Department of the University of Alberta, and assisted by grants from United Grain Growers and the Alberta Wheat Pool,[28] The School of Community Life was held over the course of three weeks beginning on June 24th. It offered a series of lectures aimed at the interests of a rural audience. The lectures were open to all men and women between the ages of 17 and 50.[29] A modest fee was charged for participation, and Principal Murray offered the students accommodation in the dormitory at the nominal charge of $1.25 per day. The gymnasium was available to anyone who wished to play volleyball after class, while other attendees proved eager to try their hand at lawn croquet on the School grounds.

The lectures addressed subjects as diverse as international affairs, drama, English literature, rural sociology, citizenship and homemaking. Some of the lecturers, such as Dalhousie University's Professor of Philosophy, Dr. Herbert Leslie Stewart, were distinguished scholars. Others, such as Elizabeth Haynes and Ted Cohen, who spoke about the dramatic arts, were quickly establishing national reputations. School instructors complemented those offerings. In the first year, for example, Hugh McPhail tackled the topic of citizenship, as he often did in his normal O.S.A. classes, while the tireless Miss McIntyre summoned the energy to speak once again on "Modern Homemaking."

The School of Community Life was the O.S.A. extension library of its day. It was the brainchild of a young man named Donald Cameron.[30] A farm boy from Elnora, just south of Innisfail, Cameron had taken correspondence courses in history and economics through the Extension Department of the University of Alberta during the winter of 1925. His marks were good enough that he won a $250 scholarship to attend the Olds School of Agriculture.

Instead of coming to Olds, however, Cameron convinced the University to allow him to enrol as a freshman in the Faculty of Agriculture. He graduated with honours, worked as an agricultural field representative, and then joined the University as Agricultural Secretary in the Department of Extension. In 1933, he won a coveted Carnegie Scholarship to study educational techniques in the Scandinavian countries. So impressed was he by the folk high schools of Denmark, which stressed the need to take education to the people, that he applied the model in his own

ALBERTA SCHOOL OF COMMUNITY LIFE
O.S.A. OLDS ALTA. JUNE 24 – JULY 10. 1937

extension work upon his return to Alberta. Just as Duncan Marshall had found inspiration in the rural schools of Denmark, so too did Donald Cameron a generation later.

Cameron ran his School of Community Life at Olds for six summers. Attendance was poor at first, with only about a dozen students coming out for all of the lectures. But as word spread, the level of interest increased tremendously. In 1938, more than 100 people registered and 70 attended regularly. It helped that the lecture topics were increasingly geared towards the interests of the participants. The idea of co-operation, for instance, ran through many of the courses and resonated particularly well with rural people who believed in grain and livestock and poultry pools, and had experienced the benefits of united political action by farmers. And, as Adolf Hitler pushed Europe to the brink of all-out war, lectures about international affairs became even more popular. By 1939, Principal Murray felt emboldened to say that, "one got the impression that it [the School] was established firmly on a permanent basis."[31]

As it turned out, he was wrong. The start of the war in 1939 brought about a sudden exodus of young people from the countryside, some into Canada's fighting forces and others into the cities where they found good jobs in war-related industries. This greatly weakened rural education programs, not only in Alberta but across the country.[32] Cameron's School of Community Life abandoned Olds for a series of weeklong "community life conferences" held at various rural locations throughout the Province. This new experiment did not survive the war. Cameron, for his part, went on to found the now-famous Banff School of Fine Arts along the same Scandinavian lines. But his connection to Olds was not yet finished. In 1958, Cameron would head up a provincial review of education that was to have important implications for the Olds School of Agriculture.

Modelled on European precedents, The School of Community Life brought the arts and humanities to rural Alberta for several summers after 1937, when this photograph of the inaugural attendees was taken.

War and Recovery

The agricultural economy revived haltingly in Western Canada and recovered fully only after the start of the Second World War.

As late as 1936 the Department of Agriculture continued to lament the persistence of drought, grasshoppers and light yields in central Alberta farm districts. It found solace only in the good quality of the grain being harvested and the fact that commodity prices had recovered just enough that a farmer might make a profit from his labours for the first time in years. A bushel of No. 1 Northern Wheat that had sold for less than 40 cents in late 1932 advanced to 55 cents in August of 1939. Prices rose primarily because drought in North America and Russia, and wet conditions in Europe, had seriously depleted grain stocks. For most people on the land, however, only mixed farming saved them from destitution.

Then, as the harvest of 1939 approached, both cereal and forage crops continued to look promising for the first time in nearly a decade. And with the approach of harvest came the start of another world war. The price of wheat soared to 80 cents a bushel within two weeks of the declaration of war and climbed by another dime before grain ship navigation on the Great Lakes closed later that year. As the war cut Great Britain off from its traditional sources of meat, hog production took off in Western Canada. Soon the demand for cheese and eggs rose as well. Then expansion of the export market for beef to the United States occurred. Soon the demands of that global conflict would ripple through to the man in the field and the economic recovery would take hold.

Farm Mechanics Instructor Fred Parkinson designed this stook sweep to compensate for the lack of farm labour during the Second World War.

Fred Parkinson's Stook School

As young men left the district to train with the armed forces, many farmers found themselves short of help during haying and harvest. Freeman (Fred) Parkinson, who taught Farm Mechanics and had a reputation for being happiest when "smeared in grease or oil"[34], tried to alleviate this labour shortage by designing a better stook sweep based on the crude efforts of a number of local farmers. These sweeps, which were like manually operated forklifts, allowed one farmer to do the work of many in moving bundles to the separator. In 1943, Parkinson and O.S.A. blacksmith Bill Armstrong put on a special short course in stook sweep manufacturing for farmers and those who ran machine shops or blacksmith shops in the district. By the end of the summer, some 70 sweeps built at the School were in use in the harvest fields around Olds. Parkinson later refined the design and prepared detailed blueprints for publication in a special booklet that was distributed to district agriculturalists throughout the Province.

In 1941, the Federal Government finally grasped the vital contribution that prairie agriculture could make to the war effort, and it set both production goals and price ceilings to forestall the possibility of inflation. The administration of Prime Minister William Lyon Mackenzie King called Frank Grisdale to Ottawa to oversee much of the work of the Wartime Prices and Trade Board. Eventually, he became Chairman and Foods Co-ordinator of the Board.[33] The global hunger for reliable sources of foodstuffs highlighted the importance of efficient farm production as never before and shone a spotlight more brightly upon the applied research and practical education that made such efficiency possible. O.S.A., like the farmers of central Alberta, would be changed by this new crisis.

Optimism, heightened by the adoption of productive new farm technologies, spread throughout the farm community for the first time in many years. Since the start of the Depression, for example, district farmers had been reluctant to apply fertilizer to their fields in significant quantities. Now they did so. Yauch's pioneering demonstration plots south, north and west of Olds had proven their worth. Similarly, his research with herbicides began to pay off locally. Demand for registered seed shot up too, and of course Olds was a key producer and seller of such seed. The draught horses that had sufficed for fieldwork during the depths of the economic crisis quickly gave way to gasoline-powered, rubber-tired tractors and larger cultivating, haying and harvesting machinery. This shift in motive power happened at O.S.A. too, as the Percheron herd was reduced in favour of tractors. Even beekeeping proved more popular than ever before; so popular, in fact, that in 1941 the School brought in 99 packages of bees and acted as midwife to the new Olds and District Beekeepers'

Association. Two years later, O.S.A. established the first artificial insemination laboratory in the Province, imported both chilled and frozen semen from Ontario and British Columbia, and instructed farmers in the productivity gains that followed from such breeding. Local farmers were grateful for the School's assistance, particularly in improving the quality of their Holstein herds.

This was the positive side of the war. There were many less desirable aspects to it as well. Among them was the high rate of enlistment in the district. Many local men joined the Olds Company of the Calgary Regiment (Tank), which saw action at Dieppe and in Sicily. Once again, O.S.A. students volunteered for service in large numbers. In 1945, the Alumni Association recorded that 202 had served in the armed forces (78 Army, 24 Navy, and 100 Air Force), including 20 women. Four received the Distinguished Flying Cross and one the Distinguished Flying Medal. Nine were killed in action.

Principal Murray reflected that,

now nearly every family has representatives in uniform. Our graduates are fighting in the air, on land and on the sea throughout the world. Some have made the supreme sacrifice, others are prisoners of war and many are daily risking their lives in their country's service.[35]

But the front-line fight, he stressed, was not the only fight. As local families realized from the strict rationing of coffee, tea, sugar and other necessities, food production was a key to winning the war.

One direct effect of those many enlistments in the armed forces was that the average age of a student at O.S.A.

dropped from 19 or 20 to between 17 and 18 years.[36] A second result was a noticeable decline in the number of volunteers for Junior Club work. This was so serious that the Minister of Agriculture, D. B. MacMillan, wrote a stern letter to O.S.A. students to remind them how fortunate they were in a time of war and to cajole them into taking up what he called their "duty" to show greater leadership in their communities. In 1942, "for the sake of efficiency," the Schools of Agriculture at Olds and Vermilion were asked to assume greater responsibility for the administration of the Junior Clubs. Soon this summertime extension work, which involved nearly 4,000 students by 1944, occupied nearly all of the attention of four O.S.A. instructors, Morley Malyon (Poultry Clubs), W. C. Gordon (Stock Clubs), and Walter Benn and J. E. (Ted) Hawker (Crop Clubs).

Ted Hawker, who joined O.S.A. as Instructor in Field Husbandry two years after graduating from the University of Alberta in 1941, also led in the formation of an O.S.A. Cadet Corps. Officially, they were known as the Olds School of Agriculture Cadet Corps, R.C.A.C. Twice weekly, 86 young men assembled on the athletic field or in classrooms for instruction in drill, rifle drill, small arms use, fieldcraft, anti-gas treatments, first aid, army law and map reading. A 12-man Signal Corps was organized as well. Its members studied Morse Code and semaphore signalling. At first the cadets lacked uniforms, so marched about in their civvies. To the dismay of many when a shipment of uniforms finally did arrive, none were of a large size. Regardless of the cadets' motley appearance, when Sergeant-Major Tillisch from Calgary came to inspect them he said he was delighted by their "high degree of efficiency and discipline."

The closest many of these young men got to the war was sitting next to a returned veteran in an O.S.A. classroom. Beginning in the summer of 1942, the School began to accept applications from discharged men who qualified for agricultural training and other benefits under the provisions of the new Veterans' Land Act. This continued annually, and in 1945 Murray found it necessary to ask a number of 16-year old applicants to postpone their attendance so that the School could admit 15 veterans.

In 1941, 86 students formed the Olds School of Agriculture Cadet Corps, R.C.A.C., and drilled on the athletic fields under the command of Instructor Ted Hawker.

The Teakettle Mechanics

Fred Parkinson seemed to specialize in solving the labour problems of farmers during the difficult war years. He got yet another opportunity when a number of O.S.A. girls approached him with the request that he give them some basic training in farm mechanics so they could help out more on the farm. There were about a dozen of them in all, and they were quickly dubbed the "Teakettle Mechanics." It didn't take long for some of the O.S.A. boys to challenge the girls to a race to see who could assemble a small gasoline engine and start it in the fastest time. With a chivalrous "Ladies First," the boys stood back as the girls put their skills to the test. Parkinson kept time. The girls were efficient and the engine started without hesitation. Parkinson then had them strip the engine down again for the boys' turn. As the boys began to assemble the engine, you could almost see the difference in speed. But when they had everything bolted together and tried to start the engine, nothing happened. Parkinson declared the girls' team the winner. Only later did the boys discover that one of the girls had pinched the spark-plug points together!

At the same time, he felt certain that the need to accommodate discharged men was merely a temporary phenomenon.

In 1946, Murray, a veteran of a different kind, chose to retire. He had seen O.S.A. through a tumultuous decade and a half. Now he needed to look after a personal health issue. His calm, competent hand on the tiller would be missed. His wife would be missed, too. While Murray was never demonstrative, his wife was the opposite. She took a great interest in all the students, appeared at most social and literary functions, and opened the Principal's home to the Home Ec students every Wednesday so they might practise their social skills while enjoying tea. Clara Storch, a student in the 1940s, called Mrs. Murray the "guiding light" of all the O.S.A. girls. Mr. and Mrs. Murray eventually moved to Ottawa, where he passed away in 1973 at the age of 91.

As momentous as Murray's departure from O.S.A. was, it paled in comparison to the death of Duncan Marshall in the same year. In his 73 years, Marshall never strayed far from the intersection of politics, agriculture and education. After his defeat in the provincial election of 1921, he prepared a review of the Agricultural Instruction Act for the Federal Government, wrote several textbooks on livestock and farm management, and continued to raise and show the Shorthorns he loved. Eventually, he moved to Ontario where he served as the Minister of Agriculture for three years before accepting an appointment to the Senate Chamber from Prime Minister Mackenzie King.

Charming, irascible, always determined and often reviled, the politically nimble Marshall remained a farmer at heart. He believed firmly that the greatest achievement in the world was, as he put it, that of "making a home on the land."[37]

Ode To The Class Of 1943

(Sung to the tune of Lili Marlene)

Here we are together, standing row on row —

The School of Agriculture from fifty years ago.

A day to remember times before

The money scarce, the world at war

The tires and gas were rationed.

It didn't bother us!

No cars upon the campus

We walked or took the bus!

Things were much more simple in 1943,

When girls were girls and men were men, the way it ought to be,

And Home Economics was in style

The girls would study all the while.

They practised in the kitchen

Their dishes to prepare

In uniforms and aprons

And hairnets on their hair.

The boys were learning farming and catching up to date

Exploring new technology their fathers would debate.

But once in a while their thoughts would stray

To pleasant sights across the way

The lovely trees and gardens

The silos, barns and stock,

And girls between their classes

Out strolling on the walk.

Such a perfect set-up and soon they had to meet

For movies, dates and dances, and milkshakes down the street.

The girls signed the book when on a date

And Lord help the girl who turned up late.

Ten-thirty was the deadline

And no-one had a key.

Our school was there to teach us Respectability!

The war is just a memory, the days of school are past.

A few of us are missing, the years are going fast.

But never forgotten, come what may,

Are friends we met at O.S.A.

They may be slowly aging,

But underneath we see

Those kids we went to school with...

The Class of '43.

A Period of Uncertainty[1]

As the war came to an end, it was all too apparent the Olds School of Agriculture was aging. Sadly, it was not aging gracefully. Buildings needed repair. Wall paint was peeling everywhere. Linoleum had worn thin. Sidewalks were cracking. The heating and lighting systems cried out for modernization. Fire protection was inadequate. Sports facilities and equipment were getting long in the tooth. The orchards were overgrown. The grounds offered few parking spaces for the growing number of motorized vehicles venturing onto the campus. Meeting rooms were no longer able to handle the thousands of conventioneers and other visitors who came to the campus each summer. Office space was in equally short supply. Some traditional classes no longer seemed relevant to the increasing maturity of Alberta agriculture and rural society.

The Changing of the Guard

Even the staff was getting on. George Holeton, reflecting on the fact that he was now routinely teaching the children of his former students, said it just served to remind him that he was no longer a spring chicken.[2]

Holeton was the first to go. He left in 1944 after 31 years of teaching carpentry, blacksmithing, mechanics and mechanical drafting. A popular teacher, he would be missed in both the classroom and in the orchestra, where his clarinet playing was greatly admired. Walter Benn, fiddle player extraordinaire in the same orchestra and passionate dramatics coach and actor, followed Holeton out the door in 1947. After 27 years of instructing O.S.A. students in English and Mathematics, he was ready for a change as well. In the following year, Hugh McPhail and Art Kemp also retired from teaching. McPhail continued on with the Department of Agriculture in a different role until 1955, while the Department kindly put the ailing Kemp in the role of Assistant District Agriculturalist, an undemanding position created just for him. He was hospitalized in 1947 and passed away in the Olds Hospital in March, 1948. Another long-serving instructor, Fred Parkinson, left teaching after the 1948-49 school year to work on other Departmental extension projects. Christine McIntyre, the Home Economics instructor who had first come to O.S.A. in 1921, departed in 1951. Of all old guard, only Morley Malyon remained, and he, too, would give up his position in 1955.

The veteran Morley Malyon making a point to his class in the dairy barn in the early 1950s. Malyon was among the last of the O.S.A. old guard still teaching at the time.

The departure of these O.S.A. stalwarts marked the end of an era. A younger generation was taking up both the administrative and the teaching reins. Soon, they would be responsible for guiding the School along a new and different path in the post-war years. The transition was not swift, smooth or certain.

The first change came in June of 1946, when F. N. (Fred) Miller succeeded James Murray as Principal. A Saskatchewan native, Miller had had a varied career. He trained as a school teacher at the Camrose Normal School in 1926-27, then entered the Two-in-One program at Olds before moving on to the University of Alberta for a degree in agriculture. He then returned to

teaching, eventually becoming the school principal at Gibbons. From 1943 to 1945, he served as District Agriculturalist at Edmonton, where he specialized in the Junior Farm Clubs and Youth Training. He also conducted extensive investigational work for the Alberta Mobilization Board and the Selective Service Office on Farm Labour during the war years.

Miller was the first graduate of O.S.A. to run the School. As such, he effectively bridged the old and new eras. As one writer commented in the Alumni Association newsletter, "By training and experience he is familiar with O.S.A. objectives and tradition, and has a sympathetic understanding of present-day country youth."[3]

Miller remained at O.S.A. only until 1949, when he resigned to take up a new position as Agricultural Assistant with the Edmonton Exhibition Association. Veteran soils scientist Charlie Yauch succeeded him. Described by those who knew him as a tower of strength,[4] Yauch remained Principal until 1952 when he became the District Agriculturalist at High River. He retained this position until his retirement in 1966.

In 1952, John Everett (Ev) Birdsall took up the Principalship, a position he would fill for the next 20 years. As the second O.S.A. graduate to occupy the Principal's chair, it was something of a homecoming for him. Immediately prior to joining the School, he had

spent seven years as the Supervisor of Crop Improvement within the Field Crops Branch of the Alberta Department of Agriculture. Before that, he had been Assistant Superintendent of the Experimental Farm at Prince George, British Columbia, and District Agriculturalist at Thorsby and Red Deer.

Solidity, rather than innovation, would be the hallmark of Birdsall's administration. He undertook these new responsibilities as he did every new venture in his life, in a "practical, organized, sensible manner."[5] In what he himself called a period of uncertainty at O.S.A., Ev Birdsall epitomized determination and stability. The School was lucky to have him.

Far left: Fred Miller took up the Principal's reins upon James Murray's retirement in 1946. He was the first O.S.A. graduate to fill that role. Centre: Called a "tower of strength," veteran soils scientist Charles Yauch succeeded Fred Miller as Principal in 1949. Right: J. Everett Birdsall served as Principal from 1952 to 1972 and oversaw O.S.A.'s transition from an agricultural school to a vocational college.

New Instructors in a Changing World

In 1954, when Frank Grisdale visited O.S.A. to take part in the midsummer alumni reunion, he reminisced about many things: his admiration for the pioneering work of Principal Elliott; the impressive cluster of campus buildings; and the remarkable changes that time had brought to the appearance of the O.S.A. grounds. Fittingly, he concluded his remarks by saying that, "Buildings and grounds do not make a school as much as does the calibre of the men and women who teach the students."[6]

While the number and calibre of O.S.A. staff did not change appreciably after the war, the names of those who did the teaching did. Ev Birdsall was far from the only new face on campus in 1952. The post-war job market, which many thought would be overwhelmed by the return of armed forces veterans, turned out to be remarkably strong. By 1946, businesses were investing, consumers were buying and employment was rising across the country. The agricultural sector rejoiced at a new deal with Great Britain that provided assurances of a market for significant quantities of wheat at good prices.

When a 1947 report on O.S.A. recorded the resignations of several instructors who had accepted "more attractive positions elsewhere,"[7] the Department of Agriculture responded without surprise or concern. It was a trend that would continue. As Birdsall took up the administrative reins, he was immediately obliged to accept the unprecedented resignation of an even dozen of his instructors.[8] Many of these departures were related to the comparatively low salaries offered by the Department of Agriculture for teaching, as well as to the increasingly unwelcome annual obligation of instructors to undertake summer extension work.

Attitudes toward work were changing, and there was clearly a new sense of labour mobility in the air. When coupled with the retirement of the old guard, the post-war perspective on employment resulted in a sea-change at the Olds School of Agriculture.

Time Given to Individual Subjects, 1949-50

Agriculture

- *Field husbandry 18.2%*
- *Livestock 28.8%*
- *Farm mechanics 23.3%*
- *Academic subjects (English, Mathematics and Science) 21.6%*
- *Economics and Management 5.6%*

Home Economics

- *Nutrition 18.7%*
- *Sewing 23.3%*
- *Home Management 15.1%*
- *Agricultural Subjects 15.0%*
- *Academic Subjects 21.6%*
- *Economics 3.8%*

Top: This photograph, taken at the 40th anniversary reunion in 1953, captured the old and the new guard. Left to right: R. M. Putnam, Superintendent of Agricultural Schools; Frank Grisdale; O. S. Longman, Alberta's Deputy Minister of Agriculture; W. J. Elliott; J. Everett Birdsall.

Below: The receiving line: J. Everett and Mrs. Birdsall greeting first-year students before the first dance of the season in the 1950s. This was a tradition that extended back to Principal Elliott.

"HOME."

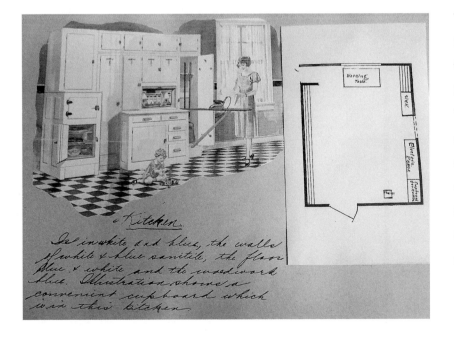

Kitchen.

Is in white and blue, the walls of white & blue sanitile, the floor blue & white and the woodwork blue. Illustration shows a convenient cupboard which is in this kitchen.

Top left: Upgrading the domestic science laboratories did little to arrest the decline in female attendance at O.S.A. in the 1950s.

Bottom left: Miss Moseson's sewing class, 1953.

This page: After the Second World War, enrolment in Home Economics at O.S.A. dropped precipitously. While O.S.A. introduced new Vocational Pattern courses for women in the 1950s, it continued to emphasize traditional domesticity as shown in this page from a student scrapbook.

The Beginnings of Specialization

Change was afoot on the agricultural front as well. Much of this change was related to the war. Rising global demand for foodstuffs, along with federal government price guarantees, encouraged prairie farmers to invest heavily in their operations.

For the first time since the 1920s, Alberta farmers expanded their holdings, enlarged their herds, planted more acreage, fertilized and sprayed their crops, and bought machinery as never before. As demobilization took place after the war, government programs such as the Veterans Land Act helped many young farmers get established by providing loans on easy terms for the purchase of land, stock and equipment.

Dealing with what would later be called farming "inputs" — machinery, fuel, lubricants, pesticides, herbicides, and the like — quickly became a routine side of life on the farm. Such knowledge became even more essential to productivity as the availability of, and need for, farm labour declined in the post-war era. Scientific agriculture was tightening its grip on rural society.

Responding to the rapid expansion of prairie agriculture demanded that students obtain a much more thorough knowledge of technology than had ever been the case. While the O.S.A. curriculum had always imparted a basic understanding of agricultural mechanics and related matters, it tended to do so indirectly and largely through the contributions of itinerant instructors.

Such was the case, for example, with the complex matter of large-scale irrigation. The topic was touched upon as early as 1913-14 as part of the Field Husbandry course, but after the drought and soil erosion of the Depression years the School began to offer more detailed instruction. In 1938, O.S.A. was fortunate to secure the part-time services of Gavin N. Houston, former Acting Commissioner of Irrigation for the Canadian government and more recently Superintendent of the Canadian Pacific Railway's Lethbridge irrigation project. Not only had he managed large irrigation

Gavin Houston, a retired hydraulic engineer, taught part-time irrigation courses at O.S.A. in the late 1930s and early 1940s. By the 1950s, however, the School was moving toward the hiring of permanent staff with technical expertise.
Courtesy Wallace Kemp

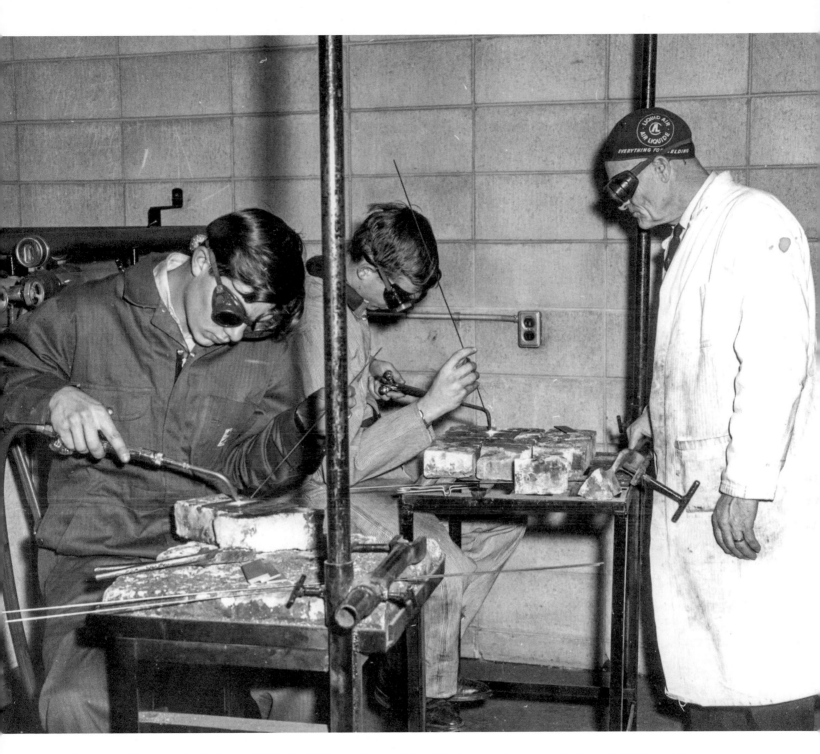

projects, but Houston had also published widely on the topic. Now retired, he had relocated to Olds to live with his daughter Dorothy, her husband Art Kemp, and their three sons. The School was able to take advantage of his fortuitous presence in the community for a decade.

When this photograph was taken in the early 1960s, acetylene welding had already been part of the O.S.A. curriculum for more than a decade.

As the 1950s began, however, O.S.A. started to move away from reliance on itinerant and part-time teachers. Instead, the administration worked to secure the services of permanent instructors with more recent training in various aspects of agricultural technology and farm management.

Cameron Kirk was one of them. A Saskatoon native, he grew up in Vancouver but then returned to his home province to obtain a degree in Agricultural Engineering from the University of Saskatchewan. He taught Farm Mechanics briefly at O.S.A. in 1949-50 before going into business at Didsbury. In the autumn of 1953 he returned to O.S.A., mainly as a replacement for that jack-of-all-mechanical-trades, George Holeton. Kirk would remain an instructor until 1962, his "contagious enthusiasm for the courses he teaches" infecting everyone around him. With Kirk, the teaching of agricultural mechanics at Olds began to shift decisively from small engine repair to heavy-duty mechanics. Acetylene welding for machinery repair also became part of the curriculum in the early 1950s.

In the following year, Dennis Radcliff joined Kirk in the staff room. Born in Calgary in 1928, Radcliff attended O.S.A. in 1947-48 before continuing his agricultural education at the University of Alberta. There he specialized in Animal Science, the course he taught at Olds, with a one-year interlude, between 1954 and 1959. Then, much to the disappointment of colleagues and students, he left for advanced training at the Ontario Veterinary College at Guelph. Radcliff would eventually return to teach Animal Science again, while seeing to it that the horse regained its rightful place on the Olds curriculum.

Stu Wilton, a Bentley boy, joined the Animal Husbandry staff in the fall of 1955 as Instructor in Poultry, Dairying and Mathematics. At the University of Alberta, which he attended from 1949 to 1953, he specialized in Animal Nutrition. Like many of the O.S.A. instructors, he had more than one job on campus. His other title in those days was Manager of the School farm. Later, he would serve as Chair of Animal Science.

In 1956, Kelowna-born Greville Harrison became a colleague of Kirk, Radcliff and Wilton. He brought with him a diploma in horticulture (1938) from the Ontario Agricultural College at Guelph and a Bachelor's degree in Agriculture (1944) from the University of Saskatchewan, where he specialized in agricultural mechanics. After graduation, he had worked with Saskatchewan's Rural Housing Committee as a Farm Structures Specialist before moving on to the Swift Current Experimental Farm where he took charge of Farm Structures Research. At Olds, he taught the course in Farm Buildings and oversaw all campus maintenance. His employment reflected the dramatic change that post-war prosperity was bringing to the design and construction of livestock shelters, machinery sheds and domestic housing.

These new instructors — and of course there were more of them hired around the same time — set O.S.A. firmly on the track to specialization. While their routine teaching still reflected the basic School of Agriculture curriculum of 1913-14, they possessed the in-depth knowledge, the determination and the ambition to focus their attention on ever-narrower aspects of Western Canadian agriculture. As the years passed and they matured as instructors, that is exactly what happened. In hiring them, Birdsall – perhaps unwittingly – secured the future of the School by establishing the academic foundation and reputation of a vocational college.

Renovating the Campus

Between 1946 and 1962, there was scarcely a year in which the campus buildings or grounds escaped renovation. Principal Birdsall said that all the Schools of Agriculture, and not only Olds, needed significant repair during that decade and a half. Age and a lack of routine maintenance had taken their toll.

Yet during much of that time the Department of Agriculture remained torn between the need to offer students and staff reasonable accommodations and working conditions, and the need to keep expenditures under control. Making the pace of improvement even less predictable was the Government's growing uncertainty about the School's future. E. W. Hinman, the Provincial Treasurer, had publicly declared the Schools of Agriculture "useless" — not a good sign — and said that in his view it would be cheaper to send Alberta students to the United States for agricultural training.[11] As a result, the many needed changes to the infrastructure of the campus usually took place in a piecemeal fashion.

The "make-do" attitude could be seen clearly as the School confronted the challenge of finding suitable space for the farm mechanics course that was beginning to attract serious attention. The Administration found an immediate solution at the former Bowden Flying School, where a 30-by-48-foot war-time drill hall had been declared surplus. It was moved to O.S.A. in 1947 and remodelled in the next year. New trusses were acquired from the former prisoner-of-war camp at Lethbridge. Sealed against the weather, insulated and connected to a new central heating plant where the old carpentry shop had stood, the makeshift structure housed both classrooms and shop laboratories.

One of Administration's priorities was to improve living conditions in the 1927 dormitory. Wear and tear was evident everywhere as some 3,000 to 4,000 students had made it their temporary home during the ensuing two decades. While Principal Murray managed to shoehorn 40 additional students into part of the dining room and had accommodated another 32 in an extension of the men's dormitory, he had lacked the resources to renovate the original student rooms — the "cells", as Art Kemp called them.

The needed changes began in 1950. The first and second floors of the boys' dormitory, and the first floor of the girls', were completely renovated and redecorated. Additional showers were installed, too. The larger investment on the boy's side of the building spoke volumes about the declining enrolment in Home Economics. Fluorescent lighting was installed in the dining room. The dormitory and all but two buildings on campus were connected to the central heating plant at the same time, which was a great improvement over the separate furnaces and stoves that Theo Moe had tended faithfully for so many years. A start was also made on tying the School buildings into the Town of Olds's sewage system. Redecoration of several rooms in the Main Building took place as well. The Animal Husbandry and Metal Work structures received a coat of stucco, and fresh paint was applied to almost all of the farm buildings. The Field Crops Laboratory benefited from new linoleum during the same wave of renovation.

In 1951, the Department of Agriculture assumed responsibility from the Department of Public Works for all School maintenance. With this change came completion of the renovations in the boys' dormitory, replacement of the battle-scarred wooden floor in the gymnasium, and a thorough refurbishing of the equipment in the large kitchen that served the dormitory dining room. At the same time, work was completed on installation of a large-capacity pump to lift dormitory sewage into the Town system.

The next year would see redecoration of the girls' rooms in the dormitory and of five classrooms, as well as continued improvements to the kitchen facilities.

And still the work continued. In preparation for the 1954-55 school year, the maintenance staff built and installed 25 bunk beds and study tables in the boys' dorm. "With the bunks completed and equipped with new mattresses," said Birdsall, "it is expected that louder bells will be needed!"[12] The Main Building, which had been stuccoed in 1948-49, now received new battleship linoleum in the hallways and on the stairs; the library and dining room in the dormitory were redecorated; naphtha gas gave way to propane in the laboratories; and the campus was connected to the Town water system as a safety measure.

Students were not the only ones to get better accommodations after the war. During the late 1940s the Principal's residence and several other dwellings were insulated

This aerial shot, taken some time after 1948, shows the 1927 dormitory at the bottom, the Main Building and water tower to the north, the renovated Bowden Flying School hangar at the top, and the farm on the bottom right. Parking lots were a new feature of the campus at the time.

and stuccoed. The Principal's house received a new heating unit at the same time. Prior to the start of the 1952-53 school year — no doubt in anticipation of the arrival of the Birdsall family — the decor of his residence was updated. Nearly a decade later, a one-car garage would be erected next to the home.

As residential renovations wound down, the Administration turned its fragmented attention and limited funds to the grounds. While the floral beauty of Art Kemp's flower beds and apple trees continued to elicit compliments from everyone who visited the campus, its roads, pathways and drainage systems now seemed outdated. They had been designed with a pedestrian and horse-drawn world in mind. Motorized vehicles now ruled the roadways.

In fact, school reports talked about "congestion" on the roads. This change was evident as early as 1946-47, when the Administration felt it necessary to remove several beautiful old trees near the main entrance to the campus in order to widen the driveway. Several serious accidents had occurred there. A series of wet years in the early 1950s then prompted the Administration to arrange for installation of four new culverts to address drainage problems. By 1960, a spacious drive looped in front of the dormitory. A new parking lot accommodated the growing number of cars belonging to students and to Olds residents who attended games at the hockey rink throughout the winter months. When completed, the wider drives and parking lot were gravelled. Cement sidewalks and curbs were replaced as well. These were the first steps in the implementation of an overall landscape plan for the campus that was prepared in 1959. Within three years, most campus roadways would be hard surfaced.

By the early 1950s many of the original School plantings were, like the retiring instructors, in their dotage. The groundskeepers routinely pruned, re-seeded patchy lawns and removed dying or dangerous trees. The School's acquisition of a large power mower made lawn maintenance much easier than in the past when everything was done by hand. But by 1956, it was clear that cosmetic changes were insufficient. Major redevelopment was in order. As a result almost the entire orchard, except for new plantings, was pulled out. The dormitory was graced with much larger flowerbeds. The sports field to the south of the dormitory was re-seeded as well.

Many of the bedding plants that filled the beds each spring now came from the School's own greenhouse. There had been a small one built in 1929 in which the staff grew tomatoes, cucumbers, lettuce and radishes, but it could no longer meet the needs of the campus. The new structure, situated immediately west of the livestock building, was begun in 1946 and completed three years later. It would serve the campus for nearly two decades.

If there was one individual to whom the School owed thanks for many of these improvements to the grounds, it was Bill Baranyk. Between 1958 and 1962, this graduate of the Vermilion School of Agriculture served Olds as Horticulturalist, Botanist and groundskeeper. He was a latter-day Art Kemp, and, like Kemp, his enthusiasm knew no bounds. In addition to his teaching duties, he became very active in the Alumni Association. Before departing to become Principal at Vermilion in 1962, Baranyk would also prove crucial in helping to define a new direction for the academic programs offered at Olds.[13]

Changes to the Farm

From 1936 to 1956, the School farm was the responsibility of Walter Ross.

He was the School's first full-time farm manager, replacing Fred Parkinson.

Working closely with his chief herdsman, Bill Burns, Ross oversaw the work of 10 farmhands and was an important member of the committee that decided to establish the Artificial Insemination lab at O.S.A.

When Ross retired, his son-in-law Gordon Ogston took his place. Ogston was a 1931 Vermilion graduate who took his third year matriculation at Olds in 1932 and then began a 41-year career in agriculture that took him across Western Canada. He came to O.S.A. in 1943 to oversee the work of the Artificial Insemination lab. In addition to managing the farm from 1956 to 1977, Ogston taught livestock judging, herdsman's practice, and coached the student hockey teams. It was on his watch, in 1956, that the School developed its first long-term plan for farm buildings.

Under the direction of these capable men, the School farm kept pace with the profound changes that affected Western Canadian agriculture after the Second World War. It continued to serve as a vital component of teaching at O.S.A., as well as being the mainstay of the dormitory kitchen. Its beef, pork, poultry, milk, vegetables and other production continued to fill students' stomachs as in years past, providing what most remembered as satisfying, if basic meat-and-potatoes, cooking.

In 1946, the farm consisted of a section of land. All but 100 acres were cultivated, as the intention was to produce the feed required for the School stock. The rest was native pasture. Now that the Ayrshire herd had been disposed of, Holsteins grazed in the pasture and produced the milk and cream for the dormitory kitchen. This breed was a local favourite and the underpinning of the School's artificial insemination program that continued until 1956. Usually a couple of dozen feeder steers were bought each fall and used for judging classes before being slaughtered, roasted and served in the dining room. A slaughterhouse had been constructed in 1944 next to the livestock classroom, and students were expected to assist their instructor in killing and butchering the animals.

It was undeniably the age of the machine. The once-large herd of magnificent Percherons was depleted now, as almost all farm work was done with tractors. While the campus drives filled with cars, the farm lane on the east side of the grounds became an outdoor showroom for the finest agricultural equipment available. Scattered about the farm were new combines and tractors with front-end loaders and forage harvesters and spray rigs and hammer mills and much more. It helped that many of the farm machinery companies eagerly loaned their latest equipment to the School in exchange for the free publicity that gave them, particularly during the annual summer field days when hundreds of farmers and their families rubbed shoulders on the School grounds.

232

The Plywood Manufacturers Association of British Columbia was another corporate donor of the School during the 1950s. In 1955, the Association supplied all the materials for construction of a large granary and two self-feeders in exchange for the School's willingness to "test their plans."

The farm continued to conduct applied research for various Departments of the Alberta Government, other educational institutions, and private companies. In 1955 and 1956, for example, School staff worked closely with the Department of Highways on a project related to the upgrading of the road to Sundre that bordered the campus on the north. The Department wished to determine the best way to reclaim gravel borrow pits. After extensive trials, the School was able to offer advice that became the model for all borrow pit reclamation in the Province.

Around the same time, School staff also co-operated with the Morden Experimental Farm in Manitoba on orchard plantings, with the Lacombe Experimental Farm on cereal and forage crops, and with the Field Crops Branch on fungicide tests.

While projects like those involved the staff directly in the design of the research, at other times the University of Alberta or the federal or provincial departments of Agriculture simply wanted to utilize farm stock, facilities or manpower as part of an experiment they had designed. Often these projects lasted half a year or less, which gave O.S.A. students a valuable opportunity to participate directly in the entire experiment.

In other cases, such as the 18-year study of long-term summerfallowing and continuous forage cropping that began in 1956, a generation of staff and students were exposed to field trials that provided greater appreciation of the negative effects of such traditional practices. This data collection work, carried out on two 80-acre fields at the School farm, was instrumental in the subsequent promotion of zero-tillage practices in Western Canada.

The Post-war Student Body

The participation of students in state-of-the-art scientific experimentation underscored two important facts. One was that the School continued to hire instructors of such high calibre that their expertise was sought frequently by the leading research institutions of the day.

The other was that facilities and programs at O.S.A. were consciously designed to give students a sensible balance of classroom and hands-on training. Throughout the decade of the 1950s, O.S.A. students continued to be immersed in the academic, practical and social aspects of the contemporary farming community. The degree to which the School remained true to the intentions of its founders was remarkable.

If the experience of being an O.S.A. student remained largely unchanged in these years, the same could not be said of the student body itself. Prior to the Second World War, it was comparatively rare for a student to have a name that was not Anglo-Saxon or northern European in origin. In this, the School population reflected the ethnic origins of most settlers in central Alberta. There were exceptions, of course, such as the 1914 graduation of Mary Wong Pond, the wife of a local businessman who later started the Public Lunch restaurant that quickly became a fixture of the community.

As the years went by, however, the School yearbook slowly began to fill with names like Skoreyko, Biamonte, Brausen, Gamache, LaPierre, Damberger, Kachuk and Pawlowski. With only two Schools of Agriculture in the Province after 1931, students now came to Olds from much farther afield than before. As the war progressed, more and more immigrants arrived from war-torn Europe; 95,000 of them settled in Alberta alone between 1946 and 1956.[14] In the next decade, an additional 90,000 would make the Province their new home. General prosperity also made it easier for a broader spectrum of students to attend. That same prosperity also translated into a larger pool of scholarship money for attendance at Olds.

The School started to attract more international students as well. During the 1946-47 school year, for example, O.S.A. welcomed Sally Cunningham from Essex, England; Christopher Marshall from Spur Tree, Jamaica; and Kevin McDowell from Bombay, India. A little more than a decade later, in 1958, the *Calgary Herald* noted the presence of Alex Sloan from New South Wales, Australia; Jaime Ellehoj from Necochea Harbor, Argentina; and Henry Wildeboer from Ovenjsel, Holland. Sloan was planning to return to Australia to put his O.S.A. knowledge to work, while Ellehoj remarked that the training he received at Olds would be particularly valuable to him because conditions in Alberta were similar to those in his home country. While foreign students certainly remained the exception, their presence made the overall student experience at Olds much more cosmopolitan.

If exposure to different ethnicities and foreign cultures helped to broaden the perspective of O.S.A. students, so too did the gradual increase of school-related travel that occurred after the late 1940s. Every second year, the senior class hopped on a bus for a weekend trip to visit their counterparts at the Vermilion School of Agriculture. Sporting and social events filled the days. Similarly, students had the chance to visit Banff each February to enjoy the annual winter carnival. After 1959 some O.S.A. students participated each Christmas in Inter-Varsity Christian Fellowship meetings at Banff that combined faith-based discussions with winter sports and an informal cultural exchange with visiting international students. The world of the O.S.A. student was expanding.

Before the 1950s, most O.S.A. students came from families with roots in Great Britain or northern Europe. Mary Wong Pond, the wife of an Olds businessman, was an exception when she graduated in 1914. The ethnic origins of O.S.A. students began to change with post-war immigration to Canada.

Those who participated in the Junior Clubs (called 4-H Clubs after 1952) had additional opportunities to expand their horizons. Occasional trips to Calgary, Edmonton and Toronto had long been the order of the day for a handful of regional 4-H winners, but in 1947 the Montana Exchange Trip was inaugurated as well. This saw four outstanding 4-H members from Montana come to Olds to take part in the annual Club Week program, and four Alberta members journey to Bozeman in return to participate in the State 4-H Congress.

As the first visit to Olds concluded, the American leader, J. Taylor, expressed his pleasure at the degree of co-operation he had encountered at Olds and hoped "this would be the beginning of the cementing of the agricultural services of Alberta and Montana." Replying on behalf of the Alberta Wheat Pool, which sponsored the exchange, Ben Plummer said he looked forward to more exchanges like this, as they provided "a chance to rob one another's brains."[15] However factitious his remark, it contained more than a grain of truth.

These were years of tremendous growth in the 4-H movement. By 1953, Alberta had 484 clubs, boasting a total of 7,456 members. The trend in membership was steadily upward throughout the next two decades, and by 1973 more than 11,000 Alberta youth would be taking part in the movement. O.S.A. students were frequently avid participants, and the School routinely hosted 4-H meetings every summer.

While many students could not get enough of learning the ropes at the Little Royal and then showing their stock, their parents often thought more about the positive change that 4-H participation brought to their children.

Alexa Church of Balzac, whose sons Gordon, Robert and Stan all took part, attributed this change to Fred Bell, their District Agriculturalist, who taught his club members how to run a proper meeting, prepare a written report and give an engaging public presentation. Many years later, Stan Church said,

> As I look back on my experience in 4-H, it has become clear that the true worth of the program had nothing to do with the agricultural project. The rewards I and others gained were in the ability to express oneself in public, a working knowledge of parliamentary procedure, an ability to work and associate with others and most important to gain self discipline and self confidence.[16]

The experience of 4-H mirrored the values that O.S.A. and the other Schools of Agriculture had worked to instil in their students from the beginning. The two efforts were complementary and mutually reinforcing.

Olds students enjoying the Banff winter carnival in February of 1958. Courtesy Jim Stone

In 1956, students at O.S.A. received yet another lesson in social awareness and cultural diversity. Through the influence of James Gladstone, a Hereford rancher on the Blood Reserve near Lethbridge and President of the Indian Association of Canada, Olds became the site of an unprecedented effort to engage Aboriginal youth in the traditional School of Agriculture programs. Gladstone had always been a proponent of integrated education. In April of 1956, special nine-week courses began for 50 young women and 70 young men from reserves in Alberta and the Northwest Territories. Funding came from the federal Indian Affairs Branch of the Department of Citizenship and Immigration.

In 1956, with funding from the federal Indian Affairs Branch, O.S.A. hosted nine-week courses for Aboriginal students from Alberta and the Northwest Territories. Source Courtesy Glenbow Archives NA-2557-8

The Little Royal and the Great Blizzard of 1955[17]

On the morning of March 30th, 1955, 1,000 people poured into town bright and early to attend the School's annual Little Royal Fair and Achievement Day. By 9 am, it was snowing heavily. Soon every road into town was impassable. The assembled guests were trapped until the weather broke. Working closely with the Town representatives and the Olds Civil Defense organization, the School staff asked everyone to attend the events and enjoy themselves despite the weather. While they did so, the Administration hurriedly made arrangements to feed and house the visitors for as long as the storm lasted. The School continued to accommodate many of the attendees for several days until the roads could be reopened. It was another great example of the School, town and district pulling together.

The students were offered basic training in home economics and agriculture, supplemented by special opportunities in community leadership and extracurricular activities. The intention was to increase their chances in the job market. To accomplish this, the School called upon its regular teaching staff, as well as instructors from Vermilion and the University of Manitoba. A Danish specialist in physical education also took part. Additional help came from three Agriculture alumni, two from Olds and one from the School at Fairview, who assisted with the laboratory work. The students did well and 400 residents of Olds turned out for the closing exercises and achievement day at the end of June.

Above: Members of the Montana 4-H Exchange on the O.S.A. campus in 1955. Reciprocal visits became customary after 1947.

Right: O.S.A. hosted meetings of 4-H Club councils annually after the Second World War. This group attended in the summer of 1955.

Framing the Future

In the 1950s Albertans, and not only those associated with the Schools of Agriculture, grew concerned about the quality of education available to their children. The economy of the Province was shifting slowly from agriculture to industry, from rural to urban, and an increasing number of citizens voiced the view that the school curriculum no longer prepared students adequately for the opportunities of this new world.

There were indeed many new opportunities to get ahead, especially for skilled workers, technicians and professionals. In response to those labour demands, the population of the Province grew by more than 40 per cent between 1946 and 1961. Now only about one in five Albertans lived in the countryside.

With this new perception of employment opportunities came a renewed interest in vocational training. Concern about skilled tradespeople was not restricted to Alberta; in fact, it was becoming increasingly common in many parts of the country. Many businesspeople of the day — especially those involved in Alberta's developing petroleum sector — felt their new workers were not well equipped to address industry's particular challenges. Those challenges were often technical in nature. They also took issue with the limited amount of money that the Government made available for school structures, equipment and teaching staff.

If that were not sufficient reason to consider reform of the educational system, a further incentive appeared in 1957 with the Soviet Union's launch of the Sputnik I satellite. To many people, it was unthinkable that a "backward" nation (and a Communist one at that) like the Union of Soviet Socialist Republics had been able to send a satellite into orbit before anyone else. The space race was on, and across North America politicians, educators and citizens alike quickly demanded higher educational standards for their children and a much greater emphasis on mathematics and science.

In Alberta, the Government responded to all these issues by establishing a Royal Commission on Education under the chairmanship of Alberta Senator Donald Cameron. This was the same Donald Cameron who had organized and run the School for Community Life at Olds beginning in 1937. After founding the Banff School of Fine Arts and then the Banff School of Advanced Management, he was appointed to the Senate of Canada in 1955. His knowledge of the Alberta educational system and business, with his longstanding interest in adult education, was excellent preparation for his new assignment.

Beginning in April of 1958, Cameron and his five fellow commissioners travelled to 17 different communities to hear the views of more than 600 Albertans and receive 189 written briefs containing 5,000 recommendations for change. The comments were wide-ranging, covering public attitudes toward education, access, matters of curricula and examinations, administrative structures, and the role, qualifications and remuneration of teachers. From this thick soup of public opinion, Cameron managed to strain 280 ideas he and his colleagues considered worthy of implementation within the overall educational system.

On the narrower issue of agricultural education, Cameron received briefs from the Faculty of Agriculture at the University of Alberta, the Farmers' Union of Alberta, the Department of Agriculture, the Alberta Institute of Agrologists, School Alumni Associations, a collective brief from the Schools of Agriculture, and a separate brief from the Fairview School of Agriculture and Home Economics. The latter, opened in 1951, had just suffered a catastrophic fire. This effectively left the teaching field to Olds and Vermilion for several years.

Fortunately for Cameron, matters were less complex when it came to provincial views of agricultural education. Those who made presentations were unanimous in believing that the day of the uneducated farmer and his wife was over. Where hands-on experience with grain and livestock once sufficed to provide a farm family with a decent living, now farmers also needed training in agricultural technology and farm management. Farming was a business and needed to be approached as such.

To succeed in that business meant acquiring more specialized education. While Cameron was utterly convinced of the need for agricultural education in the Province, he said that both the related facilities and their curricula needed extensive reorganization. For example, Alberta high schools offered a course in "agro-scientific knowledge" to Grade 9 and 10 students, yet had no effective means of delivering such content. The Farmers' Union, in particular, thought such courses impractical and argued that they should be discontinued. Cameron agreed. He recommended, instead, that high schools offer a course that created greater appreciation of the important role of agriculture in the national economy. He called this the "panoramic view."

With respect to the Schools of Agriculture, Cameron believed that the minor changes of recent years fell far short of the mark. Instead, he wished to see an expansion of the vocational training aspects of the curriculum, with a specific focus on farm mechanics, management, marketing and rural sociology. He called for greater emphasis on rural leadership training and on specialized training for the emerging jobs in agribusiness. In keeping with the views of the Farmers' Union brief, he also decried the fact that diplomas from the Schools of Agriculture no longer guaranteed their holders admission to the University's Faculty of Agriculture. Finally, he recommended the Schools be transformed into community colleges that could offer more than agricultural training and be integrated thoroughly into the wider provincial education system.

This was sweet music to the ears of the long-suffering School Principals. While being careful not to downplay the importance of agricultural training *per se*, Cameron had clearly recognized that community-based education in the skilled trades was now essential to the livelihoods of farmers and to the continuing prosperity of the Province. As Birdsall remarked to a *Calgary Herald* reporter in 1958, today's farmer was actually a "business executive in overalls."[18] Donald Cameron's perspective effectively bridged the need for traditional, hands-on training in agriculture and the demands of a job market based on specialization. If the Government could be persuaded to pursue this educational direction, the future of the Schools of Agriculture seemed assured.

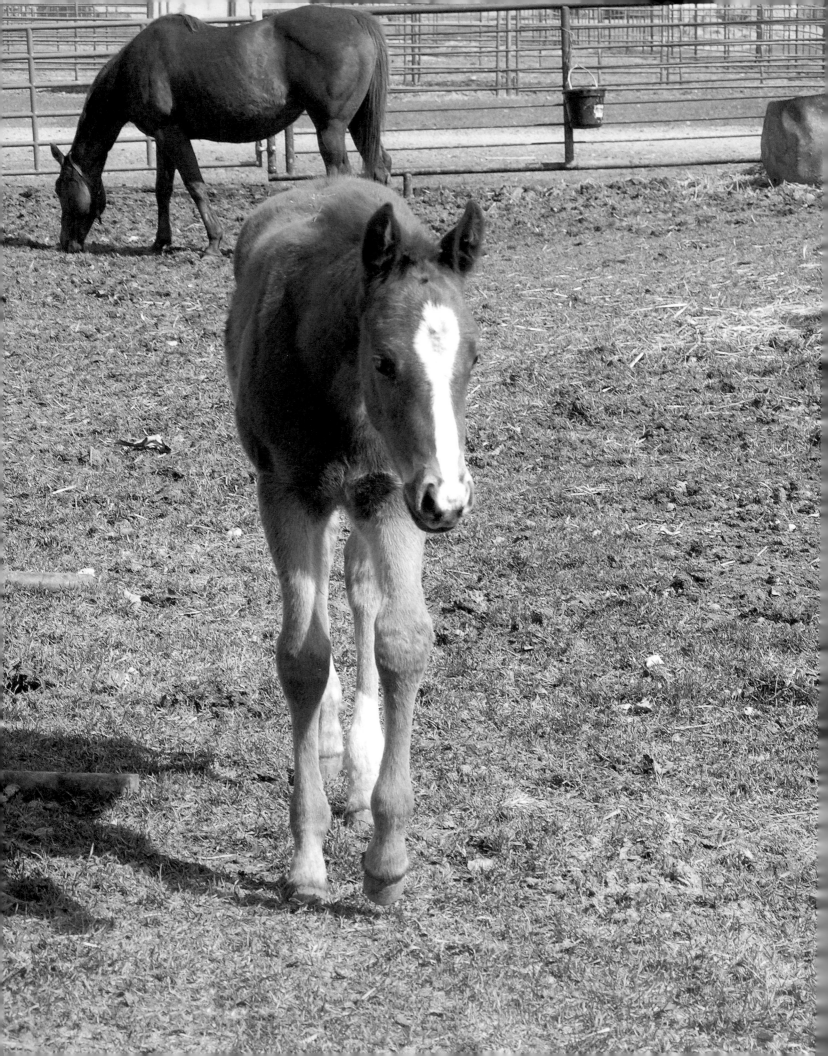

The Vocational College

They arrived in Olds on August 1ˢᵗ, 1963 amid glorious summer unshine. There had been a few drops of rain early in the day, but by the afternoon the skies had cleared and the temperature had risen into the comfortable low 70s.

7

A School To Be Proud Of

Frank Grisdale was there. So were Fred Miller and Charlie Yauch. Of the remaining former Principals, only James Murray, then resident in Ottawa, was unable to attend. The incumbent, Everett Birdsall, greeted old friends and mingled with his predecessors. Miss Christine McIntyre came down from Edmonton, and Mrs. Arthur Kemp drove up from Lethbridge. Fred Parkinson, Morley Malyon, Walter Benn and Hugh McPhail greeted each other again on campus for the first time in many years. By the time the buffet supper was ready, around 125 current and former O.S.A. staff had gathered to kick off two days of celebrations.

It was the 50th anniversary of the Olds School of Agriculture and Home Economics, a school, as *The Olds Gazette* declared, "to be proud of."[1] After Thursday's inaugural staff reunion, the party was opened to alumni and the wider community. Nearly 250 people attended the noon luncheon put together by Dietitian Thelma Graham and her staff. Then another 800 arrived to take part in a barbecue on the campus lawn.

In the evening, hundreds of well-fed people shuffled into the Mechanic's Building that had served as the campus dance hall (with removable dance floor, no less) since the end of the war. The fact that the decrepit old army hangar needed to be braced for reasons of public safety deterred no one. With Walter's All-Tones providing the music, the reunion guests danced the night away under a canopy of ultra modern red and white polyethylene streamers.

The Golden Jubilee celebrations were marked by two very special events. The first was the unveiling of an Alumni Association plaque at the Plant Science Building in honour of the memory and contribution of Arthur Kemp, whose pioneering work

in Alberta horticulture was something worth celebrating. After a moving tribute to
Kemp by Duncan Hargraves (Class of '29), Dr. Gavin Kemp, the eldest of the three
Kemp sons and an O.S.A. graduate himself, did the honours. In the 15 years since
Art Kemp's death, his fine achievements had not been forgotten.

At the well-attended Golden Jubilee celebrations in 1963, the School received a new name -
Olds Agricultural and Vocational College – that reflected its broader educational mandate.

The second event was the unveiling of a cairn commemorating the contribution of the School itself to the betterment of rural life and the advancement of farming. Harry Strom, Alberta's Minister of Agriculture and a strong supporter of the School, spoke not only of the vision and achievements of the School's founders and pioneers but also declared that the institution's name would henceforth be the Olds Agricultural and Vocational College – O.A.V.C.

Though bland in conception and awkward on the tongue, the new name was more inspired than it seemed. It captured the institution's past, present and immediate future. By 1963, almost 9,000 students had attended O.S.A., and all had studied more or less the same curriculum laid down by the Board of Agricultural Education in 1912-13. Despite its age, that curriculum had served them well. As a reporter from *The Gazette* noted:

> *The results of their training have extended far beyond their own farms, as witness their contributions to municipal and provincial affairs and the leadership they have shown in farm organizations, both provincial and federal. It is the considered judgement of the writer that these contributions to the public good have far more than justified the existence of the Schools of Agriculture, separate altogether from their great benefits to the individual's who received the training.[2]*

Yet as the School's new name indicated, the times were changing. As the 1960s approached, agricultural graduates needed new skills to cope with the new demands of their calling.

Dr. Gordon Taggart, who addressed the alumni on the evening of August 2nd, had much to say about the inevitability of educational evolution in a changing society and economy. He reminded everyone that the mechanization of farming since the war had led directly to a situation in which technical training for young agriculturalists was no longer an option. On that note, he was pleased to observe that O.S.A. had taken steps, however tentative, to introduce its students to farm mechanics and farm engineering in the 1950s.

On the horizon he foresaw a need for more technical expertise. He even appealed for greater collaboration between the fields of agriculture and medicine, as both dealt with fundamental biological processes. The School's Artificial Insemination lab stood out as an early and important example of how applied veterinary science could improve the quality of livestock, better the rural standard of living and enhance the nation's trade balance.

Finally, he focused the attention of his audience on the contribution business skills could make to success in agriculture. Not surprisingly, Olds had just introduced its first Agribusiness course. Taggart was always careful to give credit where credit was due. By the end of the evening it was clear to everyone in attendance that his speech was both reminiscence and forecast. His audience of former staff and students came away feeling they had not only been a part of something important in O.S.A. but that the future of O.A.V.C. would be brighter still.

Behind the Scenes

If Taggart's upbeat after-dinner speech made the endurance and new status of O.A.V.C. seem inevitable, Everett Birdsall was one person in the audience who knew better. Planning, persistence and more than a bit of luck had played their part in the survival of the institution into its sixth decade.

Birdsall was all too aware of the sorry shape of the School when he assumed control of the administration in 1952. Things were falling down around him. He continually heard the complaints of the new staff about outmoded facilities and poor pay. He watched, helplessly, as their turnover rate rose sharply throughout the 1950s. He saw the declining student enrolment figures, and he knew far too many alumni who looked back on their experience at O.S.A. with pleasure and gratitude yet refused to send their own children to attend. And he understood only too well that many in the Provincial Government truly believed the day of the dedicated agricultural school was over.[3] Although Alberta spent more per capita on education than any other province during the 1950s,[4] O.S.A. was in rough shape.

Rather than passively accept such a fate, however, Birdsall joined forces with his counterparts at Vermilion and Fairview, the Alumni Association, and Alberta's farm organizations to persuade the Social Credit Administration in Edmonton that agricultural education was still relevant within the rapidly changing economy of the Province. The showdown took place in Fairview in 1958. The fire that had nearly razed that campus led to much speculation that the Government would close Fairview for good, but the concerted efforts of the School Principals and others prevented that from happening. Unfortunately, the expensive rebuilding of Fairview meant that Olds and Vermilion had to make do with even less from the Government coffers.

A special Education Committee of the Alumni Association proved particularly important in transforming the Government perception of the Schools. Angus McKinnon, the 1915 Olds graduate who had organized the first O.S.A. reunion in 1934, took a leading role. Elected as an Alumni representative to the Board of Agricultural Education in 1957, McKinnon's commitment to positive change was so strong and so clear that his original two-year term was extended to 1961.

During those four years, he worked hard to diversify the School offerings by augmenting the traditional agricultural courses with programs aimed at nursing aides, laboratory technicians, farm managers, herdsmen and field technicians. He also campaigned to have the Schools of Agriculture put under the direction of the Department of Education in an effort to integrate their curricula more effectively into the overall Provincial educational system. The Alumni Association also strongly endorsed the findings of the Cameron Commission. That they achieved few of these aims took nothing away from the strength of their convictions.

Those who saw the recommendations of the Cameron Commission as a panacea were to be similarly disappointed. While few in Government disputed the Commissioner's findings about the future of the agricultural schools, no one was willing to make the needed investment to update the curriculum to reflect the vocational concerns of the emerging agribusiness sector. The few changes made were largely the initiative of the Schools themselves. Their staffs, which had been meeting annually to review course content, chose in 1958-59 to give both Agriculture and Home Economics students the opportunity to select options for the first time. The Board of Agricultural Education supported the move and simultaneously agreed to place School of Agriculture instructors under the same salary schedule as those at other provincial educational institutions. A new policy of professional development was introduced at the same time.

While welcome, these modifications were insufficient to change the situation fundamentally. Those who had worked so hard to move the Schools forward were grateful for this progress, such as it was, but quite honestly they had exhausted their store of optimism. As the 1950s drew to a close, the future of agricultural education in Alberta remained in jeopardy.

Then, in 1960, the Federal Government introduced the Technical and Vocational Training Assistance Act in an effort to relieve national unemployment and expand economic growth. Like the Agricultural Instruction Act of 1913, this new statute made generous funding available to the provinces for technical and vocational facilities.

In Alberta, where unemployment was high, this federal legislation brought about expansion and modernization of the Southern Alberta Institute of Technology (SAIT) in Calgary; construction of Edmonton's Northern Alberta Institute of Technology (NAIT); inauguration of the vocational programs that would eventually lead to the formation of Bow Valley College in Calgary; development of composite high schools with significant vocational components, and implementation of the key recommendations of the Cameron Commission with respect to agricultural education at Olds, Vermilion and Fairview. The agricultural institutions benefited further, after 1962, from the appointment of Harry Strom as Alberta's Minister of Agriculture. A farmer himself, and Premier of Alberta from 1968 to 1971, Strom proved a valuable ally of the agricultural schools and a staunch advocate of educational reform in general.

The turning point for the agricultural schools came in January of 1963. The Board of Agricultural Education presented a Cabinet committee under Strom's leadership with the following recommendations:

Recommendation No.1

That the function of Alberta Schools of Agriculture and Home Economics be now recognized as providing:

a) Vocational agricultural courses designed to give broad training for those who intend to farm.

b) Broadly based specialized vocational agriculture courses for those interested in specialized types of farming.

c) Vocational courses, designed to train students for occupations ancillary to the agricultural industry, for School of Agriculture diploma graduates or adult students as may be qualified to enter.

d) General courses in home economics (probably at one school only) designed to train students as homemakers.

e) Specialized courses in the home economics field to fit graduates for specific employment.

f) Special courses, primarily for young women, to fit graduates for employment outside the home economics field.

g) Such other courses as the Board of Agricultural Education may prescribe.

Recommendation No. 2

That required high school subjects be included in the program of studies at vocational agricultural schools at grade XI and XII level.

Recommendation No. 3

All factors considered, the committee recommends that Schools of Agriculture in Alberta continue to be operated on a regional basis provided that attendance is sufficient to justify the expenditure involved. Fluctuation in attendance will occur and it would appear realistic to establish minimal attendance of vocational students for the schools at 95 for Olds; 85 for Vermilion and 60 for the Fairview school.

Recommendation No. 4

The Committee recommends that effective if possible in

1963, the name "Alberta Schools of Agriculture and Home Economics" be changed to "Alberta Agricultural and Vocational Colleges".

Recommendation No. 5

The Committee recommends that a suitable person be commissioned to prepare an historic record of the Alberta Schools of Agriculture and Home Economics. If a suitable agency, such as a foundation cannot be found, it is recommended that the Alberta Government undertake to finance the project.

For the first time in more than a decade, the Schools of Agriculture had articulated a comprehensive and practical view of their future, one based on defensible economic forecasting rather than on tinkering and an ineffective appeal to rural nostalgia. It was a vision that Strom's Cabinet colleagues were prepared to support.

Programs to Match the Times

Cabinet approval of the new mandate focussed the School's efforts to define a more appropriate curriculum. Members of the Olds instructional staff, who had been informally discussing the need for such changes since 1959-60, were galvanized by the new emphasis on vocational training. Chief among these staff members, in addition to Principal Birdsall, were Bill Baranyk, Stu Wilton, Harlow Sutherland and Wilbur Collin. Together, they took the lead in mapping out a program of diploma studies appropriate to the times.

Home Economics was among the matters considered. By any measure, the program had been a failure for most of the previous decade. Every School Principal in the Province thought so. With enrolments at Olds down to a catastrophic low of 14 in 1960-61, radical surgery, if not outright amputation, seemed in order. That's more or less what happened. After 1962, Home Economics was offered exclusively at Vermilion and then only as a one-year (10-month) program. In its place, Olds and Fairview debuted two new diploma courses. They were intended to provide young women "with interesting employment both before and after marriage."[5]

The first, called Commercial, was a nine-month course that prepared the students for employment as secretaries, stenographers, dicta-typists and receptionists. It immediately drew 13 applicants who were exposed to the latest office technologies, including the manual typewriter, adding machine, dictaphone, dicta-belt, electric typewriter, Dilto and Gestetner, Duplicator, and Photostat.[6] This was the foundation for the Secretarial Arts program that functioned from 1971 to 1991 before becoming Office Administration. From 1963 until the mid-1970s, the course was taught by Barbara Gough, whose husband Ted worked on the College farm.

Clothing and Design was the second program. Gwen Daley instructed. A 1952 Home Economics graduate of the University of Alberta, where she specialized in sewing and laundry, Daley had done advanced training in Oregon. Returning to Alberta, she taught high school Home Economics in Lethbridge. She joined the staff at Olds for the 1954-55 school year and immediately made her mark in the School's literary activities.

Under Miss Daley's direction, the first 14 Clothing and Design (Fashion and Design after 1967) students acquired a knowledge of historical costumes, pattern making and alteration, handicrafts (such as wood carving and pillow smocking), and the use and care of textiles. In the sewing laboratory, they fabricated at least nine different garments and prepared a set of some 40 samples that illustrated various sewing techniques. Elective courses in agriculture, home nursing and horticulture were offered as well. In 1965, students would have the opportunity to tour chemical plants in Edmonton to see first-hand how modern synthetic fabrics such as Arnel and Celanese were manufactured. In reality the program was still essentially about dressmaking and tailoring. Comprising three 12-week sessions, it was intended to prepare participants for careers that involved fashion design and retailing, fabrics, sewing, tailoring and clothing selection, or simply to be more accomplished homemakers.

The College introduced many new programs in the mid-1960s, including Commercial courses designed to prepare young women for business-related careers.

The foundation of the successful Secretarial Arts program was laid in the early 1960s, as young women in particular were introduced to the newest office technologies.

The Clothing and Design program, which offered students marketable skills, was an innovative reinterpretation of the traditional sewing courses.

Learning the Lingo

Birdsall's Glossary of Terms, circa 1963

To be in the know at O.A.V.C. you need to master the terms now in use. The following listing will be of interest:

The Old	The New
Olds School of Agriculture and Home Economics (O.S.A.)	Olds Agricultural and Vocational College (O.A.V.C.)
The School	The College
School Year (5½ months)	School Year (9 to 10 months)
Fall term, Spring term	Fall Session, Winter Session, Spring Session
Mid-term exams	Mid-session exams
Diploma Course in Home Economics	Diploma Courses in Commercial and in Clothing and Design
Diploma Course in Agriculture	General Course in Agriculture • Major in Animal Science • Major in Plant Science • Major in Farm Management • Major in Farm Mechanics • Major in Agri-business • Diploma course in Horticulture

The commercial orientation of these programs led the College to direct its attention to the task of job placement for the first time. During the 1963-64 school year, Birdsall made it possible for prospective employers to interview students on campus. He arranged for a speaker from the National Employment Service to address the classes, too. The College also worked closely with the Personnel Office of the Provincial Government, which accepted applications from the Commercial graduates. Almost every graduate who sought employment was quickly hired.

The traditional Agriculture program underwent a fundamental transformation at the same time. Those wishing to acquire or improve basic farming knowledge and skills could still take a General Course. For the first time, however, students could focus on majors in: Animal Science, Farm Mechanics, Plant Science, Farm Management and Agri-business.

In 1965, a certificate course in farmland Appraisal and Assessment was introduced. Offered in April and May, this was a three-week course developed with help from the University of Alberta and professional assessors. In the autumn of 1966, a two-year Irrigation Technology course began in response to the growing demand for trained technical personnel in the semi-arid lands of southern Alberta. Like Appraisal and Assessment, this course was developed with the co-operation of an industry advisory committee. Murray Wilde of the Water Resources Division taught the course until 1967 when O.A.V.C. added permanent instructors. To supplement classroom instruction, the College purchased irrigation equipment, constructed a large dug-out, and levelled an adjoining 20-acre field.

A new diploma course in Horticulture, first offered during the 1963-64 school year, marked the beginning of the College's shift to instruction in non agricultural career options. The planning for this had begun in 1959 when representatives of the Department of Agriculture, the University of Alberta and the City of Edmonton Parks Department identified a growing need for skilled assistants in the horticultural industry.

After much discussion, a proposal for a two-year program was made to J. E. (Ted) Hawker, who was now the Superintendent of Schools of Agriculture. Its three objectives were to provide vocational training for young people, further opportunities for Diploma of Horticulture via correspondence courses from the Ontario Agricultural College, and supplemental instruction for those already employed in horticulture. While Hawker eventually approved the program, he limited its availability to O.A.V.C.

Big Valley native B. J. (Buck) Godwin, then employed as a plant science instructor at Vermilion, was brought in to launch the program. Although he insisted he would only remain long enough to get the program off the ground, Godwin eventually relented and became a permanent College fixture. His quiet inquisitiveness, superb organization and inspirational teaching soon made their mark. The inaugural class of 12 students completed their first year of studies in March of 1964 and then moved on to the on-the-job training needed for completion. As it turned out, there were three positions available for each of the students. Well-aligned with the needs of industry, the program grew rapidly. Godwin personally aided its development further by establishing the College's own herbarium and collection of insects.

B. J. (Buck) Godwin, recruited temporarily from Vermilion in 1964 to start the new horticulture program, remained at Olds until his retirement in 1987.

Olds College Herbaria

One of the lesser-known aspects of the College is its fine herbarium, located in the Land Sciences Centre. A herbarium is a collection of preserved plant specimens. Usually dry-mounted on white paper sheets, the specimens serve as reference material for the identification of plants and seeds. They are frequently used in teaching, especially as a supplement to printed descriptions and illustrations.

Horticultural Instructor Buck Godwin established the Olds herbarium in the summer of 1964. Within just two years, he had assembled more than 1,600 specimen sheets. Most of the specimens are from the Great Plains, with a focus on cultivated ornamental plants (woody and herbaceous) hardy to Zone 3 or colder. Each specimen sheet offers information on where and when the specimen was collected, its general habitat, colour and the name of the collector, among other data. Today, the College collection numbers around 30,000 and continues to be used for instructional purposes. Each horticulture student must submit a herbarium collection as part of their studies.

This is not the only herbarium to have some association with Olds College. Edward Finch Peck, a 1922 graduate of O.S.A. who went on to become a veterinary surgeon, served at various British colonial postings in Africa throughout his long career. During the nine years he spent in British Somalia, where he was the Chief Veterinary Officer to the Somaliland Camel Corps, he gathered an unprecedented collection of traditional Somali medicinal plants. In addition to documenting the medicinal and culinary uses of these plants, he pressed and preserved specimens of each. Upon his retirement, he donated his private herbarium to the Veterinary Department in Hargeisa, the colonial capital of British Somaliland from 1941 to 1960.

By 1977 Horticulture Technology, as the program became known, would be graduating more students than any other campus program. They would find jobs in tree nurseries, parks departments, golf courses, flower shops, forestry departments, commercial vegetable farms and elsewhere. Short courses on topics such as bedding plants and turf management were offered as well, and an annual "Hort Week" became (and remains) a summertime staple at the College. Godwin continued to head the program until his retirement in 1987. In 1990, he was recognized for his contribution to development of the College by being named its first Instructor Emeritus.

If there was a common thread running through the new agricultural programs launched at Olds from the mid-1960s to the mid-1970s, it was technology. In addition to Horticulture Technology and Irrigation Technology, the College soon offered Agricultural Engineering Technology, Soils Technology, Agri-business Technology, Agricultural Chemicals Technology, Animal Health Technology, and Fashion Merchandising Technology.

The Horticulture Technology program addressed a specific skills shortage and marked the beginning of College efforts to match its program content to labour market demand.

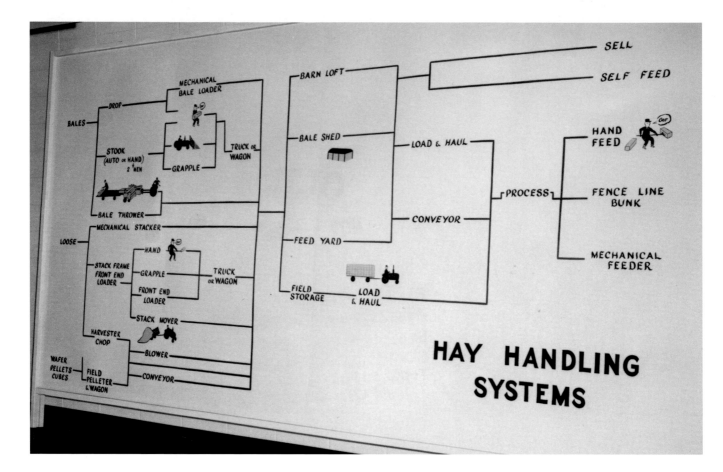

HAY HANDLING SYSTEMS

It was not simply that technology now underlay so many of the new developments in farming and the agricultural sector as a whole, nor that the academic world was rapidly being split into more and more areas of specialization. Rather, the College administrators were doggedly trying to shed the stigma of vocational education, with its implication of unskilled under-achievers. At a time when farming had lost its economic lustre and its political clout, Alberta's youth found technology much more alluring than farming. In the minds of College personnel, adding the word "technology" to any program was bound to increase its cachet and therefore its marketability. As Birdsall saw it, the age of public relations was upon them.

The same concern about the College's image could be detected in other administrative choices. For example, in 1964 Principal Birdsall chose to discontinue training for the annual Little Royal exhibition that Dave Andrews had started in 1934. When asked why this decision had been made, Birdsall replied that, "the feeling over the past few years has been that this show was putting unjustified emphasis on the show ring. It gives a wrong conception to the public. It misrepresents our belief."[7]

In an academic world now defined by technology and its many applications, even haying became more complicated than anyone on the farm had ever dreamed.

Investing in Staff

Throughout the history of O.S.A., most instructors were hired fresh out of an agricultural school or a university and thrown into the classroom or lab, where they swam or sank. Professional qualifications were seen as more important than teaching certification. Edith Collin, for example, remembers coming to Olds in 1959 as a young graduate in Home Economics and feeling less than up to the task of teaching her students about matters like child rearing, in which she had no experience.[8] If the instructors turned out to be excellent teachers without benefit of pedagogy, as happened with Collin, the School considered that a bonus. Similarly, the nurse at the School was often called upon to serve as an instructor in home nursing and first aid, regardless of whether she had any familiarity with teaching. So too with many of the instructors in carpentry, mechanics or welding, who often possessed nothing more than a trade certificate and boundless enthusiasm. Some proved to be exceedingly good instructors; others fell short of the mark.

O.S.A. was not alone in this; in fact, this was the case in most Alberta schools of the day. The report of the Cameron Commission made much of the inadequate preparation of teachers for life in the classroom. The situation did not begin to improve appreciably until the 1960s. One of the first initiatives was a new Provincial Government policy on professional development, or "improvement" as it was then called. Essentially, an instructor was able to take a leave of absence to improve his or her pedagogical standing. By 1970, all Alberta civil servants were able to apply for such time off, usually at a reduced level of pay and with a commitment to return to their previous place of employment.

There were also less formal means of professional development for staff. Until the end of the 1970s, instructors from the three agricultural colleges met annually for two or three days to learn from each other and from outside experts about current approaches to teaching and methods of evaluating students. Expert-directed workshops were held as well. These might focus on instructional techniques, testing and evaluation, or the use of audio-visual aids in the classroom.[9]

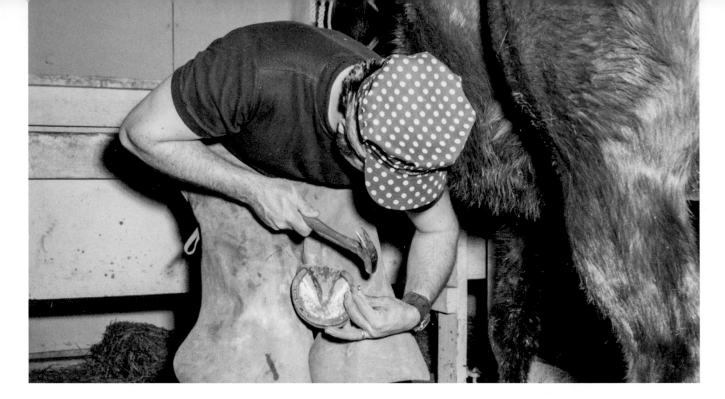

When, finally, the College was able to drop the word Vocational from its name in 1971 and become plain Olds College instead, the sense of relief among some administrators and staff was almost palpable.

But if many saw technology as the wave of the future at O.A.V.C., they looked askance at the introduction of a farrier short course in 1968. Animal Husbandry Instructor Dennis Radcliff, who was an accomplished horseman, joined forces with Wilbur Collin, then Alberta's Coordinator of Agricultural Education, and Jack Kearns of the Livestock Division of the Department of Agriculture, to prepare a proposal for a short course in horseshoeing methods. Rejected out of hand by Ted Hawker, the Director of Agricultural Colleges, the proposal then found its way to Deputy Minister of Agriculture Ed Ballantyne. As a veterinarian, Ballantyne believed the concept had merit. He approved its development on a pilot project basis.[10]

As early as 1970, the farrier course was regarded as one of the College's specialties. Soon it was a 16-week program, offered twice annually. Then the College started to receive so many requests for admission that it had to turn away applicants. By 2010, it would be a two-year Farrier Science diploma program involving eight months of directed field study. Mark Hobby, then President of the Western Canadian Farriers Association, called it the best program on the continent.[11]

Besides skill and enthusiasm, the O.A.V.C. instructors and administration of the mid-1960s brought an unprecedented interest in, and grasp of, industry's needs to the College. This expression of academic entrepreneurship, rare at the time, set O.A.V.C. on a markedly different institutional course, one that would serve it well in the years ahead.

Although mocked by some, the farrier course pioneered by Animal Husbandry Instructor Dennis Radcliff in 1968 proved tremendously successful.

Publicizing the College

In years past, a prospective student's first introduction to Olds usually came by word of mouth — they might

learn of the School from a former student and be intrigued enough to enquire and perhaps enrol themselves.

Or a parent who had attended O.S.A. might "suggest" the young man or woman could do far worse than study at Olds. Other prospective students might have noticed the small advertisements that the Department of Agriculture placed regularly in community newspapers and in the pages of the farm press. These traditional forms of introduction to the School and its offerings would always be common.

In the early 1950s the Department started to make use of radio as a means of publicity. In 1953, for example, the latest farming practices and news could be heard on six Alberta radio stations. By the following year, voices of O.S.A. students filled the airwaves of Calgary's CFAC Radio in six-minute bursts at noon every Saturday.

Fred Jorgenson, who would go on to head the Southern Alberta Institute of Technology, got the students involved. They made tape recordings every Friday afternoon on topics like their student council and yearbook activities, the school newspaper, literary events and home economics. They gained valuable on-air and public speaking experience; O.S.A. got unprecedented exposure. Later in the 1950s Dennis Radcliff and Stu Wilton also began to make radio broadcasts that often featured news of the School.

As the 1960s dawned, it was evident that new approaches to publicity were needed. The sharp increase in the populations of Calgary and Edmonton left rural Alberta without a powerful voice for the first time in the Province's history. Agricultural columnists nearly disappeared from the pages of the daily newspapers. Newspapers and other media outlets now covered agricultural news and events only if they somehow related to the interests of an urban audience. As a result, publicity at Olds grew less experimental and more sophisticated. Administrators began to talk of public relations for the first time. They were determined to get the word out to a world rapidly losing touch with the land.

Their forays into the art of persuasion included every-thing from press releases and displays at fairs and home-and-school meetings to tours of the campus and seminars with high school counsellors. All of a sudden, Old's print materials could be found on tables at the popular, new career fairs as well as at country fairs and exhibitions.

Regular participation in hosted radio and television programs took place as well. By 1964, the College was producing three five-minute tape recordings per week that were played on the Red Deer and Drumheller radio stations (CHRD and CJDV) every Monday, Wednesday and Friday under the title "College Calendar." Dennis Radcliff, who had gone on to become Farm Director at Camrose's CFCW station, returned to Olds in 1966 and assumed responsibility for broadcasting. If there were still Albertans who didn't know what was happening at Olds, it was because they weren't listening.

These efforts culminated in an award-winning film about the College. In 1971, Radcliff teamed up with John Andrew of the Radio and Information Branch of the Department of Agriculture to produce a film on the care of horse's hoofs. Called *No Hoof — No Horse*, the production focused on the equine courses then offered at Olds. Shown initially on educational television broadcasts, the film eventually became a modest hit across North America. In 1971, the Canadian Farm Writers' Association honoured *No Hoof — No Horse* with its award of merit.

It is by no means certain, however, that young people themselves were listening or even watching these exper-iments with the latest forms of publicity. Or perhaps they had heard enough at career fairs and at meetings with the

high school guidance counsellors then coming into vogue. One student said that he was appalled to learn that the inmates of the television lounge routinely shunned a fine farm show like CBC's noon-time Wild Rose Country in favour of Fred Flintstone and Barney Rubble.

Yet attendance at the College continued to increase. Between 1963-64 and 1971-72, the number of students at Olds grew markedly from 188 to more than 500. While the increase was partly due to the unprecedented capac-ity of Frank Grisdale Hall, it was also attributable to the Administration's expansion of its program offerings and its more astute handling of promotion and recruitment. More than an interest in watching the Flintstones during the lunch hour was attracting a new generation of students to Olds.

Media campaigns, including this interview with the popular "Call of the Land" radio program in 1962, publicized the College to an unprecedented number of Western Canadians.

271

Worthy of Our New Status

Writing in The Chinook as the school year came to a close in March of 1964, Principal Birdsall commented on what he saw as the more mature attitude of that year's student body. His pride in them was obvious.

They had acquitted themselves well and he appreciated both their social behaviour and their scholastic performance. He closed his message with the hope that their commendable maturation might be passed along to the next year's class so that everyone associated with O.A.V.C. in future "might be worthy of our new status."[12]

Everett Birdsall may well have seen something unusual in this group of students. He was, after all, able to bring decades of experience to the situation. His students, on the other hand, had little sense of how they differed from previous generations or of the profound changes that were swiftly overtaking the College. Yet Birdsall was right: their experience of Olds was, in many ways, different from that of the generations who had gone before them.

For a start, the College was no longer open to anyone who wished to attend. It now had entrance requirements that went far beyond the traditional declaration of interest, good health and sound moral character. The perceived need for higher admission standards had been building for some time. It had, for instance, been stated in the report of the Cameron Commission of 1958-59. In 1962, Mrs. Russell Johnston of the educational committee of the Farm Women's Union of Alberta put it plainly when she laid out the views of many in the rural community:

> *People in the farm organizations believe that the farm young people who are to remain on the farms should have adequate technical and vocational training in agriculture. They should also have an adequate academic education to develop as good citizens, aware of what is going on in the world, prepared to take responsibility, able to determine values and make wise decisions.[13]*

Birdsall felt similarly. He thought the low entrance standard encouraged academic mediocrity and gave institutions like Olds an unwelcome reputation as a place for lacklustre students. It also destined them for failure in the campaign to turn out students better equipped to fill the increasing demand for technical, off-farm positions. With the number of Alberta farmers steadily declining and the costs of establishing and operating a farm steadily rising beyond the reach of most young people, what future did old-time agricultural schools have unless they adapted?

Harlow Sutherland lecturing to his class about credit matters in his course on farm management.

273

Above: In 1963, Olds College took over the agricultural mechanics program from the Southern Alberta Institute of Technology in Calgary and revised it to suit the needs of the farm community. Pat Burton (in white coat) was the lead instructor.

Left: Office automation demanded that the College invest in the latest technologies. Here the students are processing data with punch cards.

Introduction of a new trimester system between 1962 and 1964 was seen as part of the answer. The school year, now extended from September until the end of June for the first time, was divided into three 12-week sessions. Most courses were repeated in each session. In addition to immersing students in their courses to a greater degree than ever before, the trimester system made it possible for a student to leave school for a while, perhaps to work or help out at home, and then rejoin the program without having to repeat an entire year of studies.

This did not apply, however, to the new Commercial and Clothing and Design programs; students in those programs had to attend three consecutive sessions to graduate. At the same time, the College raised its passing mark from 40 to 50 per cent.

A second part of the solution lay in new, higher admission requirements. Henceforth, applicants to Olds would need a Grade 11 diploma. Those with at least 70 high school credits (subsequently changed to 67) and a B standing in those subjects were eligible to complete the diploma agriculture program in three sessions. Those with less education would need at least four sessions to make the grade, as they had to pick up academic subjects as well. By 1972-73, all students had to have a high school diploma in order to attend the College.

Historically, none of the agricultural institutions charged admission fees. Fees were seen as a deterrent to attendance. That began to change in 1963-64 as well. While the diploma programs in Agriculture and Home Economics remained free, a charge of $12.50 per session was levied for the new Horticultural course; a charge of $20 per session for Commercial and Automotives; and a flat rate of $100 for the six-week welding course. A per-session fee for Agriculture and Home Economics students was first introduced in 1967-68, when a $20 per-session rate was levied simultaneously on all programs.

More than entrance standards and fees were changing. Principal Birdsall, looking back in his retirement years on his long career at Olds, characterized the first 50 years of the School as paternalistic and authoritarian.[14] He chalked this up to the innate conservatism and moral values of rural Alberta.

For example, liquor had always been prohibited on campus. This applied not only to students, but to staff members as well.[15] Any student caught with alcohol in their possession was suspended or expelled. In 1960, when three young men committed what the Administration called "drinking offences", they were not permitted to return to classes.

Similarly, the School did everything it could to keep the sexes apart. It did not succeed, of course, but it preferred to maintain the fiction that intimacy was unknown on the campus grounds. Birdsall observed that when Second World War veterans attended O.S.A., the Dean of the Men's Residence "turned a blind eye to much that went on so long as the veterans were discreet." As many students of that era and others have said, the veterans were hardly the first to discover how to get to the women's wing of the 1927 dormitory without being detected by a Dean. Soon the multiple doorways of Frank Grisdale Hall would make it virtually impossible for anyone to monitor the comings and goings of more than 500 students.

If O.A.V.C. students were held to a higher academic standard in the 1960s, in exchange they received a greater measure of personal autonomy. In 1961-62, a student found to be in possession of alcohol was no longer summarily dismissed but rather suspended temporarily until all the facts could be determined and a decision made. When, a decade later, the Province dropped the legal drinking age from 21 to 18, the College responded by allowing students to serve alcoholic beverages at social functions; three years later, liquor was permitted in residence rooms.

The winds of change were blowing. With them came the first sanctioned whiff of cigarette smoke on campus. It was not that no student had ever smoked at O.S.A., but as of 1963-64 smoking was permitted in designated areas for the first time. On the other hand, the traditional prohibition against gambling remained in force. In addition, students were still not permitted to visit pool halls, beer parlours, hotels or public dances in the Town of Olds; most of the decade would pass before those rules were waived. While the expansion of student privileges proceeded throughout the 1960s and early 1970s, it did so in a distinctly arbitrary manner.

With the Administration's decision to do away with Saturday classes, beginning in 1964, students could go home on weekends for the first time. Many did so if their resources permitted. This had implications for the busy weekend social calendar that had been a mainstay of the School from the start. Staff gradually relinquished much of their customary involvement in extra-curricular activities, and most took a less active role in the lives of their students.

One manifestation of this change was the radically different character of the school yearbook after about 1960. Previously a printed documentary of school activities prepared under the sharp eye of a staff member, it was quickly reduced to a glossy but mainly contentless volume of student photographs and quips.

While curriculum changes and liberalization of campus rules may have drawn more students to Olds in the 1960s, it was ironically the College's rapidly developing reputation in athletics that truly put Olds College on the map.[16] Sports had always been a central part of life at Olds, but most competitions were local and amateurish, as befitted a small college with short-lived teams.

This began to change with the hiring of Al Qually in 1964. Born and raised at Rocky Mountain House, Qually had always been athletic. He brought tremendous skill and unbridled enthusiasm, if not formal training, to his new position as Assistant Dean of Men and Recreation Supervisor. By 1965, athletics were his only teaching responsibility at the College.[17]

Although not understood as such at the time, this was yet another form of academic specialization. It reflected the growing commercialization of sport across North America in the 1960s, and the pervasiveness of professional athletes, rising salaries and televised broadcasts. Everyone had become a spectator.

During his 30 years of service, Qually continually upgraded his qualifications to match his intuitive sense of the value of this new role in academic life. Eventually he became a passionate advocate of the importance of

training the whole student and not just his or her mind. His dedication would lead Olds to strengthen its sporting reputation through intramural leagues that led, in turn, to participation in the Alberta Colleges Athletic Conference and in national championships. In 1983, Olds College was one of the hosts for the Alberta Summer Games as well. Qually himself earned awards as a coach-of-the-year, not once but twice. His efforts and persistence did much to make the well-rounded Olds College brand of education highly desirable.

Coach Al Qually (far right) and the Olds College Broncos. Qually put sports on a professional footing at the College during his three decades in charge of athletics.

Phoenix from the Ashes

The many changes that began in 1963-64 could not be accommodated within the existing infrastructure of the College. It was still more or less the same campus that had served students since 1927. Classroom facilities, administrative structures, and the landscape all needed to adapt to modern needs.

The catalyst for re-development came in 1960 when the original Livestock Pavilion, situated north and east of the Main Building, burned to the ground.[18] In recent years, it had accommodated classes in field crops, soils, botany, horticulture, animal husbandry, as well as providing space for the School abattoir and meat locker. The fire began just before midnight and, aided by a shipment of paint stored in the basement, left nothing but a smoldering heap of stucco and wire by early morning. It burned so furiously that the Town fire brigade, under Chief Pim Watkin and Deputy Chief Earle Leask, chose to focus its efforts on protection of the nearby Farm Mechanics Building. Surveying the damage on the following day, Principal Birdsall lamented the wholesale destruction of the horticultural library, teaching equipment, and photographic slides. He said little about the building itself.

Birdsall was less concerned with loss of the structure because it had outlived its utility.[19] To him, it was a relic and merely reflected the sorry state of affairs on the campus as a whole. Now the Provincial Government would be obliged to stop waffling about its commitment to invest in Olds.[20]

While the Government immediately agreed to rebuild, it seemed to have no idea how to proceed. Horticultural Instructor Bill Baranyk and other staff members took matters in hand and developed a building plan that asked for the moon on the assumption they would receive far less. To their surprise, the Government gave them everything they asked for. A temporary facility in which to hold classes was erected for the fall term, and work on the new concrete-block building began in the following spring.[21]

Premier Ernest Manning came to Olds to open the new Plant Science Building officially on Saturday, March 24th, 1962. Waiting to hear from him was a crowd of about 1,000 people who had come to see the annual Little Royal Exhibition and Achievement Day.

In his address, the Premier advised all the young people in the audience to give a life of farming full consideration when choosing a career. "We hear a great deal about the world's 'population explosion,'" he said. "This seems to indicate that the future holds high promise of satisfactory prices for farm products. Production of food to feed a hungry world will become more and more important."[22]

As if to emphasize the point, the Government soon paid for two 50-foot greenhouses situated adjacent to the Plant Science Building. Additional office space followed. Once the College adopted a formal building naming policy in 1967, the Plant Science structure became known as the James Murray Building.

Construction of the Plant Sciences Building, later renamed the James Murray Building, marked the true beginning of the School as a modern college.

Next came the razing of the Farm Mechanics Building. This was the original blacksmith and carpentry shop. It stood directly east of the Main Building and was a firetrap like its contemporary, the Livestock Pavilion. Birdsall was not sorry to see it come down. It was replaced by a modest, concrete block structure whose official opening coincided with the Achievement Day celebrations in March, 1965. Most people would refer to it as the Metals Shop or the Metals Laboratory.

The Plant Science Building and the Metals Shop were both designed by staff of the Department of Public Works. They were, in Birdsall's view, "plain and functional."[23] Plain or not, he was pleased to see them erected. They represented a tangible breakthrough in the lukewarm relationship that had existed between the institution and the Provincial Government for most of his tenure as Principal.

The planning for the next building on campus — a new Animal Science facility — marked the beginning of O.A.V.C.s architectural renaissance. For the first time, a consulting architect was chosen to design the structure. He was Albert Dale of Calgary, whose firm, A. Dale & Associates, had just begun work on the Husky Tower that would define Calgary's skyline for years.

Born in England in 1927, Dale received his Diploma in Architecture at Nottingham in 1949. In 1954 he emigrated to Canada and settled at Calgary. During the next decade, his company would become synonymous with the new Olds campus.

Built at a cost of $450,000, the Lachlin McKinnon Building was officially opened to the public on March 11, 1967.

Its name honoured the contribution of a southern Alberta rancher whose three sons and nine grandsons had attended O.S.A. over the years. Several of them had gone on to become prominent farm leaders themselves.

Construction of the building was something of a godsend, as O.A.V.C. had found it difficult to accommodate livestock classes since the 1960 fire. Just as important, its completion signalled the first step in a $3 million revitalization of the campus announced by Public Works Minister Fred Colbourne on the same day.

When the politicians and dignitaries were finished their speeches, the 200 visitors in attendance strolled around the campus to see what else was being done. Immediately south of the Main Building, a wrecking crew was taking down the 1927 dormitory that had housed thousands of students over the years. When the condition of the structure was assessed in 1964, the inspectors quickly determined that the needed renovations would be cost prohibitive. Even if renovated, it would have been unable to accommodate the current student population, let alone any future increases. As it was, between 1965 and 1968 many students had been obliged to board in town again. Those who could not find rooms to rent were distributed among various disused campus buildings and in the women's wing of the 1927 dormitory. Even with assurances that adequate barriers had been erected, that decision raised a few eyebrows.

Construction of a new residence began in 1967 under the watchful eye of Albert Dale. At an estimated cost of $2.9 million ($3.5 million with equipment and furnishings), Frank Grisdale Hall was thoroughly unconventional. Resembling an exuberant capital H from the air,

the residence was all angles. "There isn't a square room in the place," wrote a reporter for *The Calgary Herald Magazine*,[24] a feature that made it almost impossible to arrange furniture satisfactorily.

The Lachlin McKinnon Building, which housed Animal Science, opened in the spring of 1967. It was the much-needed replacement for the original Livestock Pavilion that burned in 1960.

The end of an era - the 1927 dormitory being demolished after 40 years of service to thousands of students.

Above: This postcard of
Frank Grisdale Hall, the new
student residence in the
heart of the campus,
captures the radical design
of architect Alberta Dale.
Right: In 1970 Duncan
Marshall Place – another of
Albert Dale's designs for
the new campus – arose
near the site of the original
Main Building.

Albert Dale had no intention of creating another barracks-like "home" for the students. Instead, he had chosen to offer them a relaxed and fully integrated residence surrounding a core of administrative functions. Included were a gymnasium, library, cafeteria, health services office, chapel, space for the Emergency Measures Organization, Deans' suites, and a rotunda initially called Times Square in which students could relax before a large fireplace while playing billiards or listening to an emerging talent like Balzac-born country singer LeRoy Anderson.[25] The complex provided accommodations for 500, usually with two students to a room. Near the front entrance, Calgary sculptor Bob Oldrich fashioned special, low-alloy steel into figures of "Man" and "Nature".

Some College administrative functions were housed in Frank Grisdale Hall until a new administration building was completed in 1970. This structure, called Duncan Marshall Place, was another of Albert Dale's creations. Located just north of the residence, it began to take shape in November of 1968. It was immediately stymied by cold weather and a carpenter's strike, and only completed at the end of March, 1970. Harry Strom, Alberta's Premier, laid the cornerstone. The two-storey, 63,000-square-foot structure, which accommodated administrative functions on the main floor and classrooms on the second, cost $1.2 million to construct.

The last major building erected as part of the overall A. Dale & Associates redevelopment concept was the W. J. Elliott Building, the new home of Agricultural Mechanics. Opened in March of 1971, it honoured the memory and service of the first Olds Principal.

This decade of construction utterly transformed the appearance of the campus. In the early 1960s, the campus still resembled nothing so much as a large farmstead. The buildings were few in number and small in scale. While the Main Building and the 1927 Dormitory made up what might be called the residential part of the campus, all of the rest was dominated by farm buildings, fields and plots. When Albert Dale was finished his work, the four new buildings filled the grounds and the farm retreated into the background. The emphasis had shifted, in no uncertain terms, from the barnyard to the classroom.

For Everett Birdsall, who retired in 1972 after overseeing the most radical era of change in the history of the College, the transformation of the Olds campus was a most fitting legacy.

Construction of the W. J. Elliott Building, which housed Agricultural Mechanics, brought to a close the $10 million capital investment in new College facilities begun by the Social Credit government in the mid-1960s.

Alberta in Transition

On the night of August 30th, 1971, Albertans did a most unusual thing: they elected a provincial government led by Progressive Conservatives.

New Political Masters

This had never happened before. Since Alberta became a province in 1905, its enfranchised citizens had trusted only three parties with power: the Liberals, the United Farmers, and the Socreds.

The latter, first under the leadership of William Aberhart and then of Ernest C. Manning, had formed the government in every general election — nine in all — since 1935. Their majorities were usually overwhelming. In the intervening 36 years, only 14 Conservatives had ever won seats in the Legislature. Things usually went so badly for the Tories that they had only a couple of Members sitting in the House at any one time. Even in 1965 this was a political party, with "no seats, no money, no organization, and no presence in the minds of voters."[1]

Things changed with the selection of Peter Lougheed as Progressive Conservative leader. Lougheed was a lawyer, a businessman, the son of a lawyer, and the grandson of influential federal Conservative Sir James Lougheed. He was the antithesis of everything that the Social Credit Party represented. Its base was rural Alberta; he was Calgary-born and Harvard-educated. Its image was comfortably rumpled; his was sharply creased, with clothes to match. It reached voters through radio broadcasts; Lougheed studied the campaigns of President John F. Kennedy and soon became adept in front of the television camera.[2] As the Province's answer to the charismatic Pierre Elliott Trudeau, Peter Lougheed radically altered the political landscape and led Albertans down a very different political road.

Alberta was ready for a change. In the 43 years since Lougheed's birth, the Province's rural roots had withered.[3] The cities and a few large towns were growing, often as a result of new revenues from petroleum exploration and development, while smaller places continued to lose residents year after year. Seven of 10 Albertans lived in urban centres in 1966. By 1967, 1,500 farmers were leaving the land annually. Caught between rising costs for land, machinery, fertilizer and labour, and ever diminishing incomes, they had little choice. Only large farms made economic sense anymore. It was no wonder O.A.V.C. had altered the focus of its programs in the early 1960s to prepare young people for off-farm employment. The writing was on the wall for rural Alberta.

Manning's Social Credit Party understood and sympathized with the growing plight of Albertans who preferred to till the soil. In response, it announced ambitious plans to bring electricity to more farms, pave more country roads, extend low-interest loans to farmers, and raise the standard of rural education. In the County of Mountain View, for example, students at five rural high schools received instruction in biology via a closed-circuit television broadcast made at a studio in Didsbury.[4] Similarly, O.A.V.C. became a centre for new, Government-funded studies in farm management and records management.[5] These were progressive gestures for the time.

To the extent that these programs were designed to shore up the rural base of the Socreds, they failed miserably. It did not help that after Manning resigned in 1968, the Party replaced him with a reluctant, uncharismatic and uncalculating leader. This was Harry Strom, the former Minister of Agriculture who had long supported O.A.V.C. The contrast between him and the dynamic, young Lougheed was great, and Strom suffered in the comparison. As Albertans marked their ballots on that August night in 1971, they ushered in a 40-year political dynasty whose policies on education and the economy continue to have ramifications for Olds College.

A Place for Agricultural Education

Beginning in the 1960s, every Canadian province re-examined its educational system. In Alberta, where school taxes had been increasing steadily along with the size of the educational bureaucracy since the 1950s, people were beginning to question many of the uses to which those dollars were put. Before being dislodged from power by Lougheed's Tories, the Socreds had appointed a one-man commission to define the future of education in the Province by the fall of 1972. At the request of the new Tory administration, Walter Worth delivered his report ahead of schedule in May.

To the relief of the retiring Everett Birdsall, Worth's small section on Olds held no surprises. In fact, Worth clearly enunciated the College's traditional purpose and existing mandate before exaggerating slightly by describing it as unique. He wrote,

> Olds College has a novel role to play as the only institution in Alberta specializing in agricultural education. Accordingly, it should feature more sophisticated programs in technology, marketing and management suited to the rapidly changing agricultural industry.[6]

He went on to say,

> As a logical extension of its central role in agricultural education, this College could serve as the major continuing education center for farmers and persons in other occupations related to agriculture. This would, in fact, be a return to a significant and familiar role played earlier in the century.

The initiatives of Birdsall and his staff during the previous decade had paid off. Olds would retain its role as a centre for extension work while increasing the technical content of its offerings to ensure that they remained current.

With that settled, the more immediate debate focused on provincial administration of the College. Who was going to run things with this new regime in place? The Progressive Conservatives, who reorganized much of the Government as they took power, chose to establish a new Department of Advanced Education to oversee the delivery of all post-secondary education. This included responsibility for adult agricultural and vocational education, long the purview of the Department of Agriculture.

One of the first measures undertaken by the new Department was creation of a Regional Colleges Division to administer Olds, Vermilion, and Fairview. Under the direction of Olds veteran Ted Hawker, the Division not only provided administrative direction but also co-ordinated the activities of the agricultural colleges with those of other advanced education institutions in Alberta.

For example, Olds provided instruction to students in a new meat-cutting program, although the program itself had been developed by Red Deer College. Similarly, in 1972 Olds College and Lethbridge Community College approved a transfer agreement that allowed students to take the first year of Agricultural Mechanics at Lethbridge before transferring into the final year of the program at Olds.

Administrative realignments at the provincial level also affected the name of the colleges. As of 1973, Olds became known as Olds Regional College.[7] Few people seemed to like or adopt the new name, however, and within a year even the Regional Colleges Division was referring to it as Olds College.

This marked the first time that Olds College was within Alberta's educational mainstream. While some observers wondered whether the transfer of jurisdictional oversight would harm the role of the College, a general continuity of personnel suggested this would not happen to any appreciable extent. In fact, the continued involvement of individuals like Ted Hawker and W. J. Collin — people who knew Olds and its ambitions intimately from their previous College and Provincial roles — did much to smooth the transition from one department to another. If anything, removal of the long-standing uncertainty about the College's mandate seemed likely to enable it to progress more swiftly and serve more effectively. And while the historical administrative tie to the Department of Agriculture had been severed, the relationship would continue in terms of applied research.

By 1972, Olds College had not only found a new place for itself within Alberta's larger educational system, it had also captured the attention of many people as the place to attend for specialized agricultural training.

Diversifying the Mandate

During the 1970s and 1980s, with limited means, Olds College carved out a distinctive niche for itself in agricultural, continuing, and international education.

The achievement was all the greater for the lack of Government focus on farm issues during these years. Oil, not agriculture, now fueled the economic engine of Alberta and propelled policy discussions in fundamentally new directions that had little to do with the Province's agrarian past.

That said, the Tories were so preoccupied with diversifying the economy and battling Ottawa for greater provincial rights that they passively accepted the ambitions of institutions like Olds College. If they were rarely willing to pay the costs of those ambitions, particularly during the recession of the early to mid-1980s, their reluctance was related more to general economic conditions than to political indifference or interference.

In 1972, administration of the College passed into the hands of a former O.S.A. student, instructor and Birdsall protegé, Wilbur Collin. His educational path paralleled the general trend toward administrative professionalism in Alberta. This had begun in the 1950s as consolidated schools and larger school districts demanded enhanced management skills. The growth of the agricultural colleges created the same need for better leadership in those institutions. The combined student population at Olds, Vermilion and Fairview grew from 238 in 1957 to 650 by 1971.[8]

Anticipating this trend, the University of Alberta Faculty of Education teamed up with the Kellogg Foundation in 1953 to develop a series of short courses in educational administration. By 1955, the University had established its own Department of Educational Administration, a pioneering effort that soon drew students from across Canada and around the world.

Collin was among those who took a leave of absence to study at the University of Alberta Department of Educational Administration. His interest in educational reform and administration had long been evident, as he was one of the four key instructors who laid out the O.A.V.C. curriculum adopted in 1963-64. When not teaching, he studied for and received his Bachelor's degree in Education. In 1967 he resigned his teaching post to join the Provincial Government as its first Co-ordinator of Agricultural Education. Four years later, he received his Master of Education degree in Educational Administration, and soon began work on his doctorate in the same field.

What Principal Collin lacked in years — he was just 37 — he more than made up for in determination and vitality. His goal, as he stated it, was to turn Olds into a comprehensive community college that focused on the needs of modern farm businesses. During his five-and-a-half years in office, he strove to expand the College's offerings while completing the specialization of coursework that had begun so tentatively in the 1950s when he was still an Olds student.

The situation that Collin inherited from Birdsall was as good as it had been in years. By the fall of 1971 the $10-million investment that the Socreds had made in campus buildings accommodated more than 300 students per session and 76 staff. In an academic world now measured in sessions, the College taught an average of more than 100 correspondence course students per session and more than 300 continuing education students per session. It offered between 25 and 33 short courses per session and provided meeting space for 273 events. By most scholastic yardsticks, Olds College was thriving.

Lougheed's Tories expanded the area of continuing education, honouring what Walter Worth had called the

noble goal of "lifelong learning". The concept had been gaining momentum before they took power, and they supported its continued progress. During the 1971-72 school year, for example, the new Department of Advanced Education funded 37 school systems in their quest to develop 253 credit and 1,284 non-credit school extension programs. These programs included academic courses, business education courses, home economics, industrial and technical arts and crafts, and general interest courses.

W. J. (Wilbur) Collin, an O.S.A. graduate himself, was the first Principal to bring professional management techniques to the position.

Olds College provided space and instruction for many continuing education courses. Much of the impetus for these courses came from a joint committee formed by the County of Mountain View and the Olds Extension Office of the provincial Extension and Colleges Division.

The courses fell into four basic categories: upgrading, skills acquisition or improvement, life enrichment, and recreation. The College became home to students of all ages who were interested in subjects as diverse as leather-working, car repair, interior decoration, aviation, and languages and literature. Continuing education courses went some way toward achieving Collin's goal of pedagogical thoroughness. As the Alumni Association wrote at the time, Olds College sought to provide "not only specialized employment-oriented training, but also life-enriching programs."[9]

Correspondence courses came to the College via a different route. The first course was in farm accounting. Previously offered by the University of Alberta, the course was suffering from declining enrolment. It had, in fact, dropped to the point where the University no longer considered it worthwhile to continue. Members of the farm community disagreed, however, and pressed the College to take it on.

A new course was drawn up and offered in 12 lessons, to be completed at a time convenient for each student. There was no time limit, which made it much easier for many participants. The fee was $25. By October of 1971, 104 students had enrolled; by December, the number had risen to 196. The total for 1972 was 309. In addition to Albertans, many students from Manitoba, Saskatchewan and British Columbia also took part. As the 1970s wore

In the 1970s, the College became increasingly involved in international educational work with groups such as the Alberta-Japan Dairy Exchange program.

on, the College improved its method of delivery and expanded its offerings to include other courses in farm management, horticulture, farm law, agricultural mechanics and soil management.

Throughout the 1970s, Collin and his colleagues continued to diversify the traditional College programs. By 1976, they were able to offer many programs that were the only ones of their kind in Western Canada; some were unique in the country. The programs included:

- Agricultural Chemicals Technology
- Agricultural Engineering Technology
- Agricultural Mechanics apprenticeship program
- Commercial Floriculture
- Fashion Merchandising Technology
- Horse Husbandry
- Horticultural Technology

Largely because of its specialized programs, Olds soon hosted more out-of-province students than any other agricultural school in Canada; about one-fifth of its students were now non-Albertans. Indeed, several programs proved so popular that the College was unable to accommodate more than half of the applicants. In addition, the yearly enrolment of thousands of continuing education and community service students at Olds was the most successful agricultural college of its type in Canada.

The alignment between Olds College programs and the needs of the business community had never been greater. In Fashion Merchandising Technology, for example, the input of an external advisory committee since 1965 had created tremendous opportunities for students. Most graduates of the two-year program (after 1971) readily found employment in retailing. A number of those who persisted in their careers became senior buyers or departmental managers. Around 60 young women enrolled in most years, and one young man graduated as well in the 1970s. The name of the program after 1972 reflected the buoyant job market in retail sales, although Olds did continue to offer some training in clothing design. Beginning in 1977, the advisory committee recommended that all students also complete two months of on-the-job experience prior to graduation.

The nine-month Secretarial Arts program continued to train women and men for careers as secretaries, dicta-typists, and receptionists. It, too, benefited from the advice of an external advisory committee. In addition to studying typing and shorthand, students now took courses in human relations, accounting, and communications as well. They also participated in an "office simulation" course in which they undertook clerical work for faculty, students and the wider community. It was seen as an opportunity for the students to gain experience in a realistic setting. No doubt it offset a few routine administrative costs as well. Some 30 to 40 students took the Secretarial Arts program annually.

The growing complexity of teaching responsibilities led to the formalization of *de facto* leadership roles at the College. Perhaps it is not surprising, given Collin's focus on educational administration, that the concept of Departmental heads truly came into its own under his leadership. Soon Olds had a Coordinator of Agricultural Economics (Ian Hall); a Chairman of Agricultural Mechanics (Pat Burton); a Chairman of Animal Science (Stu Wilton); a Chairman of Plants and Soils Science (Robert

Hill); a Chairman of Continuing Education (Bruce Martin); and a Chairman of the Learning Resource Centre (David Poole).

The Administration now placed greater emphasis on collaboration with other teaching institutions. The Animal Health Technology program introduced in 1975 is a case in point. Although based at Olds College, the program required that its students spend their first 24 weeks at Calgary's Southern Alberta Institute of Technology (SAIT), and their last 12 weeks at the Western College of Veterinary Medicine at Saskatoon. They also did a month-long clinical stint with a practising veterinarian.

With such practical experience complementing their classroom studies, graduates of the program more easily found employment in small animal practices, meat inspection, disease control, and diagnostic services in both the private and public sectors. Working hand-in-hand with government, industry and complementary teaching institutions, while not an original concept, would prove vital to the future of Olds College.

Under Collin's administration, the College greatly extended its international reach as well. In years past, international work was largely incidental to the mandate of the College. Now it emerged strongly. By 1976 Olds had become the seat of operations for the International Agricultural Exchange Association, the Alberta-Japan Dairy Exchange Program, the Korean Agricultural Workers Program, and the Mexican Students Visitation Program. It soon became common for delegations from as many as two dozen countries to visit Olds College during a single school year. Its influence was spreading around the globe.

O.S.A. in Ethiopia

While the international reach of Olds College increased greatly in the 1970s, that was not the first time the school had made its mark on the world.

One of the most significant and least known examples of its global impact occurred in 1947 at Jimma, an important market town in southwestern Ethiopia. The country, situated on the Horn of Africa, had been overrun by Italian fascists in the 1930s. Liberated by Allied forces in 1941, Ethiopia embarked on major reconstruction and modernization projects under the leadership of Emperor Haile Selassie. One was the United Nations Relief and Rehabilitation Association School of Practical Arts, established at Jimma. Nine Canadian missionary families, including Howard Thompson and his wife Olive of Innisfail, ran that project during its first year.

At the request of Emperor Selassie, Thompson subsequently drew up plans for a brand new agricultural college at Jimma. His model? The Olds School of Agriculture and Home Economics. The curriculum at Jimma included motor mechanics, carpentry, first aid, field and animal husbandry and the local Amharic language. The Ethiopian college thrived, eventually becoming the Jimma University College of Agriculture and Veterinary Medicine.

Charting a New Course

In the spring of 1978, the Progressive Conservatives altered the status of Olds College from that of a government-administered institution to that of a public college. Henceforth, it would be run by an independent Board of Governors.

This important change, coming as it did on the heels of the Alumni Association's diamond jubilee and just in time for the College's 65th anniversary celebrations, was appreciated at the College like a long-desired and generous gift. In theory, it promised independence in matters of administration and fundraising without severing direct communications with the departments of Advanced Education and Agriculture.

Many greeted the decision with relief, as the previous few years had been filled with frustration. Although Olds was formally a college within the Department of Advanced Education, the Government tended to consider it and its counterparts at Vermilion and Fairview no different from the five vocational centres across the Province. As trades-based facilities catering to the unskilled and chronically under-employed, Alberta Vocational Centres had little in common with the increasingly technology- and pedagogy-driven agricultural schools. Yet, to the enduring chagrin of people like Wilbur Collin, the bureaucrats in Edmonton seemed to draw little distinction between the two types of institutions.

Government intransigence had been another daily challenge. Mountains of bureaucracy had to be scaled for even the simplest of requests. Requisitions for $20 repairs often disappeared for months on end and occasionally for years. On a more serious note, building needs went unaddressed despite the tremendous increase in enrolment. The Plant Science Building, for instance, was bursting at the seams. So was the residence. Re-development of the College farm had stalled. Long-term plans languished for lack of funding. Progress was unacceptably slow; in fact, it was difficult to do more than stay the course.

Particularly galling to the Administration and the Alumni Association was the Government's stubborn refusal to acknowledge and support the College as a regional learning centre. The Alumni Association argued strenuously that Olds had served as such a centre in years past and was well situated to do so again in the future. But accomplishing this goal in the 1970s implied new investment in the College, investment that was simply not forthcoming.

For example, the situation with respect to the College library was nothing short of disgraceful. Poor planning had meant it was shoehorned into Frank Grisdale Hall during the rebuilding of the mid-1960s. Then it was shifted unceremoniously to wholly inappropriate space in the old mice-infested dairy barn (the librarians quickly got a cat). Edmonton's seeming lack of concern about such an essential teaching resource was inexcusable.

Less than a decade after opening, Frank Grisdale Hall was overcrowded because of climbing enrolments.

Governance by a board representing the public interest directly implied independence from what many saw as the indifference of the provincial bureaucracy. Surely that would mean greater responsiveness to local needs and to the wider farming community. The College administration and faculty was further heartened by the membership of the first Board of Governors.

Appointed in April of 1978 by A. E. Hohol, the Minister of Advanced Education and Manpower, the Board included four Olds alumni (Donald Robertson, Larry Edwards, Gordon Church, and Keith McKinnon), and Dr. Richard Wray, an Olds family physician. There were also two women with backgrounds in home economics and local politics (Edna Clarke and Marilyn Sharp), which provided assurances to those who felt Olds must continue its longstanding support of the educational needs of young women. In addition, Dr. Hans Flatla of the Department of Animal Science represented the Faculty Association and Gerald Donkersgoed represented the Student Association. These people understood agriculture and the communities it supported.

Everyone was pleased to see Don Robertson, who farmed near Carstairs, as the Chairman. A 1951 O.S.A. graduate and one-time instructor, he had served as President of the Alumni Association, on the Alberta Board of Agricultural Education from 1968 to 1972, and as a member of the Alberta Advisory Committee on Agricultural Education and Rural Extension from 1972 to 1975. He knew his way around the College, the Government, and the agricultural industry.

Coincident with the announcement of board governance, Wilbur Collin resigned his post and returned to Edmonton to work with the Department of Advanced Education in the Advanced Education Planning Secretariat. The new Board of Governors would start with a fresh slate and a new College leader.

In clarifying the role of Olds College within the overall educational system of the Province, the Board believed it desirable for Olds to be promoted as the "Agricultural Centre for Alberta." It would preserve its traditional, central role in agricultural instruction while branching out into complementary programs of interest to rural society, maintaining its status as a community and research centre, and working collaboratively with agricultural departments, institutions and organizations. In addition, the established relationship with industry and business would be not only maintained but also enhanced.

Soon a list of priorities was drawn up. The Board identified a pressing need for a modern facility to be called the Learning Resource Centre to replace the inadequate College library. Wilbur Collin had called for its construction back in 1972. More generally, the Board sought a comprehensive survey of campus structures to ensure that classroom, administrative and research facilities were appropriate. This was prompted, in part, by the imperative need to address the overcrowding at the Plant Science Building. A review of the College farm was implicit in the decision to carry out this survey. Finally, there was agreement that the College needed additional recreational facilities as drug and alcohol use among the student body had become a matter of considerable concern.

Chairman Robertson saw the deliberations and decisions of the Board as a logical next stage in the evolution of Olds College as it sought to come to grips with the challenges of modern farming and education. In a thoughtful guest editorial in the *Alumni Review*, he said

Reassessment has to be, at this stage particularly, a number one priority of the Board. The introduction of the Board has brought about a fundamental change in relationships from top to bottom. We must look closely

at our external links with the Department of Advanced Education and Manpower and our traditional links with Agriculture, we must look at our internal structure and the roles individuals will play in that structure. We must look at internal communication in the light of both the Colleges Act and enlightened human relations and decide how best to set up advising councils and informal communicating links to receive the best and most complete information possible for decision making. We must look at long-range planning attempting to judge as clearly as possible our most likely direction while keeping as many options as possible open to us.

The change to Board governance does not represent a radical departure from past practice, nor will it necessarily herald a change of direction, nor will it be a panacea for all the real and imagined ills of the institution. It is a natural step in the developmental process of our college and has been enthusiastically welcomed as such by the great majority of the public. It affords us unprecedented opportunities to be flexible and responsive to the needs of our many 'communities'. We must all, collectively and consciously guard against setting up our own self-imposed regulations and structures that will, in the end, prove no less onerous and restricting.[10]

It was a well-crafted message, sensitive to the concerns that naturally accompany significant change yet cautiously optimistic about the future. As far as many frustrated College alumni were concerned, it struck just the right chord.

Lacking sufficient capital redevelopment funding, the College temporarily housed the library in a mice-infested dairy barn. The librarians responded by getting a cat.

Setting Sail

In the decade and a half after 1978, Olds College embarked on what may be described charitably as an eye-opening voyage of discovery.

The destination may have been reasonably certain, but under the guidance of three very different presidents the College found it difficult to stay on course. It left more than one person to wonder if there was any significance in the fact that the Lougheed Government had relinquished administration of the College to the Board of Governors on April Fools' Day.

Perhaps it was too much to expect that those in charge could simultaneously develop and provide quality programs, build new infrastructure, refurbish the College farm, raise essential funds, forge closer ties with industry, establish mutually rewarding relationships with federal, provincial and local governments, and pursue international collaboration on many fronts. Nevertheless, that was the task at hand.

Glenn Crombie, who arrived in town with his family in August of 1978, was the first Olds College leader to bear the title of President. A forester by training, he had spent the previous 10 years as Principal of the Lindsay Campus of Sir Sanford Fleming College near Peterborough, Ontario.

During his tenure at Lindsay, he oversaw significant growth as the population rose from a total of 150 students to 850 daytime and 1,300 evening students. Most of his administrative experience involved managing

programs in the liberal arts, forestry, fish and wildlife, and cartography, although he liked to joke that he also ran "the smallest agriculture program in the world," with just 25 students.[11] He felt ready for a new challenge and saw the Presidency of Olds College as a "step up."[12] Those who knew him well, like his Lindsay colleague Dorothy Rowles, said he "had a personality that had an impact."[13]

Soft-spoken yet stern-willed, the 43-year old Crombie was determined to manage growth at the College during what he saw as an era of fundamental change. He soon laid down a series of goals.

As a school with 700 full-time and 3,000 continuing education students, Olds needed more and better facilities. This would become even more important if, as expected, enrolment topped 1,000. Crombie's plan was to ask the Provincial Government for $9 million with which to build additional student housing and a Learning Centre, renovate and expand the Plant Science and Animal Science buildings, construct new sheep and swine facilities as a first step in remodelling the farm, and develop an agricultural park that could be used by the College, the Olds Agricultural Society, community groups and provincial organizations.

The College also needed better relations with residents of the Town of Olds and the County of Mountain View. The proposal for a joint agricultural facility would go some way to addressing that concern, but Crombie also promised to do everything in his power to accommodate the educational needs of the farming community and the agricultural industry. "If we have 10 people who want something," he said soon after arriving, "we'll set up a course."[14]

The College's first Board of Governors (L-R): Dr. Hans Flatla, Keith McKinnon, Marilyn Sharp, Gordon Church, Donald Robertson, Glenn Crombie, Gerald Donkersgoed, Edna Clarke, C. Larry Edwards, Dr. Richard Wray. Opposite: Glenn Crombie, the first Olds College administrator to bear the title of President.

He was careful to point out that Olds had already done that with new short courses in pesticide use, horticulture, land appraisal, and artificial insemination. But more than that, he recognized the limitations implicit in a community the size of Olds. With only 4,000 residents, it lacked services as basic as recreational facilities. Here he suggested the College might work with the Town on developing a common swimming pool, racquetball and squash facility. Plans were already afoot, in any case, to establish a common library facility in the proposed Learning Resource Centre on campus.

Crombie's timing, through no fault of his own, was terrible. The Alberta economy, having generated tremendous wealth during the petroleum boom of the 1970s, was about to crash along with oil revenues and any semblance of federal-provincial civility as Alberta and Ottawa tangled over the National Energy Policy. By 1980 the economy was in recession and ambitious plans such as Crombie's didn't have a chance. Although he moderated his request by focusing on funding for the $3.2-million library, to be known as the Olds Community Resource Centre, the Provincial Government consistently turned him down.

Repeatedly stymied by Edmonton, Crombie turned his attention to the Olds College Foundation, hoping that the private sector would provide enough money to fund the major capital projects. The estimate for those projects stood at $30 million.

Begun through the efforts of Everett Birdsall and Wilbur Collin in 1973, the Olds College Alumni Foundation, as it was originally registered, enabled the College to accept individual and corporate donations for activities and projects not normally funded by the Provincial Government. In December 1981, the College hired Robert Redpath, former Finance Director of the Montana Department of Health, to head the Foundation. As an autonomous body with its own board of directors, the Foundation was also able to pursue opportunities denied post-secondary institutions. As Redpath said, "If we're separate from the college we can go out and be very enterprising where sometimes government restrictions wouldn't allow a college to do so."[15] In some cases, donations to the Foundation were matched by Provincial contributions through the Advanced Education Endowment Fund. That was all well and good, but everyone realized that it would take a long time to generate significant funds through the Foundation.

Deservedly or not, Crombie was seen by some as the main reason for the College's failure to secure major funding from the Provincial Government during his four-year tenure. There were those who found his administrative style authoritarian and his personal style cold and distant.[16] They claimed he rubbed both College staff and bureaucrats in Edmonton the wrong way.

To his critics, Crombie responded that they never had to be accountable for their decisions prior to the introduction of board governance, and now often fell short of what was expected of them.[17] Perhaps Don Robertson expressed the situation best when he summed up Crombie as "direct" and "if you're going to be direct you're going to get flak."[18]

Although the state of Alberta's finances precluded much College progress between 1978 and 1982, a number of matters did improve significantly while Crombie was in

office. Even his most grudging admirers had to admit that he proved a great champion of many of the agricultural programs. He supported the fledgling equine program, revitalized parts of the farm, started an Innovative Instruction Fund that allowed instructors to reinvest revenue they generated, and expanded faculty development. He also introduced a number of new programs, including surface land agent courses, a seed and grain program, heavy-duty mechanical apprenticeships, and surveying technology.

In 1982, Crombie was invited to become President of Cambrian Community College at Sudbury, an institution five times larger than Olds College. He eagerly accepted. In leaving Olds, he thanked the Board, the staff and the alumni for their commitment to excellence and expressed his belief that the College now had the experience, the faculty and the plan that would enable them to become a truly independent institution with a world-wide reputation. "Olds College," he said, "is ready to take on the challenge of the '80s."[19]

At The HEAD of its Class...

To do this he rallied representatives from groups across campus and from the Program and Campus Planning Committee of the Board of Governors to form a Council on Renewal and Instructional Strategic Planning (CRISP). Its report, "At the Head of Its Class", affirmed the agricultural focus of the College. In subsequent interviews and speeches, Cornish stated the case as clearly as he could:

> *The primary mission of Olds College is to provide current quality education, training and services for people who are involved directly or indirectly in agricultural endeavours.* [22]

Sounding very much like a management consultant enunciating a mission statement, he effectively refocused the College's mandate on agriculture for farmers and industry. It would take three to five years, he estimated, to winnow inappropriate courses from the College's programming and introduce relevant new studies, but he was confident it would happen.

With the exception of those whose jobs were potentially

In a report called At The Head of Its Class, President Cornish and the Board of Governors reaffirmed the central agricultural purpose of the College.

in jeopardy, the faculty agreed with the renewed vision and gave Cornish the vote of confidence he needed to put the case forward with conviction. Meetings with farm industry leaders then cemented the new mandate.

Cornish also decided it was his job to make sure that the politicians in Edmonton understood the needs and plans of the College and their vital role as public officials in ensuring that the needed transformation took place. Behind the scenes, Cornish worked hard on the campaign of local Progressive Conservative candidate Stephen Stiles. In November of 1982, Stiles took the riding for the Tories for the first time. Now the College would have a local voice in caucus. Cornish, for his part, would ensure that Stiles and his caucus colleagues started to think seriously about a renewed agricultural sector as part of their overall economic diversification strategy for the Province.

The Learning Resource Centre, a $4.3-million facility begun in 1984, was the first significant investment in the College by the Progressive Conservative administration.

Things did not change overnight, but the renewed College mandate and positive attitude seemed to strike the right chord in Edmonton. In the late winter of 1983 Cornish led a Board of Governors delegation to the capital to press its case for funding with Advanced Education Minister Dick Johnston and Agriculture Minister LeRoy Fjordbotten. In addition to Cornish, the delegation included new Board Chair Larry Edwards, retiring Board Member Marilyn Sharp, His Worship Mayor Bob Armstrong of the Town of Olds, and MLA Stephen Stiles.

The good news from the delegates was that the recession had caused construction costs to fall. They now pegged the needed investment at around $30 million instead of $40 to $55 million. Instead of pumping most of it into a Learning Resource Centre, they now wished to see four priorities addressed concurrently — classrooms, the farm, supporting laboratories and farm equipment, and residences and recreational facilities. Thoughtful, integrated investment like that would, according to Cornish, have a profound effect on the way in which Albertans used their precious farmland.

In the spring of 1984 Olds-Didsbury MLA Stephen Stiles visited the College to deliver a cheque for $200,000 to cover the architectural fees related to the design of a $4.3-million Learning Resource Centre. At the same time, Advanced Education Minister Dick Johnston announced that funding for construction of the facility would be included in the next provincial budget. That budget would also include $1 million for farmstead improvements, $1.1 million for new furniture, $323,000 for renovations of various kinds, and $113,000 for campus maintenance. College alumni and the Student Association raised an additional $642,000 for a Student Alumni Centre to be built as part of the Learning Resource Centre.

Olds College was back in the saddle. An incident following the 65th anniversary celebrations in 1988 brought home the point. As part of the festivities, a banner had been hung outside the Learning Resource Centre. It read, "Proudly Serving Agriculture." Even when the celebrations ended, no one wanted to remove the banner.

By 1989, when Dr. Cornish moved on to become President of Camosun College in Victoria, British Columbia, the list of long-awaited capital investments at Olds College had dwindled considerably. The Learning Resource Centre-Student Alumni Centre was up and running; the farm had been redeveloped significantly and now included a new equine arena and beef handling facility; extension renovation of Frank Grisdale Hall had done much to improve the standard of campus living for students; and work was underway on a new Land Sciences Centre. In the words of his successor, Robert Bigsby, Dr. Cornish's term was

marked by strong leadership, renewed institutional purpose, and significant campus development. Perhaps the most significant legacy of the Cornish years has been the refocusing of Olds College's primary mission on the provision of programs and services for people in agriculture and related industries.[23]

Thanks to Cornish's contribution, the role of Olds College, if not the times themselves, now seemed less confusing.

The Student Alumni Centre, built as part of the Learning Resource Centre with the generous donations of College alumni and the Student Association.

Implementing the New Vision

Throughout the years of the Cornish administration, Bob Bigsby served as the President's right-hand man. Of necessity, Cornish had given most of his time to external matters as he tried to right the foundering College ship. Vice-President Bigsby, meanwhile, was charged with the equally important task of keeping the deck hands happy. And when they could not all be kept happy, as often happens in an organization with hundreds of members, Bigsby strove to keep them from mutinying. With their complementary styles, "Dan and Bob" made a good team.

After Cornish moved to Victoria in 1989, Bigsby became President and his responsibilities broadened accordingly. Over the course of the next six years, he would of necessity devote himself to fleshing out the College's new mandate.

Bigbsy had served as Academic Dean of the College prior to being appointed Cornish's Vice-President. He was particularly interested in pedagogical and organizational issues. This concern was evident, for example, in the change he brought to responsibility for budgeting. Instead of spending authority residing with a financial administrator, Bigsby placed it on the shoulders of departmental academics, feeling that the authority and the responsibility had to reside at the same level. Similarly, he moved the College farm into the academic sector so that it would be valued more for its instructional potential than its productivity. Changes like these, which did not always elicit compliments, were aimed at strengthening the overall learning environment at the College.

He brought the same spirit of reform to the relationship between College programs and the agricultural industry. He did so largely by introducing the concept of the review committee at Olds. His inspiration was the Develop A Curriculum (DACUM) system of program development pioneered by Holland College in Prince Edward Island. A form of occupational analysis, DACUM allowed instructors and administrators to identify the tasks that must be performed by persons employed in any occupational area.

Of course there had been external advisory committees for decades, but their role was basically confined to verifying the relevance of course content. Industrial review committees of the sort envisioned by Dr. Bigsby took a different view.

Consisting of perhaps 15 to 18 members, a review committee brainstormed to identify the skills, or "core competencies" as they were called in the jargon of the day, that industry leaders expected of each College graduate in a specific field, such as the farrier program. When the results of these brainstorming sessions were overlaid on an independently generated list of competencies created by existing courses, the gaps were obvious. Those gaps could then be addressed by developing new courses or refining the content of existing ones.

This new planning tool allowed for much closer alignment between the College and the external business community. It also increased the odds that graduates would find employment sooner and in their chosen field. And for the first time, instructors were not only permitted but also encouraged to build and sustain relationships with leading agricultural businesses and industries.

The work of the review committees was soon evident. By 1988-89, more than 30 program reviews had been completed or were underway. They had an immediate effect on program development at the College, particularly in the areas of land and plant sciences.

In response to input from industry, market analysis and an emerging focus on environmental management, Olds developed the Land Resource Management Program that offered majors in Soil and Water Conservation, Integrated Pest Management, Land Classification and

Reclamation, and Agronomy. At the same time, the ground was broken for a much-needed $6-million Land Sciences Centre. Work then started on a new Agricultural Fieldman major that would be introduced in 1990.

Dr. Robert Bigsby, President from 1989 to 1995, was instrumental in integrating the skill needs of industry into the College curriculum.

Within two years of taking office, President Bigsby also signed the first of what would eventually become many joint ventures between the College and agribusinesses. Greenleaf Products, a well-known manufacturer and seller of topsoils, peats and fertilizers, joined forces with the College to develop a manure and compost bagging facility.

Then the new Olds Forage Centre began producing compressed hay bales for international markets, particularly in Japan. By 2001, Alberta would have 16 facilities like this and most of the operators received their training at Olds. Stanley Industrial Consultants Ltd. (later SENTAR) was chosen to conduct a feasibility assessment for a composting applied research facility. Operated with support from Procter & Gamble, the facility processed campus and municipal waste and soon allowed the College to offer diplomas and certificates in compost technology.

More partnerships came into being. In 1989, the College's longstanding commitment to turfgrass research was formalized as the Prairie Turfgrass Research Centre. The Centre assisted the golfing community of Western Canada with course design and would go on to become a leader in the development of low-maintenance grasses and weed control. Four years later, an agreement was signed with the Canadian Mushroom Growers Association and Agriculture Canada to develop a new Mushroom Growth Chamber facility. As early as 1992, Bigsby was able to report that one-third of the College's annual budget of some $18 million came from revenues generated on campus.

New international relationships blossomed in these years as well. In addition to the fledgling entrepreneurialism apparent in the hay sales to Japan, the College sought consortium agreements for international training contracts. In particular, they looked for new opportunities in Africa, India, Central and South America and China. Such agreements were seen as vital for staff development as well.

After 1992, much of this work was done through the CanEd International Inc. consortium of colleges, whose goal was to provide training in agriculture to clients around the world. By the time Bigsby left office in 1995, Olds instructors and administrators had worked in at least 30 countries, including Thailand, Korea, Nicaragua, the Philippines, Russia, Mexico, Japan and Costa Rica. As he said, "We cannot, and should not, settle for insularity."[24]

This outward looking view was also evident in the trio of articulation, or credit transfer, agreements signed during Bigsby's tenure. By the spring of 1992, Olds College had agreements in place with the University of Alberta, Montana State University and the University of Hawaii at Hilo.

Ironically, success was harder to achieve closer to home. Over the years the relationship between the College and the Town of Olds had swung, as Everett Birdsall once put it, between enthusiasm and indifference. At times, animosity came into it. Usually the character of the relationship depended on the personalities of the leaders of the day and the degree to which they could identify mutual gain from working together.

Research conducted by staff and students at the Prairie Turfgrass Research Centre contributed greatly to the development of low maintenance grasses and weed control.

While everyone understood implicitly that the presence of the College was a tremendous economic boon to the Town (and this would be confirmed beyond doubt by a 2001 socio-economic study), it was not always easy to find common ground on specific issues. They tried for years — in vain as it turned out — to join forces to build a common library and an agricultural arena. On the other hand, the Town eagerly teamed with the College to sponsor the Jerry Bremner chuckwagon in the Calgary Stampede during the College's 75th anniversary in 1988.

In 1993, the College and the Town altered their formal relationship through an annexation agreement. While the College farm remained as part of the County of Mountain View, the campus proper was annexed to the Town of Olds. Fittingly, the change took place on November 21st, the 80th anniversary of the institution's founding. The new relationship provided almost immediate benefits as the Town and the College co-operated in utilizing the composting facility.

Another relationship that changed significantly in the Bigsby era was that between the College and its student body. The dramatic shift toward agribusiness programs in these years reflected the fact that comparatively few students now intended to make farming their sole occupation. They were also older, on average, than in the past. One-fifth of the students were now married and half of them had children, which prompted the College to look into the provision of a married students' residence (which opened in 2001) and daycare facilities. As Dean of Student Services Sharon Carry was pleased to note, the College was now concerning itself with the "whole person."[25]

More of the students were choosing to come to Olds because of its growing reputation for academic excellence, its links with industry and its success in placing graduates. Along with those achievements came a clearer sense of the College's purpose. In 1992, the Board of Governors approved a new Mission Statement which read, in part:

> We are a responsive, innovative and client-centred educational organization dedicated to excellence in careers education, adult development, applied research and services, primarily in the areas of Agriculture, Horticulture, Land Management, Applied Business and Environment.[26]

The College now conveyed these attributes through more sophisticated marketing and recruitment campaigns. It paid off. By 1994, more than 1,000 students were attending the College. Many of its 75 instructional staff also had roles in educating the 1,500 part-time learners in Home Study programs and the 2,400 part-time learners in Extension education programs. In addition, some 20,000 people came to conferences on campus each year. It was becoming increasingly difficult to miss the fact that Olds College was prospering while many other agricultural education centres were foundering.

Through its new composting facility, Olds College led the way in the responsible disposal and recycling of municipal waste.

Tory Bookends

If the election of Alberta's first Progressive Conservative government in 1971 had obliged Olds College to confront its shortcomings as a modern educational institution, it remained for another Tory administration — that of Ralph Klein — to compel the College to refine its approach to success within a climate of unwelcome austerity.

No sooner had Don Getty won the Tory leadership following Peter Lougheed's resignation in 1985 than a tide of red ink began to wash over the Province. Energy revenues sank. Real estate prices fell. Unemployment rose. Two Alberta-based banks failed, many credit unions were on the verge of collapse, and before long a major trust company would go under, taking with it the savings of 67,000 Albertans.

When the Getty administration presented its first budget in debt-free Alberta in the spring of 1986, it made rural Alberta, and specifically agriculture, its centrepiece. It provided assistance to drought-ravaged parts of the Province and eased borrowing costs, while providing costly loan guarantees to the petroleum industry. It was no coincidence that the College was able to find the funds to construct the Learning Resource Centre and the Land Sciences Building during this era.

But when the price of oil failed to rebound as expected, the Province slid rapidly into debt. Although the Government began to base its budget projections on pessimistic oil prices, by 1992 Alberta would have an unprecedented net debt of $7.1 billion. In the intervening years, Premier Getty cut services, raised existing taxes, imposed new ones, invested public funds in one money-losing venture after another, and watched his popularity drop like a stone. The limitations of the policy of economic diversification begun by Lougheed and continued by Getty were apparent, and Alberta's prosperity was once again hostage to the world price of oil.

Enter Ralph Klein. An unlikely candidate for the leadership of the Province if ever there was one, he won the Tory leadership after Getty stepped down in 1992 and never looked back. In his previous life, he had been an Air Force recruit, vocational school student, radio and television reporter, Mayor of Calgary and, since 1989,

Minister of the Environment in Don Getty's second Cabinet. Once in the Premier's office, he distanced himself from Getty and decreed that Alberta would focus on eliminating the deficit, reducing the debt, and shrinking the civil service until the provincial books were balanced. He never tired of talking about these three points. It was the kind of mantra that E. C. Manning would have loved, and it played well throughout the Province. Wrapped up as the new Deficit Elimination Act, it became the Tory platform for the 1993 election. Klein won handily.

Klein's fresh mandate enabled him to act quickly and decisively. Every Albertan would feel the pain and help bring the Province back into the black. Nothing was spared — health care, education, municipal funding, the civil service, even the Cabinet, took a hit.

At Olds College, the Administration was only too aware that two-thirds of its funding continued to come from provincial sources. It had already tried to cut costs through discontinuation of, for example, the Agricultural Engineering Technology Program. Now far greater restraint would be needed.

In 1993 Bigsby sombrely announced the Government's intention to cut the College's grants by 21 per cent over the next three years, starting with 11 per cent in the first year, seven in the next, and three in the third. The caveat was that the College had to achieve this target without decreasing the quality of its education or limiting its accessibility.

This was a definite concern, as the usual difference between the actual annual revenue and spending at the College was around four or five per cent. There were those who thought an average annual cut of seven per cent impossible, while others believed that although achieving such a target was possible, it would wipe out the significant gains of the previous two decades. Once again, Olds College would be obliged to confront the vagaries of politics to ensure its survival.

Community Partner

The Administration was not amused. It was one thing for the Provincial Government to ask a bloated, spendthrift institution to trim the fat by 21 per cent; it was quite another to ask the same of a College that had been working conscientiously to get its house in order for years.

9

Looking Outward

The Administration followed its cost cutting measures with a look at new or more effective means of generating revenue. Prior to 1993, revenue generation at Olds College was incidental to its main purpose; now it was imperative to its survival. Accordingly, the Board created an internal task force to develop and implement a long-range plan to maximize future revenue generation. The intent was not merely to meet the Government's fiscal targets but also to ensure continued growth at the College.

The Olds College Foundation, which operated at arm's length from the College, was once again seen as part of the solution. Its effectiveness was already proven, as it had raised more than $6 million in cash, gifts-in-kind, and matching grants towards endowments since being established in 1982. The Board now encouraged it to assume an even greater role in fundraising.

Having spent several years raising funds for the new Land Sciences Centre, the Foundation took on the challenge of completing that capital campaign in a time of general economic downturn. It contributed in less dramatic ways as well. Its annual Golf Classic event, for example, now attracted around 100 golfers to campus and raised tens of thousands of dollars that were allocated to needs such as the purchase of audio-visual and computer equipment. In addition, the cash amount equal to the five per cent AUPE/OCFA wage reduction between April and July of 1994 was shifted into the Foundation coffers where it could be used with more discretion than was granted to the College.

Development of the Land Sciences Centre was a direct result of the College's efforts to address contemporary stewardship issues such as soil and water conservation, pest management and land reclamation. The Olds College Foundation played a major role in the capital campaign that raised funds for its construction.

John Deere has long made its latest equipment available for the hands-on education of Olds students. Establishment of the John Deere Training Centre in 1997 marked the first time that the machinery company offered training at a post-secondary institution in North America.

Supporting the Leaders of Tomorrow

Throughout the long history of the College, private citizens, companies, service clubs, professional organizations, staff and alumni have generously supported the success of its students and its capital projects.

Scholarships were among the earliest gifts that made a difference in the lives of many deserving students. Companies with a close connection to the land, such as P. Burns and Company, the United Grain Growers and Swift Canadian, offered annual prizes for achievement in everything from the two-year Agricultural program to proficiency in stock judging.

In 1955, for example, a Warner farm boy named Wilbur Collin won an Alberta Wheat Pool scholarship that allowed him to continue his education. It proved a good investment. Seventeen years later, Collin would return to Olds to serve as one of the youngest Principals in its history.

The Alumni Association, which has been active at Olds since 1917, often directed its surplus funds towards student scholarships as well. In 1976, an Olds College Alumni Association Special Projects Fund was established to receive donations from which scholarships would be paid. The Association was also instrumental in creating Alberta's first charitable college foundation, the Olds College Alumni Foundation, that soon became the model for all other college foundations in the Province.

While many companies have provided scholarships and bursaries over the years, some have also ensured that Olds students were able to hone their skills on the latest equipment. These donations have ranged from De Laval's installation of cream separators in 1913 to John Deere Limited's ongoing contribution of the latest farm equipment to assist apprenticeship and industry training programs. In 1997, the farm machinery manufacturer also funded the construction and furnishing of the John Deere Training Centre on campus.

While the College sincerely appreciates every contribution, none is more gratifying than a personal donation from someone who believes wholeheartedly in its educational mission. This generosity of spirit was never more evident than in the one-million-dollar gift the College received from Jack Anderson in 2007. This was the single largest donation by an individual in the history of the College.

Anderson, a successful businessman and rancher, had quietly given to many worthy causes over the years. When he looked into the breadth of the educational programs offered by Olds College, he came away very impressed. He also appreciated the College emphasis on managing assets properly, whether cattle or greenhouse plants or water. Knowing his contribution would be managed with similar care, he placed no conditions on its use.

As it turned out, the donation was earmarked for a variety of important purposes, including support for the Bell eLearning Centre of the Community Learning Campus, the Botanic Garden, the Landscape Pavilion, and a bursary endowment fund. Importantly, Anderson's contribution allowed the College to leverage another $600,000 in matching donations.

Anderson is pleased to have been able to further education in a town that doesn't have the corporate base of a big city like Calgary. "It's harder for a college in a smaller place like Olds to raise the money it needs," he says.

But more than that, Anderson believes those fortunate enough to be financially successful have an obligation to support the larger community that made them what they are today. It's a basic value shared by his whole family. "When I first went into business, I borrowed $5,000 from my aunt. She told me to be sure to help someone in return when I was able to do so. That lesson stuck with me all my life."

Jack Anderson, who donated one million dollars without restrictions to the College in 2007, astutely realized that rural educational institutions are not able to draw upon the larger donor base of urban schools. His generous contribution helped the College complete several important capital developments. Part of Jack Anderson's donation to the College went towards completion of the Landscape Pavilion, an indoor facility where students can hone their horticultural skills regardless of weather conditions.

With the appointment of 43-year old Dr. Robert A. Turner as President in 1995, the push to forge stronger relationships with industry and the rural community accelerated.

Born in Saskatoon and raised in Manitoba and Alberta, Turner knew his way around the college world. He had been a part of it for 20 years. Before coming to Olds, he served as a counsellor at Fairview and at the Alberta Vocational Centre in Grouard, as Dean of Student Services at Fairview, as Director of the Kitimat Campus of Northwest Community College in Terrace, British Columbia, and as a Vice-President of Capilano College at Vancouver. Administration was in his blood.

Chosen as President in 1995, Dr. Robert Turner brought tremendous enthusiasm and focus to the development of Olds College as an entrepreneurial institution.

Turner liked to talk about "networks" and "partnerships". In one of his first messages to the campus community he stressed that, "It is my own consideration that networking with industry, technological innovators and community is of utmost importance."[4] He believed firmly in the tenets of public relations and marketing, and wasted little time in telling the Board of Governors that Olds College needed to improve its game on both fronts.[5]

As though to show everyone what he meant, Turner immediately joined the Olds Community Development Committee and attended the first meeting of the Regional Economic Development Committee. He also had plans to join the Olds Chamber of Commerce. We need more and better alliances, he said, "not only in Alberta, but throughout North America and beyond."[6]

The College forged new co-operative agreements with other institutions, both domestic and foreign. It entered into an agreement that made it possible for residents of Okotoks and district to gain access to agricultural, horticultural and business management classes, workshops and seminars on the grounds of the Okotoks Agricultural Society. In concert with Alta. Genetics Incorporated, Olds delivered training in dairy farm management to Chinese learners. It worked with Grant MacEwan Community College to offer training in curriculum development to educators from Ukraine. And it became the first Canadian school to collaborate with The Gorbachev Foundation on advising Russian institutions about free-market ways to define and run educational programs.

Articulation agreements proliferated. A partnership with Fairview College allowed students enrolled in its two-year

Agricultural Technology program to transfer directly to the Olds College Agricultural Production program, and vice-versa. New exchange partnerships were signed with Alfred College in Guelph, Ontario and with College of the Rockies in Cranbrook, British Columbia. A formal transfer agreement with Kirkwood Community College in Iowa covered many programs. New agreements with the University of Saskatchewan, the University of Alberta and Medicine Hat College expanded the transfer, exchange and continuation options available to Olds students.

Approaching education in this way lowered the cost of delivering many courses, and allowed the College to offer a wider variety of programs in more locations — including international destinations — while satisfying the Government call for non-duplication within the educational system.

If building relationships was one key element of Turner's approach to administration, doing deals was another. He was always ready to talk about Olds as an "entrepreneurial

college". He felt that the College was, unfortunately, sending out mixed signals about its long-range plans, and worked with staff to develop what he called a "partnering plan" that would offer a more consistent message to industry, government and the community. "Our aim," he declared, "is to work with our networks toward maximization of opportunity for our graduates."

Eventually, under the new motto of "Education That Works," Turner and his colleagues declared that Olds College was open for business.

Agricultural Production has been a mainstay of the Olds curriculum from the beginning, when it was usually referred to as Animal Husbandry and often taught by the Principal himself.

Efforts like these resulted in a balanced set of books at the College at the conclusion of the 1996-97 school year, and generation of a $1.4-million operating surplus. The latter was designated for much-needed capital reinvestment.

Minister Dunford thought Savage's example of self-sufficiency was particularly commendable and added how pleased he was to hear repeated mention of the word "entrepreneurial" during the day's discussions. He felt certain the private sector would continue to respond favourably to the College's entreaties. He also liked the references to greater co-operation with other institutions. Olds College was on the right track.

He noted, as well, the College's tremendous achievement of the recent enrolment increase of 17.5 per cent. Letting down his guard as an elected official for a moment, he said this was remarkable given his Government's extensive cuts to post-secondary education since 1981-82. Olds College, in his view, was clearly one of the jewels in the crown of Alberta's post-secondary education.

Joint ventures were not the only measures of success in those days of fiscal restraint. Key Performance Indicators (KPIs) were discussed with Dunford as well. KPIs were now the yardstick for determining the comparative success of colleges. There were three of them: Responsiveness, measured by student satisfaction and the

graduate employment rate; Accessibility, which sought an increase in the number of students working for credit; and Affordability, which looked at administrative expenditures and revenue from enterprise.

By 1996-97, Olds had received the maximum number of points available using the Government's KPI report card. Turner was particularly pleased that more than 40 per cent of their revenue was already coming from non-governmental sources and that the Student Satisfaction rate had hit 99.1 per cent.[8] This also translated in larger Government grants. In the early days of what became known as "The Klein Revolution", all progress on the funding front depended on measurable performance.

Olds College contributed land and financial resources to the Town of Olds to assist with the construction of an Aquatic Centre to serve both the community and the college.

Opposite page: The College trains students in all aspects of meat processing - from slaughterhouse to stuffing sausage casings. Beginning in the mid-1990s, Olds students were able to incorporate new technologies such as Global Positioning Systems into their studies.

Teaching and Learning

As Sharon Carry noted as early as 1990, the students at Olds College were changing. More mature, more career-focused and more harried, they were now seeking greater flexibility from educational institutions.

An increasing number took courses while they worked; they often sought part-time courses. They also wanted to be able to take courses when it was convenient for them to do so, which was frequently outside normal classroom hours. Weekend classes, which had been discontinued by Principal Birdsall's administration in the early 1960s, were now in demand. Some students preferred to live off-campus; attending scheduled classes in traditional classrooms did not suit them either. Institutions like Olds College had to juggle a wide variety of concerns as they sought to maintain or increase enrolment levels.

Many students also sought greater specialization in academic programs. They were quite willing to shop around until they found an institution with a program that suited their needs. Part of their expectation was that colleges should be aware of the trends in the job market and design programs that enhanced the possibility of employment upon graduation. Just as the College was beginning to act like a market-driven enter-prise, a growing number of students were beginning to act like discerning consumers.

This perspective had its counterpart in the Administration itself. In 1993, the College took the view that students would have to shoulder greater responsibility for their education. This was about much more than paying higher tuition fees. "Faculty roles will change from information providers to learning facilitators and coaches, and students will be more responsible and accountable for their own learning," read the Summary of Recommendations for Re-Organization of Olds College Academic Division.[11] It went on to recommend that instructors teach 15 per cent less and focus more on providing an environment in which learning might be optimized.

Much of this change, it was believed, could be achieved through the use of technology. While no one was advocating the abandonment of traditional classroom or field

studies, the College had clearly begun to incorporate a greater degree of self-directed education into its curricula.

Computer technology rapidly became the new pedagogy. As in years past when Olds College eagerly embraced new technologies ranging from silent films to electric typewriters, it now accepted the challenge of providing online instruction to a generation of students who were born at the same time as the personal computer.

President Turner was a great advocate of technology. In 1997, for example, he had taken the then-unusual step of inviting an Industry Canada expert on the so-called Information Highway to address the Olds and District Chamber of Commerce about the impact of the Internet on small business operations.

In 1994-95, the College joined with Assiniboine Community College, Lethbridge Community College, and Wascana Institute/SIAST to develop and deliver an online course for forage and livestock producers and range managers called the Forage and Range Management Program. During the 1998-99 school year, it launched its first pedagogical experiment with Web-based technology when it developed three Internet courses — Introduction to Soils, Weeds and Weed Management, and Soil Fertility. These were marketed to farmers, ranchers and agribusiness professionals who wished to learn at home or work via the Internet.[12]

Olds College embraced digital technologies with the same zeal it had exhibited in previous eras for pioneering technologies such as film and radio.

If the methods of delivery were changing at the College, so too were its programs. In 1996, for example, the College introduced a two-year Seed and Grain Technology diploma program. It was one-of-a-kind in Western Canada, offering highly specialized training that gave its graduates an excellent shot at a new range of jobs emerging in biotechnology, precision farming, specialty crop production, and global seed and grain marketing. Just as importantly, the program was transferable to the University of Lethbridge where students could gain two years of credits toward the four-year Bachelor of Agriculture degree.

In the same year, Olds received the approval of Alberta Advanced Education and Career Development to offer a four-year Bachelor in Applied Horticulture Technology. There was nothing else like it.

It rested on two majors: Garden Centre and Arboriculture. The Garden Centre program, developed with the co-operation of the industry, was unique in the country. Aboriculture, a new two-year diploma program, focused on the technical, managerial and entrepreneurial skills required in the urban horticulture industry. Importantly, the degree program saw instructional staff working closely to design a customized program of study for each student based on their experience and aspirations. It, too, was transferable.

A new two-year Land Information Systems diploma program depended heavily on state-of-the-art technologies. Incorporating Geographic Information Systems (GIS), Global Positioning Systems (GPS), computer-assisted drafting and design (CADD), and precision farming and land administration software, the program enabled graduates to transfer into the University of Lethbridge's degree program in Geographic Information Systems and then continue in a Masters level program at the University of Calgary.

Aboriculture, a two-year diploma program, prepared Olds students for employment in the urban horticulture industry.

Academic Core Programs, 2010-11

Animals
- *Animal Health Technology*
- *Equine Science*
- *Advanced Farrier Science*
- *Veterinary Medical Receptionist*
- *Meat Processing*
- *Meat Industry Management*
- *Certified Racetrack Groom Training*
- *Exercise Rider & Jockey Training*

Plants and Horticulture
- *Production Horticulture*
- *Turfgrass Management*
- *Environmental Horticulture*
- *Arboriculture*
- *Landscape Management*
- *Bachelor of Applied Science*
    - *Production Horticulture*
    - *Landscape Management*
    - *Golf Course Management*
- *Landscape Gardener Apprenticeship*

Machinery & Trades
- *Agricultural and Heavy Equipment*
- *Heavy Equipment Operator*
- *John Deere Technician Program*
- *Apprenticeships:*
    - *Agricultural Equipment Technician*
    - *Carpentry*
    - *Heavy Equipment Technician*
    - *Welding*
- *Pre-employment Trades*

Fashion
- *Apparel Technology*
- *Fashion Marketing*

General Studies
- *General Studies*
- *Transitional Vocational Program*
- *Career and Academic Preparation*

Land & Environment
- *Land & Water Resources*
- *Land Agent*
- *Land Administration*
- *Environmental Reclamation*

Business
- *Business Administration*
- *Office Administration*

Agriculture
- *Agricultural Management*
- *Bachelor of Applied Science*
- *Agribusiness*
- *Agricultural Finance*

Continuing Education

While innovative programs and facilities like these took direct aim at industry needs that were not being met well by other educational institutions, other initiatives echoed changing Governmental policies.

After two years of cutting to the bone, Premier Klein had balanced the Province's books. This occurred one year ahead of schedule. Opportunely, rising petroleum prices and lottery revenues produced a large budget surplus at the same time. It was time for reinvestment.

In the world of Alberta agriculture, the new buzzword was "value-added". Value-added meant producing and marketing farm products in ways that appealed directly to the needs and wants of consumers and selling them at higher profit margins. It included everything from raising free-range chickens to developing nutraceuticals to the production of biofuels. The Progressive Conservatives vowed to create an agricultural value-added sector worth $20 billion a year. Olds College embraced the concept with a passion.

"The future in agriculture is in the value-added sector and innovative, efficient operations. And it's a bright future for those with the right training," said Bob Lockwood, Dean of Agricultural Production, Business and Animal Science at Olds. "The reality is that in today's evolving agriculture industry the only way to succeed is to learn to be innovative."[13]

Beginning in the fall of 2001, the College offered a new Bachelor of Applied Agricultural Technology and Entrepreneurship degree. Comprising two semesters of classroom study and two of internship, the program was intended to appeal to those who wished to add value to existing products, develop and commercialize new products or technologies, or manage agricultural enterprises more effectively. While Olds hosted the program, the colleges at Fairview, Lakeland and Lethbridge fed students into it.

Under Turner's administration, Olds College came to terms with the new world of students, agribusiness and politics. It firmed up sagging relationships with the Town and the County, revamped its programming to suit the demands of a new generation of learners, embraced the instructional potential of digital technology, refined its political game, and began to tell its story to the world.

Growing Great Ideas

On March 5ᵗʰ, 1999, Premier Klein took part in a celebratory dinner at the Alumni Centre. The theme was "Partners in Innovation".

In his address to the largely industry crowd, Klein had nothing but praise for the College. In particular, he lauded the institution for the newfound entrepreneurial drive that enabled it to find industry partners to support its expansion.

Not coincidentally, President Turner used the occasion to announce publicly the start of a business incubator on campus. To be called the Olds College Centre for Innovation (OCCI), its purpose was to conduct applied agricultural research and help to take the products of that research to market.

Turner was particularly pleased to be able to say that the College had succeeded in bringing together a plethora of private investors and public funding agencies to fund the OCCI. He noted the contributions of the Alberta government, the Federal Government, the Town of Olds, Scotiabank, George Weston Limited, Federated Co-operatives Limited, Banner Pharmacaps, and many others.

In reality, more than four-fifths of its $3 million in start-up money had come from the Alberta Value Added Corporation (AVAC), the arms-length, not-for-profit agency that the Klein Government seeded with $35 million in 1997 (with an additional $10 million from the Federal Government) to promote the Province's agricultural value-added sector.

For all that, the OCCI was an impressive achievement. Barbara Duckworth, writing in the *Western Producer*, hit the nail on the head when she asked "how do you make a centre of innovation?" and then answered her own question with,

> *At Olds College, they started with a government vision to create a $20 billion a year value-added processing sector, blended in an innovative agriculture college, stirred in willing business partners, and mixed it with the desire to catapult research from the lab to the commercial world.* [14]

In its first year alone, the OCCI would tackle 25 projects that ranged from studies of natural fibres from exotic animals to applied research in composting. The existing Composting Technology Centre found a new home at the OCCI as well. In the years ahead, scientists, students, entrepreneurs and industry partners would all utilize the facility to their advantage. As O.S.A. alumnus and internationally renowned scientist Dr. Robert Church would later remind the Board, "we need to be in the value added side or we won't survive." [15]

Eventually housed in a $1.25-million facility that would later be named The Dr. Robert Turner Research Centre, the OCCI symbolized the President's legacy. Achieved through adroit partnering and politicking, it combined

academe with applied research and commercialization. In the world of colleges there was nothing quite like the value chain that now extended outward from Olds. It enabled the College to stand out from the crowd while reaffirming its status as Western Canada's pre-eminent school of agriculture.

In co-operation with the horticulture industry, Olds College developed the Botanic Gardens that provide a beautiful setting in which to teach students about new floral and other plant species. Study of natural exotic fibres was an important part of the earliest value-added investigations conducted at the Olds College Centre for Innovation, later renamed the Olds College School of Innovation.

373

376

Applied Research at Olds College

*Applied research — the practical application of science —
found a home at Olds College with establishment of the Olds
College Centre for Innovation in 1999.*

*Now called the Olds College School of Innovation (OCSI),
this facility undertakes confidential research for private
clients, collaborates with other Canadian and international
research institutions, trains researchers, and helps clients
secure research funding. The OCSI focuses on research in
sustainable agriculture and bioprocessing. At any given time,
15 to 25 staff work at OCSI under the direction of Dr.
Abimbola Abiola, an internationally respected soil scientist.*

Among the many recent successes of OCSI are:

*The BioFuel Technology Centre — a research and demonstra-
tion facility that converts Alberta field crops such as canola
into biodiesel fuel for an energy-hungry world. The fuel is
biodegradable, non-toxic and suitable for use in diesel
engines with minimal modification. As part of the pilot
project, several school buses and service vehicles from
Chinook's Edge School Division, the Town of Olds,
Mountain View County and Olds College were run
successfully on a blend of 80 per cent regular diesel and 20
per cent biodiesel. When fully operational, the OCSI facility
is expected to produce up to one million litres of biodiesel
annually.*

*Botanic Gardens and Treatment Wetlands — this $4.8-
million, 12-acre constructed wetlands facility and arboretum
comprises 20 ponds for the treatment of storm water,
municipal wastewater, 'produced water' from oil and natural
gas facilities, and run-off from intensive livestock operations.
Its potential for removing contaminants via a dynamic
aquatic environment has advanced research in this area
while providing Olds College students with a unique outdoor
laboratory in which to study perennial plants and trees.
Research conducted at the wetlands has many important
implications for the treatment of domestic, agricultural and
industrial wastewater. According to Dr. Abiola, "Ultimately,
we will also be able to drought-proof our campus and create
healthy green ecological environments to be enjoyed by our
community and all Albertans."*

*More than anything else, the OCSI epitomized the shift
from farm to factory in the world of commercial agriculture
and society's new emphasis on land management and
environmental sustainability.*

It was only a year after hitting that high note that Turner chose to leave for a new challenge as President of Sheridan College near Toronto, one of the largest colleges in the country. Even as he departed, he was aggressively helping to reshape the College strategic plan to emphasize growth, innovation, entrepreneurship and quality.

Being at Olds had been "absolutely wonderful," he said. "Olds College is an extraordinary institution. It is absolutely head and shoulders the best group of professionals I have ever worked with and likely ever will."[16]

Above: Dr. Abimbola Abiola, Director of the Olds College School of Innovation, leads a tour of the new Treatment Wetlands site on the eastern edge of the campus. The BioFuel Technology Centre, a joint venture of the College, the Town of Olds, the Chinook's Edge School Division and the County of Mountain View, converts field crops into biodegradable vehicle fuel. Right: Dr. Ken Fry in his campus lab.

Charging from the Gate[17]

As the new millennium began, Olds College was riding high. It achieved superb scores on the Key Performance Indicators each year.

Despite government cutbacks, enrolment had increased dramatically, rising from 959 FLEs or full-load equivalents (the mandated standard in Alberta) to 1,260 in 2000. Industry and international relationships were multiplying. Community and government relations had seldom been better. The Foundation was bringing in more than $1 million a year in donations. As Board Chair Jim Smith said with noticeable pride, "We are confident that this organization will make a significant contribution to the education and applied research needs of Albertans."[18]

If there was a fly in the ointment, it was that the College budget had slipped into the red. Throughout the 1990s revenues usually kept one step ahead of expenditures, but beginning in 1996-97 the annual accounts showed a deficit as often as not. For the College to continue to grow, while reining in costs or finding new sources of income, would require greater discipline.

In 2001 the Board found that discipline in a new President, H. J. (Tom) Thompson. Thompson brought an unusual breadth of experience to management of the College, as well as a deep-rooted passion for rural society and effective governance.

A Saskatchewan native, Thompson enjoyed a career in public school teaching, administration, and university coaching and lecturing before turning to professional sports coaching and marketing in the 1970s. Beginning in 1986, he taught business administration at Grande Prairie Regional College. He soon advanced to the position of Vice-President of Instruction and Enrolment Management, then Acting President, and finally President in 1997. While at Grande Prairie, he also organized and served as President of the 1995 Canada Winter Games and was recognized by the local Chamber of Commerce as its Business Citizen of the Year. Systematic, collaborative and, above all, focused, Thompson would introduce a healthy dose of intellectual discipline and organizational rigor to Olds College.

As Thompson began his tenure, the Government of Alberta was laying out a 10-year strategy for development of the agricultural sector. More than 1,500 stakeholders had taken part in a province-wide brainstorming process called Ag Summit 2000. Together, they examined the challenges and opportunities before Alberta agribusiness and developed a list of 10 priority areas around which to build new strategies for development. A number of these areas had direct implications for the future of Olds College. The priority areas were:[19]

1. *environmental stewardship;*
2. *sustainable rural communities;*
3. *food quality and safety;*
4. *research, innovation and technology;*
5. *global market development;*
6. *diversification and value-added;*
7. *building an innovative, entrepreneurial learning culture;*
8. *new business strategies;*
9. *future of farm business; and*
10. *image of the agriculture and food industry.*

Many of these issues were already being explored at the College because the Board had had the foresight to engage Dr. Robert Church and Brian Heidecker, who chaired Ag Summit 2000, to prepare a strategic positioning paper on the College's future.

That the College was in a position to affect most of these key issues was more than fortuitous; it meant that previous Board members and administrators had responded to challenging Government policies in a manner that positioned the College well.

By 2001, it was not so much a question of whether or not the College could play a significant role in the transformation of rural Alberta, but rather how best to contribute to that process. Over the next few years, President Thompson and his colleagues would directly or indirectly address the matters identified by Ag Summit 2000 and, in the process, greatly strengthen their institution.

Saskatchewan native H. J. (Tom) Thompson became President of Olds College in 2001 and set out to redefine its wider relationships in order to provide equal educational opportunities for Alberta's rural residents.

Reaping the Harvest

The new President was passionate about the rural way of life.

He shared its deeply held conservative and co-operative values, its fundamental belief in fairness, and its vision of a better life through individual initiative and responsibility. To his way of thinking, rural society was special, something to be treasured and supported for the good of all Albertans. In this, he was the direct heir to the philosophy and strategy first deployed with great effectiveness by Daniel Cornish.

Ever the coach, Thompson strove to build what he called a culture of collaboration among the College's diverse constituencies and, in doing so, gain the leverage he needed to foster a more sustainable rural society. While some of Thompson's predecessors had found it expedient to accept the crumbs from the Provincial Government's table, he would never willingly settle for less than a whole loaf.

Thompson wasted little time in consolidating the gains of his predecessors: the emphasis on the technical aspects of agribusiness initiated by Birdsall and Collin, the redefinition of the College's mandate begun by Crombie, the strengthening of community and political relationships championed by Cornish, and the focus on institutional and business partnerships sharpened by Bigsby and Turner. All became grist for Thompson's mill.

Yet while each earlier initiative had played a part in shaping a new identity for Olds College, none truly linked the institution to a broader sense of purpose. Thompson, with his gift for being able to see the big picture, would draw these disparate threads together and fashion them into a comprehensive development strategy aimed at nothing less than the renaissance of rural Alberta.

The first overt sign of basic change at the College came during its 90th anniversary celebrations in 2003. A new four-year business plan, called "Four Horses for the Future," offered a high-level vision of what Thompson saw in the College's immediate future. He anticipated a $26-million capital campaign built upon partnerships that would lead to new investment in a Community Learning Campus, the OCCI, a Canadian Centre for Equine Excellence, an Arboretum and Landscape Pavilion, and a satellite campus at Calgary.

Behind the scenes, Thompson had been working to reorganize critical College functions and reorient the thinking of his colleagues so they would be equipped to deal effectively with changes of this magnitude. The Olds College Foundation, for example, was replaced by a new Office of Advancement that oversaw fundraising, marketing and government relations.

The Board of Governors, in particular, became immersed in the tenets of good governance, with all its implications for strategic partnerships, fiscal responsibility, best practices, and managed growth. Once the College leadership

had a clearer sense of its role and new stewardship tools at its disposal, it would be in a much better position to define and lead change.

The widely acclaimed Community Learning Campus (CLC), on which construction began in 2005-6, was the keystone of the Thompson era. Epitomizing the President's emphasis on broad-based collaboration, the CLC harnessed the strengths and ambitions of the College, the Chinook's Edge School Division, the Town of Olds, the County of Mountain View, outlying rural communities, business and industry, agricultural organizations, the University of Alberta, and the Provincial Government.

While Thompson's approach was not unlike those of his predecessors in pairing government policy with infrastructure needs, it differed vastly in scale. He began with

analysis of current government policy, which told him the Province would likely support a major initiative that allowed it to show significant progress on the matter of enhancing the quality of rural life, and built his approach outward from there.

In addition to the Go Alberta Strategy that stressed value-added production, Klein's administration had released a major policy document on rural redevelopment called "Alberta: A Place to Grow." This called for everything from promoting economic growth to expanding learning and skill development opportunities for rural youth. It suited Thompson's purposes perfectly.

In 2007, construction of the Bell eLearning Centre made digital long-distance learning a reality for thousands of remote students who wished to study at Olds College.

A third policy component incorporated into the Community Learning Campus was that of Campus Alberta, an idea that had been kicked around for more than a decade with few tangible results. Campus Alberta was a learning initiative based on connection of all Alberta communities to the Internet via a project known as the SuperNet. While the needed infrastructure was in place, no one had stepped forward with a sound idea about how best to utilize this barely used information superhighway.

With its many partners, Olds College delivered a comprehensive, integrated 110-page planning document to the Provincial Government in March, 2005. A little more than a year later, Alberta's Minister of Education, Gene Zwozdesky, came to town for the official CLC groundbreaking with a commitment from his Government to fund $38 million of the anticipated $52.3-million cost.

In his remarks, Zwozdesky noted the degree to which the new facility would address the intent of the Go Alberta strategy to make Alberta the "best place to work, to live and to visit." He continued:

> *This particular project will certainly fulfill that.*
> *We in Alberta Education are very proud to be one of*
> *your partners. This fits so extremely well with our overall*
> *rural development strategy. What you are doing here*
> *is so integral, it speaks to the heart of what that strategy*
> *is all about...*[20]

The Community Learning Campus embodied the ethic of co-operation and the pursuit of progress that had animated an earlier generation of politicians and educators. The close integration of its four main components — a 700-student high school, a fine arts complex, a wellness-recreation centre, and an eLearning centre — established Olds College as the Canadian model for the seamless movement of high school students into a post-secondary institution. And through its eLearning facility, the CLC harnessed the power of the digital age to satisfy the educational, training and information needs of residents in some 20 outlying Community Engagement Sites. As Thompson had hoped, being rural no longer had to mean being second best in educational matters.

Not all matters went as smoothly as construction of the ambitious CLC or the $10-million commitment of the Provincial Government commitment toward the Equine Centre in 2006. The fortunes of Olds College remained tied to the health of the provincial economy, and President Thompson's road to the future was fraught with twists and turns.

In the summer of 2008 petroleum prices, which had boomed since 2003, peaked and then fell markedly. This brought about a serious downturn in the Province's revenues – never good news for Olds College — that was followed in the autumn by a catastrophic worldwide economic collapse. The latter affected the College's long-term investment strategy as well. Suddenly the College was once again tightening its purse strings and seeking ways to cope with declining income and no increase in provincial operating grants for at least the next three years.

The Importance of Local Relationships

*Relationships — personal, political, and economic — have always been a
source of the College's enduring success.*

From its earliest days, the College enjoyed a special relationship with the Town of Olds and with the wider farm community.

The connections were numerous: good-natured sports rivalries, the sharing of urban utilities and recreational facilities, a significant contribution to the Town and County tax bases, staff and students living in town (especially before a new dormitory was built in 1927), promotion and guidance of the annual school fairs in dozens of rural communities across central Alberta, staff participation in local service clubs, the provision of farm extension services, leadership of 4-H clubs, and serving as a showcase for best farming practices.

Paddy Munro, the Reeve of Mountain View County and an Olds College alumnus himself, expresses the view of many when he says that the College has always been part-and-parcel of everyday life in central Alberta. It has always instilled a striving for excellence in its students and, in his case, the attitude contributed much to a highly successful business career. The County counts a number of Olds College graduates among its employees and would hire more in a heartbeat.[21]

The College has also served as a community centre from the beginning, offering free or inexpensive meeting space to all sorts of organizations, including the United Farmers of Alberta and the Women's Institutes. And when it came to farm children, the College not only educated them academically and agriculturally but encouraged many to remain on the farm rather than abandon a life on the land for one in the city. The development of the Community Learning Campus between 2005 and 2010 is simply the latest expression of this close-knit relationship between College and community.

"There's no doubt that Olds College is the progressive leader in the Town of Olds," says Olds Mayor Judy Dahl. "We work closely with them on so many initiatives and as a community we benefit significantly from the sense of partnership and collaboration that the professionals at the College always bring to the table."[22]

Hopes of a satellite campus for equine studies as part of a racetrack development near Balzac failed to be realized as water management issues stalled the overall proposal. The plan to establish a permanent Calgary satellite foundered on the rocks of rising costs and declining revenues, and Olds eventually settled for shared teaching space. Much of the existing campus infrastructure was showing its age and demanding precious capital reinvestment. Every leader of the College had been confronted by unpredictable political and economic circumstances; as these mixed results showed, Thompson's experience was to be no different.

Olds College, 2009-10: A Snapshot

Annual operating budget	*$44 Million*
Full-time equivalent learners	*1,294*
Full-time equivalent faculty	*85*
Full-time equivalent support staff	*144*
Employment rate of graduates	*95.1%*
Satisfaction rate of graduates	*93.9%*

397

Epilogue: Coming Full Circle

"I am confident," said President Thompson, "that the visionaries who founded Olds College would agree that we remain true to our roots."

When we cast an eye to the past, we look back upon almost a century of accomplishment and service to people and industries that are fundamental to society. In many cases, the values and skills that established Olds College as a national resource to agriculture and horticulture remain relevant and visible today.

Yet, the needs of individuals and society change. At Olds College, we choose to continue with our historic strengths while at the same time working diligently to ensure our relevance in the years ahead.[23]

Indeed, much has changed in the world of agriculture since Christena Marshall fixed her grip upon that breaking plough in the autumn of 1912.

Farming is no longer a matter of scratching a living from furrows in a quarter section, as it was in 1913. Alberta farms now average more than 1,000 acres and cost hundreds of thousands of dollars to buy and operate. They are sizeable commercial enterprises. To run a farm successfully, the owner benefits from formal training in management and marketing, and more than a measure of computer literacy.

Most farms are no longer a family affair, handed down from generation to generation without fail. The family farm is now the exception, not the rule. The interest of youth in staying on the farm, which had declined steadily since the Second World War, continues to do so. And as the interest of young people declines, the average age of Alberta's farmers rises. Most are now more than 50 years of age. They represent only three per cent of the Province's population. Where once there had been two or three farms on a section of land, there are now few neighbours.

Money is often tight — which is certainly not new — but now many aging farmers also have no choice but to sell their farms if they are to enjoy their retirement years in comfort. Children who choose to stay on the land find it increasingly difficult to secure the capital needed to buy out their parents, let alone modernize their operations. Many family farms are lost in the bargain. And of those who stay on the land, nearly half work off the farm for part of every year to augment incomes and pay down debt. In a world of $75,000 tractors and $300,000 combines, an annual income of $130,000 doesn't go very far.

For many Olds College students, being primary producers is no longer possible or even desirable. Their goal is not necessarily farming. While they know they want to work with the land somehow, they are not certain they want to be on the land. Consequently, they seek training that will prepare them for work in related fields — in meat processing, equine training, animal health, artificial insemination, horticulture, golf course development, soil reclamation, water management, farm financing and accounting, commodity marketing and equipment maintenance and repair. The opportunity to take part in the wide world of agribusiness, first spotted by Everett Birdsall some 50 years before, is now the ordinary state of affairs for many Alberta youth with an interest in stewardship of the land.

The triumph of the Community Learning Campus, completed in 2010, rests on the fact that it plays to the institution's traditional agricultural strengths while accommodating the diverse needs of modern rural society. Without for a moment sacrificing educational goals, the integrated CLC satisfies political goals, economic realities, and community needs. It is a timely reminder that no successful school exists unto itself; rather, each reflects the shifting imperatives of its most important constituencies.

To all who know something of the College's history, it is clear that the principles behind the Community Learning Campus reflect and reaffirm the staunch values of the institution's founders.

One hundred years before, those founders believed the best hope for their beloved countryside lay in co-operation. They grasped that educational progress rested on political vision and personal will. And they understood that rural residents needed not only opportunity but also the latest thinking and the finest tools if they were to enjoy the prosperity and advantages of the great world beyond Alberta's pastures and fields.

Most important of all, they saw knowledge of agriculture, past and present, as the best way of ensuring that young people seek, respect and cherish the deep satisfactions of a life on the land.

408

A Note on Sources

Documenting the history of Olds College presents special challenges. The main difficulty is that few of its historical administrative records were retained. According to long-time Principal J. E. Birdsall most pre-1970 records succumbed to the ravages of fire; more recent records were likely the victims of overzealous housekeeping in the 1980s. Gaps in the historical record are abundant and often hard to fill.

Fortunately, Principal Birdsall possessed a strong interest in history and particularly in the history of the institution he administered for 20 years. The results of his labours — *The Sixth Decade at the Alberta Agricultural Colleges, 1964-1974*, and *Sixty Years of Service, 1917-18 to 1977-78: A Brief History of the Olds College Alumni Association* have much to offer the historian, particularly from an administrative point of view. Birdsall also produced an unpublished autobiography, "Son of the Soil," (1982) which presents a more personal view of his experiences at the College. The other work of note is E. B. Swindlehurst's 1964 volume, *Alberta's Schools of Agriculture: A Brief History*. Together, these books establish the basic chronology of Alberta's Schools of Agriculture and Home Economics while providing considerable administrative and anecdotal information.

The available records of College life vary by period. Generally speaking, those covering the half-century before 1960 offer much more on the day-to-day activities of staff and students than do those of the following 50 years. The annual yearbooks of the College, housed at the College library, provide an extraordinarily full record of ordinary events. The history reflects this basic division in information sources, as is evident from the greater emphasis on political and administrative matters after 1960.

Government records are important in documenting College events. The annual reports of the departments of Agriculture and Advanced Education, which administered the College until it became a board-governed institution in 1978, are invaluable to the historian. After 1978, the College published annual reports of its own, although it has not been possible to locate those from 1978 to 1988. The minutes of the Board of Governors form another key source of information for the years after 1978.

Much information can be gleaned from a close reading of *The Olds Gazette*, which has published continuously since 1907. *The Calgary Herald* and *The Edmonton Journal* also frequently covered major events on the campus.

Photographically, the College is well served. Its own collection, in the Olds College Alumni Museum, contains thousands of outstanding images from every era. Other important images are housed at the Provincial Archives of Alberta at Edmonton and the Glenbow Museum at Calgary.

The reminiscences of former staff and students, many now deceased, have been of great assistance in preparing this history. Many of these first-hand accounts were gathered for a volume called *Golden Echoes* that was prepared for the 50th anniversary of the College in 1963; others are scattered throughout the collections of the Alumni

Museum. The College also possesses an idiosyncratic anonymous typescript entitled "The Story of Olds College". Dating from about 1989, and apparently compiled from extensive staff interviews, it deals subjectively with the internal politics of the College in the 1980s.

Finally, the recollections of living alumni have been an inestimable resource in confirming specific aspects of the documentary record or in adding personal colour to the story. The generous assistance of these individuals, who are noted in the endnotes, cannot be overestimated.

Endnotes

Chapter 1

1) *The Olds Gazette*, 27 September 1912, p. 1.

2) John H. McCulloch, "A Tribute to the Hon. Duncan Marshall," *Farmer's Advocate and Home Journal*, December 14, 1921.

3) Provincial Archives of Alberta, PR1969.0329. Olds College Fonds.Acc. 69.329 SE, and
J. E. Birdsall, *Sixty Years of Service,*
1917-18 to 1977-78: A Brief History of the Olds College Alumni Association. Olds: The Olds College Alumni Association, 1978, p. 59.

4) *Annual Report of the Department of Agriculture of the Province of Alberta*, 1911. Report of the Superintendent of Demonstration Farms.

5) *Annual Report of the Department of Agriculture of the Province of Alberta*, 1914. Report of H.A. Craig, Superintendent of Demonstration Farms, p. 28.

6) "The Minister of Agriculture Discusses Agricultural Education and Other Public Matters in the Legislature," *The Olds Gazette*, 22 December 1911.

7) Canada. *Debates of the House of Commons*, Speech by the Honourable Martin Burrell, 24 January 1913, pp. 2146-47.

8) National Library of Canada, Microfiche CC-4, No 82875. C. C. James. *Administration of the Agricultural Instruction Act*. Ottawa, Commission of Conservation, Committee on Lands, 1915.

9) "In the Legislature," *The Olds Gazette*, 2 February 1912.

10) *Dominion Aid To Agricultural Instruction In Canada: A Review Of The Work Performed By The Provinces With The Moneys Granted Under The Agricultural Instruction Act During The Four Year Period, 1913-1917*. Ottawa: Department of Agriculture, 1917.

11) *The Olds Gazette*, 2 November 1934.

12) Provincial Archives of Alberta, PR1977.0009, Frank Sidney Grisdale Collection.

13) Canada. *Sessional Papers for 1916*. Volume LI, Number 11. Report on the Agricultural Instruction Act, 1914-1915, prepared by Commissioner C. C. James.

14) *Birdsall, Sixty Years of Service*, p. 59.

15) *The Olds Gazette*, 24 October 1913.

16) "John Boosts Some," *The Olds Gazette*, 10 October 1913.

17) "O.S.A. History," *The O.S.A. News*, January 1935.

18) Provincial Archives of Alberta, PR1977.0009, Frank Sidney Grisdale Collection.

19) James, *Administration of the Agricultural Instruction Act, op. cit.*

20) E. B. Swindlehurst, *Alberta's Schools of Agriculture: A Brief History*. Edmonton: Alberta Department of Agriculture, 1964, p. 48.

21) "Local and General," *The Olds Gazette*, 12 September 1913.

22) Provincial Archives of Alberta, PR1977.0009, Frank Sidney Grisdale Collection.

23) "Opening of School of Agriculture," *The Olds Gazette*, 28 November 1913.

Chapter 2

1) "The Provincial Schools of Agriculture," *The Olds Gazette*, 3 October 1913.

2) "Large enrolment of Students at Agricultural School," *The Olds Gazette*, 31 October 1913.

3) Alberta. Department of Agriculture. *Report of Demonstration Farms & Schools of Agriculture of the Province of Alberta*, 1914, pp. 3-4.

4) "Agricultural Schools to Open on November First," *The Olds Gazette*, 27 June 1913.

5) *Report of Demonstration Farms & Schools of Agriculture of the Province of Alberta*, 1914, p. 76.

6) *Swindlehurst, op. cit.*, p. 41.

7) *O. S. A. Magazine*, 1957.

8) Catherine C. Cole and Ann Milovic, "Education, Community Service, and Social Life: The Alberta Women's Institutes and Rural Families, 1909-1945," in Catherine A. Cavanaugh and Randi R. Warne (ed.). *Standing on New Ground: Women in Alberta.* Edmonton: University of Alberta Press, 1993, p. 20.

9) "School of Agriculture," *The Olds Gazette*, 13 June 1913.

10) "Household Science Course Commences on Tuesday Next," *The Olds Gazette*, 2 January 1914.

11) *A. S. A. Magazine*, March 1916.

12) *Olds: A History of Olds and Area. Olds: Olds History Committee, 1980*, p. 79.

13) *Annual Report of the Department of Agriculture of the Province of Alberta*, 1919.

14) *Annual Report of the Department of Agriculture of the Province of Alberta*, 1922. Report of the Olds School of Agriculture, p. 124.

15) *O.S.A. Magazine*, 1925, p. 53.

16) *O.S.A. Magazine*, 1929-30, p. 22.

17) *O.S.A. Magazine*, 1928-29, p. 22.

18) *O.S.A. Magazine*, 1925-26, pp. 26-27.

19) Reminiscences of former OSA Students (letters in red binder in Olds College Alumni Association Archives & Museum).

20) *Swindlehurst, op. cit.*, p. 94.

21) Provincial Archives of Alberta. Premiers' Papers. 69.289. File 495, Boys Settlement Scheme, 1928-30.

22) *O.S.A. News*, 1 October 1934, p. 3.

23) *Golden Echoes, 1913-1963*, printed by the Olds School of Agriculture, c.1963, p. 50 cf.

24) *O.S.A. Magazine*, 1925-26.

25) *Annual Report of the Department of Agriculture of the Province of Alberta*, 1929. Report of the Olds School of Agriculture, p. 88.

26) *Annual Report of the Department of Agriculture of the Province of Alberta*, 1919.

27) *O.S.A. Magazine*, 1937-38, p. 4.

Chapter 3

1) *Annual Report of the Department of Agriculture of the Province of Alberta*, 1917.

2) Report of Demonstration Farms & Schools of Agriculture of the Province of Alberta, 1914, p. 80.

3) Canada. *Sessional Papers for 1917.* Volume LII, Number 8. Report on the Agricultural Instruction Act, 1915-16., prepared by Commissioner W.J. Black, pp. 84-5.

4) *Ibid.*

5) Glenbow-Alberta Institute and Archives. Me 4049. S. Longman Fonds and Agricultural Collection. "Pioneer and Pioneering in Western Canada," unpublished autobiography, 1963, p. 95 cf.

6) http://awi.athabascau.ca/About/Mary%20 MacIsaac/index.php#_jmp0_

7) *Annual Report of the Department of Agriculture of the Province of Alberta*, 1915. Report of Provincial Agricultural Schools for 1915.

8) Canada. *Sessional Papers for 1922*, p. 91.

9) *Annual Report of the Department of Agriculture of the Province of Alberta*, 1921. Report of the Olds School of Agriculture, p. 110.

10) *Annual Report of the Department of Agriculture of the Province of Alberta*, 1923. Report of the Olds School of Agriculture.

11) *A.S.A. Magazine*, March 1915.

12) Dominion Aid to Agricultural Instruction in Canada, 1913-17.

13) *Annual Report of the Department of Agriculture of the Province of Alberta*, 1917.

14) Canada. *Sessional Papers for 1919*. Volume LIV, Number 5. Report on the Agricultural Instruction Act, 1917-18, prepared by Commissioner W. J. Black.

15) *Golden Echoes, op. cit.*, "Memories," by F. C. McIntyre.

16) *O.S.A. Year Book*, 1932-33.

17) *Annual Report of the Department of Agriculture of the Province of Alberta*, 1922. Report of the Olds School of Agriculture.

18) *Alumni Association Newsletter*, 1 May 1926.

19) *Ibid.*

20) The Alberta 4-H Council. *4-H and Alberta: 75 Years of Growing Together*. Calgary: McAra Printing Limited, 1992.

21) *Alumni Association Newsletter*, 1 May 1926.

22) *A.S.A. Magazine*, March 1915.

23) *O.S.A. Magazine*, 1925-26.

24) *Annual Report of the Department of Agriculture of the Province of Alberta*, 1923. Report of the Olds School of Agriculture.

25) *Annual Report of the Department of Agriculture of the Province of Alberta*, 1924. Report of the Olds School of Agriculture.

26) *Alumni Association Newsletter* 1 May 1926.

27) *O.S.A. Magazine*, 1949.

28) Provincial Archives of Alberta, PR1969.0329. Olds College Fonds.

29) *Olds Alumni Association Review*, February 1977.

30) E. S. Hopkins, "Agricultural Research in Canada Its Origin and Development," *Annals of the American Academy of Political and Social Science*. 1923 (107) pp. 82-87.

31) *Annual Report of the Department of Agriculture of the Province of Alberta*, 1915. Report of Demonstration Farms.

32) *Annual Report of the Department of Agriculture of the Province of Alberta*, 1921. Report of the Olds School of Agriculture.

33) *Alumni Association Newsletter*, 1 May 1926.

34) *O.S.A. News*, 1 July 1926.

35) *Annual Report of the Department of Agriculture of the Province of Alberta*, 1911. Report of the Superintendent of Demonstration Farms for 1912.

36) *Annual Report of the Department of Agriculture of the Province of Alberta*, 1914. Report of George Harcourt, Deputy Minister of Agriculture.

37) David Spector, "Animal Husbandry on the Prairies, 1880-1925," Parks Canada Manuscript Report Series, pp. 60-61.

38) *Farmer's Advocate and Home Journal*, 14 December 1921, p. 1437.

39) *Annual Report of the Department of Agriculture of the Province of Alberta*, 1920. Report of the Farms and Agricultural Schools.

40) Clinton L. Evans, *The War of Weeds in the Prairie West: An Environmental History*. Calgary: University of Calgary Press, 2002.

41) *Annual Report of the Department of Agriculture of the Province of Alberta*, 1917.

42) *Annual Report of the Department of Agriculture of the Province of Alberta*, 1914. Report of H.A. Craig, Superintendent of Demonstration Farms, p. 57.

43) *Annual Report of the Department of Agriculture of the Province of Alberta*, 1914. Report of George Harcourt, Deputy Minister of Agriculture, p. 56.

44) *Ibid.*

45) *Annual Report of the Department of Agriculture of the Province of Alberta*, 1928. Report of the Olds School of Agriculture.

46) *Alumni Association Review*, February 1977.

47) Provincial Archives of Alberta. 69.289 Premiers' Papers. Roll 4, File 20.

48) *Olds: A History of Olds and District*, pp. 411-12.

Chapter 4

1) Swindlehurst, *op. cit.*, p. 40.

2) *Annual Report of the Department of Agriculture of the Province of Alberta*, 1914. Report of George Harcourt, Deputy Minister of Agriculture.

3) Swindlehurst, *op. cit.*, p. 40.

4) *O.S.A. Magazine*, 1923.

5) *A.S.A. Magazine*, March 1917.

6) *O.S.A. Magazine*, 1924.

7) *O.S.A. Magazine*, 1928-29.

8) Birdsall, *History*, p. 59.

9) *O.S.A. Magazine*, 1920-30.

10) *O.S.A. Magazine*, 1921.

11) *Golden Echoes, op. cit.*

12) *A.S.A. Magazine*, March 1916.

13) *A.S.A. Magazine*, March 1915.

14) *A.S.A. Magazine*, March 1916.

15) *O.S.A. Magazine*, 1926-27.

16) *O.S.A. Magazine*, 1929-30, p. 33.

17) *A.S.A. Magazine*, 1918.

18) *O.S.A. Magazine*, 1953.

19) *A.S.A. Magazine*, 1918.

20) *O.S.A. Newsletter*, 1 March 1921.

21) *O.S.A. News*, 1 November 1923.

22) *Annual Report of the Department of Agriculture of the Province of Alberta*, 1923. Report of the Olds School of Agriculture.

23) *O.S.A. News*, 1 July 1926.

24) *O.S.A. Newsletter*, 1 October 1922.

25) *O.S.A. Magazine*, 1923.

26) *Alumni Association Review*, June 1978.

27) *O.S.A. Magazine*, 1924.

28) *O.S.A. Newsletter*, 4:11 (November 1st, 1924).

29) *Alumni Review*, Winter 1980.

30) *Ibid.*

31) *O.S.A. News*, 1 June 1927.

32) These contents are now in the Provincial Archives of Alberta.

33) Provincial Archives of Alberta. 69.289 Premiers' Papers. Roll 4, File 20.

34) *O.S.A. Magazine*, 1927-28.

35) *O.S.A. Magazine*, 1927-28.

36) *O.S.A. Magazine*, 1925-26.

37) *Annual Report of the Department of Agriculture of the Province of Alberta*, 1930. Report of the School of Agriculture, Olds.

38) *O.S.A. Year Book*, 1932-33, p. 41.

Chapter 5

1) *Olds: A History of Olds and Area, op. cit.*, p. 429 cf.

2) Interview with Wallace Kemp, 12 July 2011.

3) J. E. Birdsall, "Son of the Soil," unpublished autobiography, p. 34. A copy is available at the Olds College Library.

4) Swindlehurst, *op. cit.*, p. 68.

5) *O.S.A. News Letter*, November, 1930.

6) *Sixty Years of Service, op. cit.*, p. 22 cf.

7) *O.S.A. News*, 1931.

8) *The Olds Gazette*, 16 November 1934.

9) *The Olds Gazette*, 23 November 1934.

10) *Annual Report of the Department of Agriculture of the Province of Alberta*, 1935. Report of the Schools of Agriculture.

11) *Annual Report of the Department of Agriculture of the Province of Alberta*, 1944. Report of School of Agriculture, Olds.

12) Reminiscences of former O.S.A. Students. Alumni Association Museum.

13) Reminiscences of former O.S.A. Students. Alumni Association Museum.

14) *O.S.A. Magazine*, 1935-36.

15) *O.S.A. Magazine*, 1948.

16) *O.S.A. Magazine*, 1925-26.

17) *O.S.A. Magazine*, 1944-45.

18) *Annual Report of the Department of Agriculture of the Province of Alberta*, 1933. School of Agriculture, Olds.

19) *Annual Report of the Department of Agriculture of the Province of Alberta*, 1942. Report of School of Agriculture, Olds.

20) William H. Vanden Born and Jack F. Alex, "History of the Canadian Weed Science Society aka the Expert Committee on Weeds, 1929-2002."

21) When Murray left Medicine Hat for the principalship of Olds, he received a new set of golf clubs as a farewell gift. He was then President of the Medicine Hat Golf Club. See *The Calgary Daily Herald*, 30 June 1930. His wife was also an avid golfer.

22) *Alumni Association News*, October 1932.

23) *Golden Echoes, op. cit.*

24) Nanci Langford, *Politics, Pitchforks and Pickle Jars: 75 Years of Organized Farm Women in Alberta*. Calgary: Detselig Enterprises Ltd., 1997, p. 85.

25) *The Alberta 4-H Council. 4-H and Alberta: 75 Years of Growing Together*. Calgary: McAra Printing Limited, 1992. p. 17.

26) *Alumni Review*, June 1964.

27) *Olds: A History of Olds and District, op. cit.*, p. 457.

28) *O.S.A. Magazine*, 1937-38.

29) *The Calgary Herald*, 27 May 1939.

30) See David and Peggy Leighton, *Artists, Builders and Dreamers: 50 Years at the Banff School*. Toronto: McClelland and Stewart Limited, 1982, p. 34 cf.

31) *Annual Report of the Department of Agriculture of the Province of Alberta*, 1939. Report of the Olds School of Agriculture.

32) John M. Parsey and John K. Friesen, "Folk Schools in Canada," *The School Review*, 61:3 (March 1953), pp. 141-50.

33) National Archives of Canada, RG 64. Wartime Prices and Trade Board. Series 1050, Frank S. Grisdale Files.

34) *O.S.A. Newsletter*, July 1932.

35) *O.S.A. Magazine*, 1942-43.

36) Annual Report of the Department of Agriculture of the Province of Alberta, 1942. Report of School of Agriculture, Olds.

37) *O.S.A. Magazine*, 1921.

Chapter 6

1) J. Everett Birdsall, in *O.S.A. Magazine*, 1958.

2) *O.S.A. Magazine*, 1943-44.

3) *O.S.A. Magazine*, 1946-47.

4) "Son of the Soil," *op. cit.*, p. 93.

5) Reminiscences of J. Everett Birdsall, by David Birdsall, no date. A copy is available at the Olds College Alumni Museum.

6) *O.S.A. Alumni Review*, September 1954.

7) *Annual Report of the Department of Agriculture of the Province of Alberta*, 1947. Report of the Schools of Agriculture Branch.

8) *Annual Report of the Department of Agriculture of the Province of Alberta*, 1952. Report of Schools of Agriculture Branch.

9) Connie Hunt, "My O.S.A. Story," 2011. A copy is available at the Olds College Alumni Museum.

10) *Annual Report of the Department of Agriculture of the Province of Alberta*, 1957. Report of the Schools

of Agriculture.

11) *The Sixth Decade at the Alberta Agricultural Colleges,* *op. cit.,* p. 5.

12) *The Chinook,* Christmas 1954.

13) Wilbur Collin, correspondence of 20 April 2011. A copy is available at the Olds College Alumni Museum.

14) Howard and Tamara Palmer, *Alberta: A New History.* Edmonton: Hurtig Publishers, 1990, p. 304.

15) *The Olds Gazette* 17 July 1947.

16) Stan Church, quoted in Nancy Millar, *Alberta Bound: A Church & Black Family History,* privately printed, 2001, p. 103.

17) In *Olds: A History of Olds and District,* this incident is incorrectly dated to 1959. For details, see *Annual Report of the Department of Agriculture of the Province of Alberta,* 1955. Olds School of Agriculture and Home Economics.

18) "The Olds School of Agriculture: Training Ground for Scientific Farming," *The Calgary Herald,* 22 March 1958.

Chapter 7

1) *The Olds Gazette and Mountain View News,* 1 August 1963.

2) *The Olds Gazette and Mountain View News,* 1 August 1963.

3) *The Sixth Decade at the Alberta Agricultural Colleges,* *op. cit.,* p. 4 cf.

4) Amy von Heyking. *Creating Citizens: History and Identity in Alberta's Schools, 1905-1980.* Calgary: University of Calgary Press, 2006, p. 92.

5) W. J. Collin, "Fashion Merchandising at Olds College," *Olds College Alumni Review,* February 1977.

6) "The Commercial Class," *Alumni Review,* March 1965.

7) *The Chinook,* 1964.

8) Interview with W. J. Collin and Edith Collin, 7 June 2011.

9) *The Sixth Decade, op. cit.* p. 53 cf.

10) W. J. Collin to Dr. Tom Thompson, 31 December 2009. A copy of this correspondence is available at the Olds College Alumni Museum.

11) *Olds College Horizons,* April 2010.

12) *The Chinook,* March, 1964.

13) *The Calgary Herald,* 2 June 1962.

14) *The Sixth Decade, op. cit.,* p. 99 cf.

15) Interview with W. J. Collin, 7 June 2011.

16) *The Sixth Decade, op. cit.,* p. 12.

17) *Ibid.,* p. 115.

18) *The Olds Gazette,* 4 February 1960.

19) *The Sixth Decade,* op. cit., p. 6.

20) W. J. Collin to Kerry Moynihan, 20 April 2011. A copy is available at the Olds College Alumni Museum.

21) *Annual Report of the Department of Agriculture of the Province of Alberta,* 1961. Report of the Schools of Agriculture and Home Economics.

22) *The Calgary Herald,* 27 March 1962.

23) *The Sixth Decade, op. cit.,* p. 198.

24) *The Calgary Herald Magazine,* 12 July 1968, p. 3.

25) Interview with Laurinda Parkinson, 3 June 2011.

Chapter 8

1) Peter Lougheed, quoted in Bradford J. Rennie, *Alberta Premiers of the Twentieth Century. Regina: Canadian Plains Research Center,* 2004, p. 207.

2) Perhaps he also realized that Albertans were abandoning their radios for televisions *en masse.* By 1971, when the election was held, more than 95 per cent of Alberta owned televisions. See David G. Wood. *The Lougheed Legacy.* Toronto: Key Porter Books, 1985, p. 76.

3) Max Foran, "1967: Embracing the Future...At Arm's Length," in *Alberta Formed Alberta Transformed*, Volume 2, edited by Michael Payne, Donald Wetherell, and Catherine Cavanaugh. Edmonton and Calgary: University of Alberta Press and University of Calgary Press, 2006, pp. 613-643.

4) *Ibid.*, p. 632.

5) *O.A.V.C. Alumni Review*, March 1969.

6) Walter H. Worth, "A Choice of Futures," 1972.

7) *Annual Report of the Department of Advanced Education for the School Year 1971-72*.

8) *The Story of Olds College*, p. 4-9.

9) *Sixty Years of Service, op. cit.*, p. 100.

10) *Alumni Review*, June 1978, p. 4.

11) *Olds College Review*, Spring 1982.

12) *Olds Alumni Review*, October 1978.

13) Dorothy Rowles, quoted in Bruce Winning, "Olds College head works to encourage 'quality growth'," *The Calgary Herald*, 26 January 1981.

14) *The Edmonton Journal*, 12 December 1979.

15) *The Calgary Herald*, 23 December 1981.

16) "The Story of Olds College", p. 4-16 cf.

17) *The Calgary Herald*, 20 July 1982.

18) Quoted in Bruce Winning, *op. cit.*

19) *Olds College Review*, Spring 1982.

20) Daniel Cornish, "Olds College - The Vision", *Olds College Review*, Winter 1983.

21) Bob Warwick, "Cornish warms up expansion issue," *The Calgary Herald*, 9 September 1982.

22) "Olds College eyes its roots," *The Calgary Herald*, 28 April 1986.

23) *Olds College Annual Report*, 1988-89.

24) *Olds College Alumni Review*, Spring 1992.

25) *Olds College Alumni Review*, Fall 1990.

26) *Olds College Annual Report*, 1992/93.

Chapter 9

1) Les Sillars, "The Colleges Jostle for Money," *Alberta Report*, 21: 1 (1993).

2) Olds College. Minutes of the Board of Governors, 18 November 1993.

3) Interview with Al Qually, 6 June 2011

4) *Olds College Annual Report*, 1994-95.

5) Olds College, Minutes of the Board of Governors, 19 October 1995.

6) *Ibid.*

7) Olds College, Minutes of the Board of Governors, 1997.

8) *Olds College Annual Report*, 1996/97.

9) *Olds College Annual Report*, 1999.

10) Alberta Intergovernmental and Aboriginal Affairs. "Mission Report, Alberta's Participation in Team Canada '98, January 10 to 23, 1998", p. 4.

11) "Summary of Recommendations for Re-Organization of Olds College Academic Division," Board of Governors Minutes, 1994.

12) *Olds College Annual Report*, 1999.

13) *Olds College Alumni Review*, January 2001.

14) Barbara Duckworth, "Centre of innovation in research," *The Western Producer*, 24 May 2001.

15) Olds College. Minutes of the Board of Governors, 25 January 2001.

16) Carla Victor, "Olds College president resigns, heads to Ontario," *The Calgary Herald*, 19 December 2000.

17) "Message from the President and CEO H. J. (Tom) Thompson," *Olds College Annual Report*, 2003-2004.

18) *Olds College Annual Report*, 2000.

19) Ag Summit 2000. *Catalyst for Growth, Framework for Change: Key Findings from Ag Summit 2000*, December 2000.

20) The Hon. Gene Zwozdesky, quoted in "Million dollar announcement made at official CLC groundbreaking ceremony," 25 May 2006. Olds College press release.

21) Interview with Reeve Paddy Munro, 18 July 2011.

22) Interview with Her Worship Judy Dahl, Mayor of the Town of Olds, 5 July 2011.

23) *Olds College Annual Report*, 2006/7.

Copyright © 2012 Olds College
All photography courtesy Olds College except where noted.

Written by Barry Potyondi

Designed by Eric Graham & Heather Cooper
Cooper Company Creative Design
www.coopercompany.com

Project Director Kerry Moynihan
General Manager, 2013 Centennial
Office of Advancement

Published by Olds College
4500 - 50th Street
Olds, AB, Canada T4H 1R6
www.oldscollege.ca

ISBN 978-0-919609-60-0
Printed in Canada

OLDS COLLEGE
100 years
1913-2013